THE REMARKABLE TALE OF
RADIO 1

THE REMARKABLE TALE OF
RADIO 1
THE HISTORY OF THE NATION'S FAVOURITE STATION 1967–95

ROBERT SELLERS

OMNIBUS PRESS

London / New York / Paris / Sydney / Copenhagen / Berlin / Madrid / Tokyo

Acknowledgements

I'd like to thank all the DJs, broadcasters, presenters, producers and backroom staff who worked at Radio 1 for sharing their memories, views and experiences, and for bringing the station's golden age back into vivid life:

David Atkey, Johnny Beerling, Pete Brady, Bruno Brookes, Tim Blackmore, Ric Blaxill, Tony Brandon, Paul Burnett, Dave Cash, Martin Cox, Trevor Dann, Gary Davies, Pete Drummond, Noel Edmonds, Paul Gambaccini, Jeff Griffin, David Hamilton, Paul Hollingdale, Adrian Juste, Phil Ward-Large, Chris Lycett, Paul McKenna, John Miles, Frank Partridge, Andy Peebles, Chris Peers, Mike Read, Paul Robinson, Emperor Rosko, Jonathan Ruffle, Keith Skues, Gary Stevens, David Symonds, Robbie Vincent, Johnnie Walker, Tony Wilson, Steve Wright, Jeff Young.

1

It's hard to imagine today, with music readily accessible on so many different platforms, from YouTube and iTunes to a plethora of digital radio stations catering to all manner of musical tastes, that in the early sixties there were few opportunities to hear your favourite records played.

With the UK one of the few countries in the world without commercial radio, the BBC monopolised the airwaves and heavily restricted the amount of pop music played, preferring classical music or light, middle-of-the-road sounds. The only station available feeding this thirst was Radio Luxembourg, which operated from the continent on an unreliable medium wave signal that notoriously faded in and out. 'When rock'n'roll began to really be noticed,' says radio producer Tim Blackmore, 'people of my generation started to listen to Radio Luxembourg, which had been going since the 1930s but all of a sudden switched to embrace rock'n'roll because the BBC were very nervous of it.'

When 'Heartbreak Hotel' was released in 1956, marking Elvis Presley's debut on the UK chart, Anna Instone, then head of the BBC's gramophone programmes and one of the few women in a senior position within the corporation, was chairing a producers' meeting. 'Has anybody heard this record by this new Elvis Presley person?' she asked.

'Yes,' they all said. 'We've heard it.'

'Well, I suppose you can play it if you must,' she went on. 'But I can't see anybody wanting to.'

This was typical of the BBC's attitude at the time. And it didn't get much better.

By 1964, the year of Beatlemania, vast swathes of the population, especially the youth, classed the BBC as stuffy and outdated. 'We used to laugh at the BBC, they were just complete idiots,' recalls DJ Johnnie Walker. 'They were so old-fashioned. All this great music had come along and they'd sort of done nothing about it. They hoped it was a fad, a fashion that would go away after a couple of years. I remember Douglas Muggeridge, when he became controller of Radio 1, saying to me once, "Johnnie, I think, in hindsight, the BBC totally underestimated the impact of the Beatles."'

It wasn't just the Beatles that the BBC tried to disregard. Until its popularity was such that it couldn't be ignored, black music rarely featured on the network. Tim Blackmore recalls record pluggers telling him that until Radio 1 got underway there was a real racial bias against black artists within the BBC. 'Motown was a no-no. And the records that Atlantic and Chess were issuing through the London American label were also, by and large, no-nos.'

The BBC did attempt to address the rise of pop music with the introduction of programmes such as *Saturday Club*, playing skiffle, rock'n'roll and country music, along with *Top Gear*, which was a little more progressive in the musical acts it chose to feature, and *Pick of the Pops*, based on the Top 20 singles chart. However, this was tokenism at best. Indeed, *Top Gear* only lasted a year and was axed in 1965, despite its popularity.

Producers who valued pop music, such as Bernie Andrews, were similarly looked down on. 'You were regarded as a completely mad person. Most people in the BBC, particularly in management, put no value at all to pop music... They regarded it as a necessary evil, in a rather patronising way. And they would much rather not have had to bother with it.'

Put simply, the BBC were oblivious to any innovation or departure from the norm that would interfere with the cosiness of the monopoly they had enjoyed for all these years.

Everything changed over the Easter weekend of 1964 with the launch of Radio Caroline, the first of the pirate stations. The brainchild of Irish businessman Ronan O'Rahilly, Caroline began broadcasting from a former passenger ferry off the coast of Felixstowe, anchored in international waters and so beyond the reach of UK legislation. At last the British public had access to a non-stop output of pop music, delivered by a young bunch of disc jockeys.

For DJs like Keith Skues, who spent weeks at a time on board ship, life was 'a combination of isolation, claustrophobia and a kind of deprived, hip euphoria'. With, of course, no computers or mobile phones, the DJs were cut off from the rest of the world. 'We lived for correspondence from our listeners who wrote to us in their thousands,' remembers Keith. 'Never in my sixty-plus years in radio have I experienced that sort of friendship with listeners. They were our lifeline.' Food parcels were sent, along with cuddly toys, scarves, socks, gloves, woolly hats and sweaters. During calm weather, the station itself became a tourist attraction with boatloads of people sailing over on day trips to catch a glimpse of the DJs taking a stroll on deck and to shout out requests for records.

The weather was changeable. One day sunny, with calm seas, on other occasions force eight gales would toss and pitch the ship from side to side. 'During rough weather it was difficult to control a programme,' recalls Keith. 'The records would jump off the turntable when a heavy wave hit the ship. So, when a storm was brewing, we used to place heavy coins on the stylus of the turntable. This did no good whatsoever to the stylus, but it kept the record playing.'

That winter, Caroline was followed by Radio London which started broadcasting from an old World War Two minesweeper anchored off the Essex coast, just a mile from Caroline. On a clear day, both ships could see each other and they shared the tenders that went back and forth with provisions.

Thanks to an American owner, the formula and presentation style of Radio London adhered closely to the format of Top 40 American radio, with records interspersed by chat, ads and jingles, something new to the ears of British listeners. There was also a quick burst of news on the hour. Since the station had no news-gathering facilities, the DJs used to monitor BBC bulletins, do a bit of rewriting, and then present it as if it had just come hot off their own presses. The BBC eventually twigged what was going on and deliberately read out a piece of false news, only to hear it repeated minutes later on Radio London.

The American DJ Emperor Rosko went one step further during his spell on Caroline. 'I took the BBC's live broadcast of the Henry Cooper championship fight with Muhammad Ali, plugged it into our console and pretended that we were ringside with the BBC reporter, because you could hear the other guy as well, and I was saying, "Radio Caroline is bringing you this fight live, folks!"'

Just like on Caroline, accommodation on Radio London was adequate at best. Everyone had to share a cabin, with barely enough space for a wardrobe, a metal basin and a desk. With no baths, everyone made do with a shower block consisting of tin cubicles which, during rough seas, bounced the DJs from one wall to the other.

As for the studio, it was located in the bilges, the lowest part of the ship's hull, and was poky and claustrophobic, with an overpowering odour of damp. Most of the electronics in the studio, such as the turntables and the RAC cartridge machines that played the jingles and promos, were run from a single generator.

The DJs on Caroline and Radio London became household names, the likes of Tony Blackburn, Kenny Everett and Dave Cash. John Peel was a late arrival to Radio London, going on air in March 1967, having returned from living and broadcasting in America. He was offered the midnight-to-two shift, which gradually developed into a programme called *The Perfumed Garden* and garnered a huge following, as fellow DJ Tony Brandon recalls. 'Students used to swot up on their papers in the early hours of the morning listening to Peel in his *Perfumed Garden*. And it certainly was "perfumed" on board ship because what it was that he was smoking, I cannot imagine. It was pretty pungent stuff. You went into the studio at the same time at your peril.'

Amongst the more inexperienced DJs was a young Kenny Everett, who'd landed his first professional job with Radio London. Kenny didn't hang out very much with his fellow DJs, and was extremely shy and naive. One afternoon he was relaxing on deck with Ed Stewart when the Beatles track 'Yesterday' came on the radio. 'Ah, that's a great piece of music, beautiful song,' said Stewart. 'Do you know, Kenny, it's like a musical orgasm.'

Kenny looked puzzled. 'What's that?'

'Well,' said Ed, 'it's like, every time I hear this record, I have an orgasm.'

The next day Kenny was presenting his early evening show and, playing 'Yesterday', announced into the mic, 'You know, listeners, every time Ed Stewart hears this, he has an orgasm.' The word 'orgasm' had never been uttered on live radio before and Kenny was instantly dismissed, only to be reinstated twenty-four hours later when the bosses realised that he genuinely didn't know the meaning of the word.

Kenny was a law unto himself, as Keith Skues found out. Skues often ended up with the weekend shifts and dreaded having to sit opposite Kenny to read his news bulletin, 'because I knew he'd be up to some trick or other. He'd either start removing his clothing or on one occasion setting fire to my script!' Skues managed to get through the headlines, but during the sports announcements had to pound on the paper to stem the flames.

Following the success of Caroline and London, the North Sea became a battleground of competing pirate stations. There was Radio Essex, Radio Scotland and Radio England. Radio 270, broadcasting from a converted Dutch lugger positioned off Scarborough, was smaller than its rivals and therefore even more uncomfortable in rough seas. DJ Paul Burnett once threw up live on the air in the middle of reading a script advertising the delights of a bacon breakfast.

The pirate DJs all worked on a rota system: fourteen days and fourteen nights with no time off before being let loose on the mainland for a week's break. The tender picked them up from the ships and deposited them on shore, where a minibus would be waiting to take them to the nearest railway station. From there they'd catch a train to Liverpool Street Station to be greeted, more often than not, by crowds of screaming girls. 'At the time, we took it all in our stride,' says Keith Skues. 'We never believed we were as famous as some of the recording artists we played.' The cult of the celebrity disc jockey had begun.

In 1966, a national opinion poll found that 45 per cent of the population was listening to pirate stations. They had been not just a breath of fresh air but a musical revolution, broadcasting loud and proud in open defiance of the stuffy old Beeb and the establishment. There really was a sense of pioneering adventure about the whole thing. 'We didn't know how much change we were creating to broadcasting,' says DJ Pete Brady. 'And not only in the UK but in Europe, too, where we had a massive audience.' In many ways the pirates came to symbolise the new, youthful, post-war Britain and the huge cultural change that was happening – the whole Swinging Sixties vibe. As John Peel put it: 'The pirates provided the soundtrack to a lot of young people's lives.'

2

It was the then incumbent Labour government, presided over by Harold Wilson, that sounded the death knell for the pirates. The government's attitude towards independent radio had consistently been one of suppression, and part of a determined plan to maintain the BBC's monopoly in radio broadcasting. 'They were totally against any form of commercial radio,' says DJ Paul Hollingdale. In a bid to undermine the pirates, the government leaked to the press unsubstantiated stories about the pirates' unlicensed transmissions not only interfering with legal broadcasters throughout Europe but with the emergency services. 'It was absolute rubbish,' argues Hollingdale. And there were other attempts to shut them down. DJ Dave Cash recollects at least two police drug raids on Radio London.

In the end, Wilson knew that the only way to smash the pirates was to draw up a new law that banned them. Thus, the Marine Broadcasting Offences Act was drafted early in 1967, which effectively sought to make it illegal for anyone subject to UK law to operate or facilitate a pirate station.

At the same time, the government were smart enough to realise that the landscape of radio and the listening habits of the nation had changed dramatically. 'The Labour government also knew that if they silenced the pirates, they'd be really unpopular with young people, because millions were tuning into these stations,' says Johnnie Walker.

'So, the only way they were going to get away with taking them off the air was to ask the BBC to do a substitute pop station.'

The BBC, however, were totally uninterested. 'The government put huge pressure on the BBC to prepare for this and the BBC fought it tooth and nail,' according to Tim Blackmore. Producer Johnny Beerling confirms that the BBC couldn't have been less interested about running a pop station. 'They would much rather have been doing Radio 3 with culture, that was what epitomised the BBC in those days, not broadcasting all day popular music with gramophone records. They didn't see that as part of their function.' Indeed, the BBC's chairman, Lord Norman Brook, is reported to have said: 'You can't have popular music all the time, it would be like having the pubs open all day.' Commentators beyond the halls of the BBC also decried the fact that the nation's broadcaster should be bulldozed into creating a copy of the pirates.

At the time, the BBC consisted of three national radio stations: the Light Programme, founded in 1945, provided easy listening, comedy and a smattering of pop music; the Home Service, founded in 1939, had news, discussion programmes and plays; and lastly the Third Programme, founded in 1947, prioritised classical music. 'But the reality was, the BBC had to do something,' says Paul Hollingdale. 'And once they got their act together, they did fall into line and began to carry out what they had been instructed to do by the government.'

The result was the biggest overhaul since the corporation's inception in 1927. Out went the Light and Third Programmes and the Home Service in favour of what we know today as Radios 2, 3 and 4. To occupy the space once dominated by the pirates, a brand-new 'pop' music service was to be created, known as Radio 1. There was just one problem, the BBC mandarins didn't have the first clue how to set about running such a service. The obvious solution was to bring in someone with a BBC identity but also outside experience. That man was Robin Scott, something of a mover and shaker in the world of radio and television. The fact that Scott was asked to oversee not just Radio 1 but also Radio 2 'was an indication of how unimportant Radio 1 was to the BBC,' says Johnny Beerling.

Scott had begun his radio career with the BBC European Service in 1942, dabbled a bit in the music industry, and set up his own television company in Switzerland before going to work for BBC Television in 1964, rising to Assistant Head of Presentation at BBC 1. A keen jazz enthusiast, Scott was an intelligent, erudite and unassuming middle-aged man. Handed this hot potato, he was determined to make the best of it, keenly aware that he had just the one shot to make it work. 'It was a political job, really,' says Gary Stevens, an American DJ living in London, who met Scott around this time. 'He'd been charged with providing a replacement for a service that nobody thought needed to be replaced. Somebody up there in the senior levels of the BBC obviously thought he was the go-to guy to manage volatility because when you start introducing that sort of change within an organisation, you're going to rub a lot of people the wrong way.'

Scott also brought to the job great entrepreneurial skills. 'He could sum up people quite quickly,' claims Chris Peers, a record promotions man. 'And he had a nose for talent.' He also had complete carte blanche, 'because they hadn't got a clue inside Broadcasting House,' says Paul Hollingdale. 'And it was Robin Scott's brainchild as to how Radio 1 evolved when it got on the air.'

Chris Peers was one of the first people to have a meeting with Scott after he got the job. Peers had been managing DJs for years and would later come to regret being the person who introduced Jimmy Savile to the gramophone department of the BBC. Having helped with the recruitment of DJs for Radio London and worked with Chris Blackwell during the early days of Island Records, Peers was exactly the kind of expert Scott wanted to hear from. Like any smart guy, Scott was in the process of getting as much information as he could from people who knew perhaps more than he did on a particular subject.

Peers found Scott an easy man to deal with. 'Robin was different to other BBC executives. He was willing to listen and wanted to learn. You walked into his office and, unlike a normal first meeting with a BBC executive, you were handed a glass of wine. So, he made you feel very much at home.' This genial aspect to Scott's personality certainly endeared him to the people who were to work closely with him. 'Prior to his arrival, under the old BBC, none of us had ever met a controller,' says Johnny Beerling. 'They were remote figures from another BBC planet.'

Scott was left in little doubt as to the herculean task that lay before him. 'How long have I got?' he asked the powers that be. The reply was terrifying – just six months. This was April. It wasn't long to put together a brand-new national radio station almost from scratch, something that was both fresh and different and yet a viable alternative to the sound of the pirates. It was a task, he later described, 'to fire the blood and to be the greatest challenge perhaps I'd had to face'.

For one thing, he'd been given very few resources. 'In the beginning, there was no concept of Radio 1 as an entity, in organisational terms,' says Tim Blackmore. 'Because the BBC had been forced to create Radio 1 in order to mop up the market that the pirates had created, there wasn't very much extra money made available by anybody. So everything was a make do and mend.' One consequence of the lack of money was that Radio 1 couldn't fill the hours of the day with its own programmes, resulting in its having to share a lot of output with Radio 2, a situation that lasted for years.

Another bone of contention was that out of the four new networks, Radio 1 was to be the only one not to be allocated an FM frequency. Instead it would broadcast on 247 metres on the medium wave. 'The powers that be saw fit to give FM stereo to Radio 4, which is a speech station, and a mono AM signal to Radio 1, which just seems crazy,' says Johnnie Walker. 'It really demonstrated their lack of understanding.'

The official reason for this omission was that there was insufficient space on the FM dial, despite the fact that there were no licensed independent commercial stations operating at the time. 'It really was a terrible transmitter, 247 metres,' says Johnny Beerling. 'It wasn't much better than Radio Luxembourg. It covered the country in the daytime but after dark half the nation couldn't hear it.' While Radio 1 did broadcast some limited programming on FM, it would be another twenty-one years before it was given a full FM network.

Now came the question of recruitment. Scott was acutely aware that the pirate DJs had brought a whole new style and breeziness to the airwaves; they talked the language of the sixties to a young population. For Scott it wasn't merely a question of imitation. 'It was a question of saying that is the new style of radio and that's the way to go.'

Since landing the job, Scott had been listening as often as he could to the pirate stations, sometimes for hours on end. And with a large number of pirate jocks and broadcasters soon to be out of work, he was spoilt for choice. In bringing the pirate jocks to the BBC, Scott was not only seeking to harness their considerable experience, but also the large and loyal audience that they had cultivated over the years. 'We had a persona,' says Pete Brady. 'The pirates had a huge audience, so the public knew exactly who all these people were and that's who they wanted to hear.' The plan was to mix these young guns with veteran broadcasters from the soon-to-be-defunct Light Programme, like Pete Murray and Jimmy Young, who were kept on because their shows commanded such large figures. It all made for an odd combination, but Scott needed to throw his net wide to please everyone and compromises had to be made. It was like the merging of two disparate companies.

At midnight on 14 August 1967, the Marine Broadcasting Offences Act was enacted and the pirates were dead in the water. After 14 August, anybody found to be illegally broadcasting on a pirate station faced up to three months in prison and a substantial fine.

Within twenty-four hours, Radio London shut down operations. The last record played was the Beatles' 'A Day in the Life'. Tony Brandon was on board for those last few emotional hours. 'That really was quite something,' he remembers. 'To see our boss, Alan Keen, who was not an overly emotional man, to see him literally in tears.'

Millions of listeners mourned the loss of the pirate stations. It was as if the soundtrack of their youth had been stifled without their consent. For the DJs, too, it had been a special time. 'It could never be replicated on land,' says Johnnie Walker. 'Because you had a bunch of people who had to learn to live together and get on with each other. You had all the day-to-day goings-on of the ship. Regular listeners knew when the tender arrived because it used to bang against the side of the ship and the record would jump. And when the tender arrived there was always that excitement of some people going off on leave and new people arriving. You tuned in to a family running a radio station twenty-four hours a day.'

A few perceptive DJs had already seen the writing on the wall and jumped ship early. 'We knew it was only a matter of time before they closed them down,' says Dave Cash. In any case, Dave had been forced to leave Radio London after becoming seriously ill with kidney stones and his manager had got him a job on the Light Programme. Here Cash came face to face for the first time with the intransigence of the BBC. Bumping into the Rolling Stones at a club one evening, Dave managed to persuade them all to come onto his show. Incredulously his producer said no. 'Why not?' asked Cash. 'There's five of them,' replied his producer. 'And we've only got three microphones.'

And then there was Kenny Everett. Kenny left Radio London in March, hoping to find a way into the inner sanctum of the BBC. Importantly, he had an ally in the shape of Johnny Beerling, a young, ambitious producer. When plans were first drawn up to radically alter the way the BBC was going to broadcast to the nation, every producer working in popular music and the gramophone department was asked which of the new networks they wanted to work on. Beerling opted for Radio 1 and, along with people like Derek Chinnery, Teddy Warwick and Angela Bond, began coming up with ideas and strategies for the new station.

Beerling and Kenny first met in February 1967 when Beerling paid an unofficial visit to the Radio London ship to gain firsthand insight into how the pirate stations operated. According to Beerling, it was Kenny, out of all the pirate DJs he met, who proved the most helpful. 'He was delighted to show off all the equipment and demonstrate how it worked. It was such a different way of working to those of us in the BBC.'

For starters, the pirate DJs ran their own show: there was no producer choosing the music for them or looking over their shoulder, which was the practice at the BBC. The pirate DJ sat alone in his studio playing the records and informally chatting to the listener. It was spontaneous. It was exciting. The BBC way of doing things was very different. Each record to be featured on any particular show was selected days in advance, along with a script written by the presenter that was then typed out by a production secretary and vetted. Canadian Pete Brady, who managed to land a few shows on the BBC after leaving the ships, recalls getting a phone call from his producer three days before his first programme went out asking, 'We haven't had your script yet.' Peter went into a panic and said, 'I don't do scripts.' He wouldn't know where to start doing a script. 'My agent stepped in and calmed everybody down. But on the first day I had about three people in the studio with their fingers very near to the button to take me off the air in case I strayed from whatever they thought was the norm.'

On the day of broadcast, the presenter was also required to be at the studio three hours early for a rehearsal, which meant going through each item of the programme to check timings, announcements or any alterations to the prepared script. During the show itself, a producer was always present, along with a studio manager to mix the sound. 'In those days, you didn't spin the records, you weren't a disc jockey,' recalls Pete Brady. 'You sat in a box with a microphone and you looked at the glass and there was a chap on the other side of the glass and you waved at him when you wanted the record to start.'

It was clear to Beerling, and others, that if Radio 1 were to have any credibility with younger listeners, it would need to go down the route of self-operating DJs. 'It was a whole different concept, just one man controlling everything – incredible,' says Beerling. 'The BBC had never done anything like this before.'

Something else that Beerling took away from his Radio London experience was an enormous respect for Kenny Everett. Back on dry land, he put in a call to Robin Scott that Kenny was someone they should be mining for ideas. A meeting was duly arranged at a restaurant in Regent Street, near Broadcasting House. It was a lively lunch and

Beerling remembers that 'Robin was quick to appreciate the talents of Kenny' as he explained the requirements for self-operating. As a result, Scott managed, in his words, to 'bully and bludgeon the system' into allowing him to adapt a couple of old studios in Broadcasting House, where announcers traditionally did their show links, into 'self-op' studios as close as possible to those on the Radio London ship. There were three turntables, two microphones, cartridge machines and a simple mixer, all within easy reach, so that the DJs could work the same way they did on the pirates. It was no mean feat getting them ready in time, recalls Tim Blackmore. 'When I first went inside, there were wires running everywhere and extra bits of equipment had been stuck into the old spaces in order to make do and mend. It worked, but it was several years later before it became a sleek operation. It was very much a case of "How can we make do with what we've got because we haven't got very much money to spend?"'

Another of Kenny's suggestions was that Radio 1 needed to have jingles. The BBC had never used anything as common as jingles before, but Kenny was at pains to emphasise their importance, and that the people to get them from were PAMS of Dallas, the first production company to specialise in the creation and syndication of station identification jingle packages for radio and TV. In the end, that's exactly what happened; the BBC even used a few of PAMS old Radio London jingles, re-recorded to extol the virtues of Radio 1. Beerling also entrusted Kenny with the job of making a series of jingles to saturate the airwaves that summer, plugging the forthcoming Radio 1, including one promo that ran just prior to the station going on air for the first time.

The use of jingles caused something of a backlash from the Musicians' Union, who demanded they be taken off the air until an agreement could be reached which saw this kind of material recorded by their members. At a hurriedly convened meeting, the BBC refused to budge on the matter. This left the union representative rather indignant. 'Well, if that is all you have to say,' he said, 'I don't think there's any point in our discussing the matter further.' And with that, he and his delegation left the room. Scott was to recall that at two minutes and fifteen seconds, it was the shortest meeting between the BBC and the Musicians' Union he could ever remember.

By early September, the DJ line-up for Radio 1 had been announced and many of them assembled on the steps of All Souls Church, next door to Broadcasting House, to pose for the national press. They were Mike Ahern, Barry Alldis, Tony Blackburn, Pete Brady, Dave Cash, Chris Denning, Pete Drummond, Kenny Everett, Bob Holness, Duncan Johnson, Mike Lennox, Johnny Moran, Pete Murray, Pete Myers, John Peel, Mike Raven, David Ryder, Keith Skues, Ed Stewart, David Symonds, Terry Wogan and Jimmy Young.

'What was funny about that picture,' says Beerling, 'was the older guys from the Light Programme tried to dress down and the pirate guys tried to dress up!' David Symonds recalled buying a new white suit for the occasion, getting his hair cut and having a close shave only for Robin Scott to whisper in his ear, 'A bit too straight, Dave.'

It was now just a matter of a couple of weeks before launch day and there was a flurry of activity, along with an overwhelming sense of expectation. 'We knew we were going to be part of something that was going to have significance,' says Tim Blackmore. It was a matter of putting the finishing touches to everything and there were endless rehearsals and dry runs. 'Tony Blackburn's breakfast show, for example, went on for quite a few weeks of rehearsal until they got it right,' confirms Paul Hollingdale. There was nervousness about the place, to be sure, and tension, but no panic. 'The BBC doesn't do panic,' says Blackmore.

Finally, on Saturday morning, 30 September 1967, it was all systems go. Paul Hollingdale arrived early at Broadcasting House to open the Light Programme for the final time at 5.30 a.m. with *Breakfast Special*, and he recalls a palpable sense of excitement running through the entire building. Continuity studios A and B were crowded with top brass and well-wishers. As the time approached 7 a.m., Robin Scott arrived at studio A to prepare the countdown. Hollingdale could see him through the glass, standing almost to attention as the station's theme tune, especially written for the occasion by Beatles producer

George Martin, was played. As the music faded, Scott stepped up to the microphone. 'Ten seconds to go before Radio 1, stand by for switching, five, four, three, Radio 2, Radio 1, GO!' A new era in radio had begun.

With Radio 1 as the nation's new pop music service, Radio 2 settled down as a middle-of-the-road station playing easy listening, light classics and oldies. There could be no more symbolic demonstration of how both networks were to differ musically than the choice of opening records: 'Flowers in the Rain' by The Move on Radio 1, Julie Andrews and 'The Sound of Music' on Radio 2.

It wasn't a difficult decision for Robin Scott to put Tony Blackburn in charge of Radio 1's all-important breakfast show, as he'd done the same shift on Radio London. Born in Surrey in 1943, Blackburn was ex-public school, did a course in business studies and for a while was a singer with a local dance band. He joined the BBC just a month before the launch of Radio 1 and was put to work on the Light Programme. While still on the pirate ships, Blackburn often heard people joke about a stereotypical BBC image of a dear old lady sitting in the corner of the studio knitting a jumper. Blackburn was amazed on his first day to see just such an apparition: her job was to open up the microphone for the DJ.

Blackburn was seen by some as a 'safe' option as the first breakfast jock, someone who fitted easily into the BBC way of doing things. 'The thing about Tony was that he could be relied upon to deliver a very fast-moving show,' explained Robin Scott in 1997, 'with wisecracks, some of them silly schoolboy jokes. He would appeal not only to the young audience, from the records he was playing, but he would also appeal to perhaps a middle-aged commuter-type audience sitting in cars.'

Others were to find his delivery and cheeriness a bit cheesy. This wasn't helped by having characters on his show like Gerald the Pixie, with a speeded-up chipmunk-type voice, and Arnold the Dog, whose bark he'd found on a BBC sound effects tape. Quite bewilderingly, these two characters would soon be receiving around a thousand letters every week.

Such was his instant fame that Blackburn was the victim of a prank that November when a group of students 'kidnapped' him as he left his West End flat. Bundled inside a van, he was driven round the streets of London and forced to listen to Radio 2. It wasn't anything malicious, just part of a university rag week, and Blackburn was deposited outside Broadcasting House, annoyed and late for his show.

Johnny Beerling was the producer on the breakfast show and found Blackburn very easy to work with. 'He was eager to please everyone and like many performers had a streak of insecurity which meant he needed constant reassurance,' Beerling wrote in his memoirs. He also found Blackburn to be quite shy but holding strong views on what the show should sound like: a selection of current hits, but not that many (he didn't want too much unfamiliar music) and oldies. He also highlighted a lot of Motown, of which he was a huge fan. In 1971, Blackburn was to champion the Diana Ross song 'I'm Still Waiting'. Initially intended only as an album track, Blackburn managed to persuade the record company to release it as a single where it reached number one in the UK Singles Chart.

Radio 1's first day on air continued when Blackburn handed over to Leslie Crowther for the children's request show *Junior Choice*, a hangover from the Light Programme, as was *Saturday Club* with Keith Skues, replacing original presenter Brian Matthew. It was a strange feeling for Keith, a keen admirer of Matthew's professional style. 'How on earth could I come up to his charismatic presentation?'

Keith had left the pirates months before the chop to achieve his ambition of working for the BBC, something he'd craved since he was 11 years old and built his own crystal radio set in his bedroom. The set had a long piece of wire going into an iron bedstead and another bit of wire that went out of the house to receive the transmission. 'There was enormous pressure on everyone,' Keith remembers, 'but when that green light went on, the DJs had to sound happy, friendly and, above all, professional.' The first song he played on Radio 1 was 'Soul Man' by Sam & Dave.

That first show also featured pre-recorded 'live' performances from the Bee Gees – with versions of 'New York Mining Disaster' and

'Massachusetts' – along with Billy Fury, Dave Dee, Dozy, Beaky, Mick & Tich. Other regular features included an album of the week and a golden oldie. There was also an overseas request spot in the final half hour when they were joined by the World Service and the British Forces Broadcasting Services.

Following Keith at noon was something the like of which had never been heard on the airwaves of the BBC before. Emperor Rosko, real name Mike Pasternak, hailed from Los Angeles and was influenced as a kid listening to Emperor Hudson and Wolfman Jack on local radio. His first opportunity to broadcast came while in the US Navy where he presented a show on an aircraft carrier. 'If you saw the film *Good Morning, Vietnam*,' he says, 'that was the kind of thing I did.'

After a stint on Radio Caroline, Rosko moved to Paris to work for Radio Luxembourg, which had a subsidiary operation in France. Fans would congregate in the street below the window of the studio and Rosko would sling out records for them. In time, Robin Scott was told about Rosko and made an approach, but the wages came nowhere near matching what he was earning with Luxembourg. In the end, a compromise was reached and Rosko agreed to record a show for Radio 1 from Paris and send a tape over each week.

Getting Rosko was seen as both a coup and a gamble by Robin Scott, and his debut certainly made an impact. As Dave Cash recalls: 'Mike came on doing, "Hey, baby, what's going on? Moving and a-grooving, I'll see you next week. Be there or be square. Yeah!" – all that kind of business. The show ended and you got the pips – *beep, beep, beep* – and there was a little gap after the last pip, before the announcer said, "The time is two o'clock. And now here is the news – in English!"'

By the spring of 1968, Rosko was doing his Radio 1 shows in person; it was the student uprising in Paris that changed everything for him. With riots in the streets and strikes, Radio Luxembourg's management urged Rosko to tone down his show, perhaps by playing some classical music. Instead, the first record he played was 'Dancing in the Street' by Martha and the Vandellas and he dedicated it to 'all the students out there'. Consequently, he was asked to leave. He packed his things, got in a car and drove all the way to London.

Highlights of the rest of Radio 1's launch day included Jack Jackson, a former bandleader who'd been on the BBC since 1948. His trademark practice of mixing comedy extracts and music became an inspiration to succeeding generations of disc jockeys, especially Kenny Everett. That was followed by the late afternoon show hosted by Pete Brady, who, along with Tony Blackburn, was the only presenter who was on for six days a week. 'I was just pleased beyond belief that I'd got myself a slot,' he says. 'But a daily show, that was big stuff. It was an honour to be asked, because everybody wanted to be on Radio 1.'

Following an hour of country music came *Scene and Heard*, a magazine programme featuring new music, pop news and interviews, hosted by John Moran. This first edition had an exclusive interview with George Harrison. And that was about it. The evening proved a bit of a damp squib, taken up mostly by Radio 2 programming and then Pete Murray at 10 p.m.

When it was all over, Robin Scott waited for the verdict of the public and the critics. It was swift and decidedly mixed. 'They said, "Well, it's not bad for the first day,"' remembers Paul Hollingdale. 'And "Things can only get better."'

3

Radio 1 hit the ground running, increasing the old Light Programme audience by 22 per cent within a month of its launch – not that difficult considering the fact that if you wanted to hear pop music Radio 1 was really the only option. Against much resistance, Robin Scott had done it. 'In the business we couldn't see how an organisation like the BBC could manage to recreate pirate radio,' says DJ manager Chris Peers. 'So, a lot of the success must go down to Robin Scott.'

Despite the immediate success of Radio 1, for a lot of people something was lost in translation between the defunct pirates and the new station. For them, Radio 1 never quite captured the spirit of the pirates, the madness of it, the informality of it. The BBC was just too professional an organisation to really do that. 'When we heard the BBC were going to do a pop station, we thought it was never really going to be any good,' admits Johnnie Walker. 'They might have the pirate DJs but they would shackle them with producers with clipboards and stopwatches. It would all be too organised.'

By and large, Radio 1 was welcomed and marked a major shift in broadcasting. People forget that the pirates didn't really offer a national service. Some ships lay off the coast of Yorkshire and in Scotland, but it was only the south coast that was saturated. 'Radio 1 brought something new to the whole nation,' says Tim Blackmore. 'And it saw off Radio Luxembourg.'

There were, of course, areas of complaint. Unlike the pirate ships, Radio 1 was not a 24-hour service. The BBC simply didn't see why they needed to broadcast every minute, every day; besides the budget for it was not there anyway. Another restriction was something called needle-time, largely imposed by the Musicians' Union to restrict the amount of recorded music transmitted by the BBC per day. The view of the Musicians' Union was that the playing of an unlimited number of records would deprive musicians of live work. Anything off a commercial record counted as needle-time and the BBC also had to pay performing rights to the industry each time a record was played. The pirates, being unregulated, ignored all of this.

When Radio 1 launched, the public naturally expected the kind of non-stop pop that they'd heard on the pirates, but because of the limitations of needle-time this simply couldn't be achieved, leaving many people working at the new station both bemused and angry. 'It meant we were fighting not with one hand behind our back, but both hands really,' says producer Jeff Griffin.

While it's true that an extra amount of needle-time per day was allocated, after lengthy negotiations with the Musicians' Union, it just wasn't enough and Robin Scott felt the need to go around the corporation begging for any scraps that were going spare. 'It was a question of pinching extra hours from the other channels,' he explained in 1981. 'There was an odd hour which was pinched from the Home Service. I remember banging on the door of Howard Newby's office and asking him if I could have a precious half hour from the Third Programme, and Howard being very sweet and nice saying he couldn't possibly because he was down to practically nothing already.'

As a result of these restrictions, the BBC had to carry on with the practice of using their in-house orchestras to supply cover versions of popular hits. 'The frustration with needle-time was when you can't play records all the time, what do you do about Joe Public, who have got used to hearing the songs they love the most,' says Tim Blackmore. 'For example, the Rolling Stones' "Satisfaction": the record is the definitive performance of that song, but because of the shortage of needle-time we were sometimes forced, to fill the hours of the day, to have "Satisfaction" played by the Joe Loss Orchestra. It hurt the station's credibility. It meant that people were taking the piss out of us.'

For the former pirate DJs used to working on stations which played non-stop popular music around the clock without any concerns about the amount of record music being used, joining the BBC and encountering needle-time was something of a culture shock. In a strange way, however, needle-time necessitated a different kind of approach from a DJ, not just someone who could run a tight show and play wall-to-wall music, but personalities able to sell themselves and fill time in a way that engaged the listener. All of which fitted in nicely with what Scott wanted to bring to Radio 1, and that was a clear move away from the BBC tradition of using largely anonymous announcers to using DJs who were personalities in their own right. The DJ's role now was not simply to announce, but to entertain.

For many inside the BBC, antagonism and plain bemusement over this new 'pop' station was clearly on view. 'Some of them couldn't understand what the hell was going on,' recalls Paul Hollingdale. 'They were all coming up towards retirement anyway, but they thought that the wrath of God had come in when Radio 1 started, because they didn't know anything else. One or two of them actually left saying, "I'm not staying around for this. I don't like what I hear."' In the words of Dave Cash, 'They didn't know what hit them. It was like having a bastard child foisted on you. They hated us with a vengeance.'

Robin Scott was the first to acknowledge that the atmosphere was not always an easy one. 'There was a feeling that Broadcasting House had been invaded in some way by a rather disreputable crowd who didn't dress perhaps in the appropriate way.' Of course, no one expected broadcasters to wear dinner suits to read the news any more, as was the case in Lord Reith's time, but there was still a modicum of formality to the place, with everyone required to wear a suit and tie to work. But when DJs started walking in sporting T-shirts with 'Down with Radio 4' on them and a few others wore kaftans there was a certain feeling in Broadcasting House, observed Scott, 'that the place had gone to the dogs'. As Terry Wogan observed, 'The poachers became the gamekeepers.'

One DJ in particular who caused a stir with his long hair and colourful clothes was John Peel. Tony Brandon remembers Peel turning up for work at Broadcasting House one day.

> He presented himself in the garb of the day: shoulder-length hair, the obligatory kaftan and probably sandals or flip flops – John wasn't a man given to wearing shoes. 'Excuse me, sir, can I help you?' said one of these rather officious commissionaires. 'Yes,' said John. 'My name's John Peel.' 'Oh, really, they all say that, sir.' And they wouldn't let him in. John was remonstrating, 'If you don't let me in there's going to be dead air for an hour.' Eventually he went over to the reception desk, accompanied by the commissionaire, and rang his producer: 'Can you convince this man who I am!'

This invasion of pirate DJs was a complete culture shock to the way the BBC functioned and what it had been used to. Paul Hollingdale, who worked on Radio Luxembourg in the early sixties before moving to Broadcasting House, remembers the BBC's head of presentation saying to him, 'You've got a very, very good voice, very, very good voice indeed, but I'm afraid you're going to have to be de-Luxembourg-ised.' Hollingdale wondered what he was talking about. 'You're a little bit too poppy, rocky for us,' the head of presentation explained. What came next was almost like some form of indoctrination. Paul says: 'I was put into a studio to listen to these BBC announcers who were a throwback to the last war.'

Tim Blackmore suffered a similar humiliation when he started as an announcer at the World Service in the early sixties. First of all, his voice had to be evaluated and Tim was given the mark 1B, which essentially meant that he could do anything except read the news. 'And when I asked why, they said, "Because some of your vowels are still very Northern."'

Scott and many others realised that unless the BBC responded to the tastes of listeners and moved forward, it was death to the organisation.

It had to win over young listeners and convince them that it could run a pop music service that was the equal of the pirates, if not better. And it was this new generation of producers, like Tim Blackmore and Johnny Beerling, eager to prove themselves and make a difference, that was going to make it happen. Those who had been there for years, steadfastly stuck in the past, would remain so until they left or were replaced. And only then did the atmosphere begin to truly change. 'It was stuffy behind the scenes at the BBC and it remained stuffy even when Radio 1 came on the air,' claims Paul Hollingdale. 'It was quite some years before it loosened up.'

Having previously enjoyed total control of their shows on pirate stations, the DJs now found themselves with a producer keeping them in line. Keith Skues' producer Bill Bebb was a hard taskmaster. 'He wanted a fast presentation with no errors. He stood over me with a stopwatch and would say, "You have ten seconds to announce the next record..." I would have to obey.'

Needless to say, these kinds of constraints didn't help when it came to anything approaching spontaneity. Of course, it all depended upon the individual producer's relationship with the DJ. A good case in point was Johnny Beerling, who produced the breakfast show. After a while, he realised that Tony Blackburn could be trusted and so rarely sat in the studio with him; instead he would listen driving into London from his home in Kent and afterwards they would have a meeting to discuss the following morning's show.

For Mike Ahern, who had come from Radio Caroline, it was too much and it wasn't long before he left Radio 1. 'He found it really difficult,' says Johnnie Walker. 'He couldn't stand the idea of the producer telling him what to do when he'd never had a producer before. And the producer who was telling him what to do didn't have a fraction of the musical knowledge that Mike did, because these producers had been doing all sorts of odd shows. Then suddenly, they're pop music producers deciding what music young people want to hear.'

In time, it became clear that the DJs could be trusted and the shackles were loosened a bit. 'We were allowed to revert to our old ways,' says Tony Brandon. 'And I'm certain that it made for far better radio.' However, it did remain a fact that the content of programmes and the majority of the records chosen remained the responsibility of the producer. Although this did depend on how involved the DJ actually wanted to be in the planning of his show and how flexible the producer was. Someone like Emperor Rosko was very proactive. 'My producers were always very respectful of my talents and where I was coming from and they basically let me do as I wanted, subject to good taste,' he says. 'I also listened to every single record I got. I listened to the A-side, and I listened to the B-side.' In addition, he flew back to the States twice a year to buy a whole load of 45s. Conversely, other DJs left pretty much everything to their producer, or, in the case of Tony Brandon, if he happened to be in the office when a new single arrived, the producer might play it to him and ask his opinion.

Brandon was a little different from his colleagues, having first worked as an entertainer in variety theatres and cabaret appearances before becoming a DJ for a brief time on Radio Luxembourg, then Radio London. Even today he thinks he was lucky to get the Radio 1 gig. Indeed his original contract was for just six programmes and, when the powers that be deliberated whether to keep him on or not, it was Brandon's producer who argued the case that no one could possibly establish themselves with the public in such a short space of time. Tony ended up staying with the BBC for fifteen years.

Although Tony's time on Radio 1 was 'a wonderful experience that I wouldn't have wanted to miss', it lacked the camaraderie that there'd been on the pirate ships. 'Sometimes you went for weeks on Radio 1 without seeing colleagues,' he says. This is something that Keith Skues picked up on, too: that the DJs at the station seldom mixed. 'The only time we all got together was for the photograph where we sat on the steps of All Souls Church.'

Still, Tony recalls some memorable characters working in Broadcasting House. There was the head of the sound effects department. 'He was a delightful chap. You could say to him, "Could I have the sound of some custard hitting a garden wall at the range of about thirty feet?" and he was able to bring out a selection.' Then there was this female producer who when elevated to an executive position suddenly started sending out all these jobsworth memos. These memos soon became legendary and were the talk of the department. People would say to each other, "Did you get a memo?" and the reply might be, "Oh yes, in fact I've had two today already." Then suddenly there was a hiatus. Tony recalls someone saying to him, "I haven't had a memo for about five days now."

"What do you think's wrong?" asked Tony.

"I think she's on the memo pause."

4

In order to have direct access to his people, Robin Scott presided over those early months at Radio 1 from an office on the second floor of Broadcasting House, directly above the continuity studios and the control room. 'Since I was listening a great deal of the day with the radio always on in the background, I could interfere and intervene, which I did frequently.' It was this hands-on approach and energetic demeanour that earned Scott the affectionate nickname of the 'white tornado'.

Generally liked and admired by the staff, Scott was an invaluable source of encouragement and positivity. 'He was very friendly with the young DJs,' recalls Paul Hollingdale, 'because they had no idea what it was going to be like at the BBC and Robin supported and encouraged them to become part of the team.' The pirate jocks had been working with hardly any structure at all and now they were within an organisation with a definite strict way of going about things. At least Scott ensured that they would have the freedom of the microphone and not be restricted to reading off carefully prepared scripts. 'We were all very conscious of the fact that the BBC were extending a lot of trust,' says Tony Brandon. 'Of course, it was in everybody's interest not to jeopardise their own show by saying something unsavoury or libellous on air.'

When choosing the first batch of Radio 1 DJs, Scott always intended to narrow the field down, so that only the best survived. The first casualty was Duncan Johnson, who was fired, according to a *Daily Mail* headline that October, because he was 'Too Old At 29'. Another ex-pirate weeded out was Simon Dee. The very first voice heard on Radio Caroline, by 1967 Dee had his own Saturday night TV chat show on the BBC and so was a ready-made personality for Radio 1. But juggling both jobs quickly became too much of a chore and, coupled with a reprimand for playing 'Jackie' by Scott Walker – a record then banned by the corporation due to its sexually risqué lyrics and drug references – he was gone by December. Dee continued with his TV show for another two years until a pay dispute forced the BBC not to renew his contract. The problem with Dee, some of his contemporaries felt, was the bigger he got, the more he overreached himself, with his ego often getting in the way. Moving to ITV on higher wages, he started throwing his weight around and making demands. After just a few months, with his new show failing in the ratings, Dee was dropped and his career never recovered. 'It was sad really,' says Chris Peers. 'He was the first DJ to really make the transition to television. He had so much going for him, but fame just went to his bloody head.'

One DJ who Scott was particularly keen to get on the air was John Peel, whom he counted as the most talented presenter to come out of the pirate ships. 'He was obviously the kind of slow-talking, uncompromising disc jockey that would attract an enormous cult following,' Scott said. Despite that, Peel was the last of the new DJs hired and, on the *Wogan* show in 1987, recalled his job interview with one of the BBC's top executives. 'He was very nervous,' remembered Peel, 'because he thought I was going to do something unforgiveable like rub drugs into the roots of his hair.' During the course of their chat, Peel happened to mention public schools. 'Oh,' said the BBC bigwig. 'You knew somebody at public school?'

'No,' answered Peel. 'I was at public school myself – Shrewsbury.'

'Shrewsbury! How's old Brookie?'

Straightaway Peel was in. 'From that moment on it was a case of "He may not look like one of us, but he is."'

Tony Blackburn was to tell a similar story, that one of the first things he was asked when he arrived for his interview was which school he went to.

There were many in BBC management who remained to be convinced about Peel's suitability. 'They tolerated him,' says producer Chris Lycett, who worked for years with Peel. 'They didn't understand him or the music he played. They thought he was a weirdo hippie.' Luckily for Peel, he fell into the orbit of producer Bernie Andrews. When Robin Scott decided to bring back *Top Gear*, featuring sessions from bands that were specially recorded for the BBC, he also opted to reinstall its original producer, Bernie Andrews. And Bernie's choice of presenter was John Peel. That didn't go down at all well. 'They weren't in favour of him at all. In fact, they were dead against him.'

Indeed, after Bernie booked Peel for the first show, he was told by management never to use him again. 'I'm sorry, you're too late,' Bernie told them. 'I've already booked him.' This was a complete fabrication, but by telling management that he'd already made arrangements with Peel's agent for the next eight weeks, Bernie had pulled a fast one because a verbal booking from a BBC producer was a legal contract. 'So, they couldn't get out of it, and I had hell to pay for that.'

Bernie was the perfect foil for Peel. Hailing from south-east London, he joined the BBC in 1957 as a technical operator, on the same day as Johnny Beerling, and worked his way up to a producing role on the old Light Programme. 'He was meticulous in what he did,' says friend and fellow producer Jeff Griffin. 'He allowed a lot of freedom for the musicians and most of the bands loved working with him on sessions because he would play things back to them. A lot of the previous producers had never done that. It was a case of, "OK, that's fine. Let's move on to the next one."'

Bernie's booking of the Beatles in their early days on *Saturday Club* was a significant step for the group, which they did not forget, and also the start of a friendship. 'The boys used to go round to his flat after the programme because they liked egg and chips, and Bernie used to cook it for them,' says DJ Andy Peebles. Bernie also gave the fledgling

Rolling Stones a leg up. After failing their BBC audition – 'Too black' and 'Too American-sounding' went the report, Bernie brought the group back in and gave them another chance.

There's a story that Bernie used to enjoy telling about himself, and no one has ever found out if it was true or not, of when he produced a session with Stevie Wonder. Traditionally in a BBC studio the flashing of a green light signifies 'ready to record'. To his eternal mortification, Bernie claimed to have said to Wonder, blind almost since birth, 'When you're ready, Stevie, on the green.'

Bernie lived for music, an enthusiasm he shared with Peel. And like Peel, Bernie built up a huge record library, at one time owning a collection of every 45 r.p.m. pop record released in Britain since 1958. Even more significant was Bernie's habit of sometimes taking home the master tapes of his music sessions instead of sending them to the BBC library. This was in breach of the rules, but it meant that much precious material escaped the BBC's infamous policy of wiping tapes to save money.

It was hoped that the returning *Top Gear* would feature the likes of Dusty Springfield, but Bernie and Peel had other ideas. Keen to champion the emerging prog and rock scene, they booked sessions from artists they thought worthy of recognition, resulting in a wide roster of acts appearing right through into the early seventies: Pink Floyd, David Bowie, Jimi Hendrix, The Who, Deep Purple, Fleetwood Mac, Black Sabbath, Led Zeppelin and T. Rex. The now legendary Peel sessions were born. These were bands that had yet to make it big and didn't have much hope of featuring on the more chart-leaning daytime shows. As Peel later observed: 'People at the time said, "How can you possibly play this awful stuff?" whereas now of course they're sort of pillars of the establishment.'

During the early months of *Top Gear*, several DJs were tried out, such as Pete Drummond and Tommy Vance, but Peel eventually emerged as the sole presenter. That success led to his hosting a show called *Night Ride*, which went out on Wednesday nights from midnight until 1 a.m., establishing John's reputation as a nocturnal DJ. 'This is the first of a new series of programmes on which you may hear just about anything,' he announced during that first broadcast. In fact, this was to prove something of an understatement and brought about Robin Scott's first run-in with the newly installed BBC chairman, Lord Hill.

Scott was in his office one morning when the phone rang. It was Lord Hill complaining about an interview Peel had conducted with John Lennon and Yoko Ono during which Yoko talked in great detail about a recent miscarriage. The feature included Yoko playing a cassette recording of the unborn baby's heartbeat over the air, which had caused distress to some listeners. Scott was summarily summoned to see Lord Hill and together they ran through a recording of the show. 'Well, I don't think there really is too much to worry about,' said Hill. 'But I think maybe your Mr Peel ought to be watched a bit.'

Worse was to come when Peel invited satirist John Wells onto the show to discuss the Nigerian Civil War (Biafran War). This was a major hot political potato at the time and a very emotive subject, with divided feelings on both sides. The Labour government were in support of the Nigerian government and BBC reportage favoured this position. So, when Wells and Peel argued against the official line, alarm bells rang and Scott was once again called in to see Lord Hill. Scott was made acutely aware that this was a far more serious situation than the Yoko Ono storm, given that an MP had made a complaint, and he was urged to go and see Sir John Hunt, Wilson's advisor on the conflict. 'John Peel and I were actually paraded before Hunt in his office somewhere in Whitehall and admonished,' Scott recalled. 'I remember John being absolutely taken aback by the whole proceeding. And that was a black mark against Peel, and I suppose to some extent against me, because in effect John Peel and I had been given a reprimand by the State.'

Someone else whose creative talents Scott admired was Kenny Everett, although he had not been given a regular programme on the new network. The BBC were only too aware of his erratic nature and that there'd been a series of disciplinary problems at Radio London. Instead Kenny was tucked away in a Tuesday lunchtime slot, hosting an hour-long record review programme called *Midday Spin*. And he wouldn't have got that if it hadn't been for the determination of a young producer called Angela Bond. At a production meeting she had raised the question of Kenny landing the *Midday Spin* gig to executive Mark White. 'Well, actually no,' White admitted. 'He's rather difficult to handle and we can't think of anybody who will be able to look after him.' White glanced over at Angela. 'Why, are you volunteering?'

'If it means the difference between having him and not having him, then yes, I'm volunteering,' she replied.

Angela's role in the development and success of Kenny as a DJ at Radio 1 cannot be underestimated. She brought out the best in him and as a partnership they worked brilliantly together. Like Kenny, Angela loved radio people and adored her craft. She was warm, friendly and blessed with a terrific sense of humour. She also wore colourful headgear, until a colleague told her that only lesbians at the BBC wore hats.

Stuck in *Midday Spin*, where the rigid format gave him little expression for his brand of anarchic spontaneity, Kenny felt lost and unloved. Or, as he put it: 'Seething every morning as I'd hear Tony Blackburn doing his daily breakfast show. Aaargh!' Everett never got on with Blackburn, calling him his arch nemesis, a man whom he needed little encouragement to ridicule and denigrate in public. According to Everett's friend Paul Gambaccini, Kenny's lifelong antagonism towards Blackburn began when he came to work at Radio London, having jumped ship from Radio Caroline. 'Kenny told me the story about how on the Radio London boat Tony just walked into the mess one day and announced that he was going to be a big star, and this really rubbed Kenny the wrong way. I think he just loved sending him up ever after, all from that one moment.'

Kenny wouldn't remain on the sidelines for long. After much badgering by Angela Bond, he won himself a two-hour Sunday morning show that December, and also played a prominent part in Radio 1's Christmas Day broadcast, when he was reunited with his old sparring partner on Radio London, Dave Cash. *The Kenny & Cash Show* had been a huge hit when it first went on the air in 1965, giving Radio London some of its biggest ratings, and it was a great idea bringing these mavericks back together, but, as Cash recalls, one sketch in particular ensured that it never happened again.

> Kenny comes on the mic and says, 'Can you say "bum" on the radio?' Well, by asking the question, you've said it. 'Just a minute, I'll find out. Hello, Mr Producer, can you say "bum" on the radio. Just a minute, I'll find out.' And then pre-records of different voices going all the way up five levels of management to the director-general, whose voice was godlike: 'Noooooo! I'm afraid you can't say "bum" on the radio.' Kenny says, 'Well, that's tough, I'm going to do it anyway. Bum-bum-bum-bum-bum-bum.' We thought it was a fairly funny sketch. They didn't.

For Kenny, this meddling typified his new employers. Already he was talking about the 'doomy atmosphere' at Broadcasting House, with its abundance of red tape and bureaucratic incumbents, its old-fashioned ideas and out-of-date equipment. He complained about there being more administrators on radio programmes than actual creative talent, that it was busy with people whose job it was to file voluminous typewritten data about how long records lasted and whether the programmes got out on schedule.

Nevertheless, with Angela Bond behind him, Kenny flourished in his new slot, spending hours in the studio late into the night mixing classical music or blasts of George Formby in-between the records, along with an array of comic characters, to create the most beautifully crafted and nutty soundscapes to punctuate his show. 'Kenny was a fantastic DJ,' says Johnnie Walker. 'And it didn't really matter what records he played. He did happen to play great records and he loved music, but it was the bits between the records that everybody tuned in for.'

Another DJ with rebellious tendencies was David Symonds, who'd already had his run-ins with BBC management on the Light Programme after coming up against the rigid format of *Breakfast Special*. 'You would say, "That was," or even "You've been listening to the band of the Coldstream Guards with 'The Radetsky March'. The time is six eleven, that is eleven minutes past six. And now we're going to hear..." and that was the de rigueur style. Well, obviously I wasn't going to do that.'

Instead, David brought a bit of light relief to the airwaves, a humorous take on things. This didn't go down well and he was summoned to the controller's office, a certain Dennis Morris. 'He was pacing up and down on his carpet and said, "I'm not really sure, David, that the nation is ready for humour at this time of day. I know myself, if I've been up for a while, had breakfast and been to the rear, that I'm actually ready for humour." But when they saw what the listening figures were, they withdrew their opposition very quickly.'

By the time David landed on the Light Programme, he'd already gained a great deal of experience. After reading botany at Oxford University, then dropping out just prior to taking his degree, much to the disappointment of his family, David moved to New Zealand. There he got his first radio job working for the New Zealand Broadcasting Corporation, reading the news and working as an announcer. By 1965, he was back in London, and, after a brief spell with Radio Luxembourg, landed a job with the BBC, working on the Home Service and the Third Programme, before joining the Light Programme.

Following his success on *Breakfast Special*, David took over the Sunday morning pop show *Easy Beat*, where he pulled in a regular audience of 13 million and gained the label of radio's 'Golden Boy', when, in the summer of 1967, *Nova* magazine published a feature titled 'Can you live without David Symonds? Millions can't.' All of that made him a natural choice for Radio 1. As he remembers: 'The top slot goes to the breakfast show guy and the runner-up gets the drivetime show, which is what I got.' The show, with its mixture of pop music and interviews, was really an extension of *Easy Beat*, although like many it was hamstrung due to needle-time restrictions. 'Only 40 per cent of my show came off gramophone records,' David confirms. It was also produced at Aeolian Hall in Bond Street, a venue that the BBC had originally taken over in the 1940s for the recording and broadcast of concerts and recitals. 'My routine,' says David, 'was to go in late morning where we'd discuss everything. The running order would be photocopied, and the records and the tapes, on little 5-inch spools, would be put into a hard box and I would take that and walk up from Bond Street to Broadcasting House in Portland Place literally with the show in my hand.'

Chris Peers represented David Symonds and liked him enormously. 'He was a charmer, a fascinating guy and a very good broadcaster. But he had an almost self-destructive personality.' Chris recalls one incident, in 1969, when David was doing an outside broadcast from Doncaster. Chris was in his office when he received a call from an irate hotel proprietor. David had left his suitcase behind. It contained a small trace of hash and the police had been called.

Meanwhile David was about to go out live on air from a Top Rank ballroom in the city. He'd warmed up the kids in the audience to a state of near-hysteria and Keith Skues, at Broadcasting House, was about to hand over to him, when David felt a firm touch on his shoulder. 'This guy said, "You're under arrest." I said, "Why?" He said, "For possession of illegal substances." I said, "Can I do the show?" And he said, "Yeah, OK." So, I went live on the air and had to pretend to be as enthusiastic as normal.' After the show the producer asked if he was coming out for a pint, but by then David was already in handcuffs, so made his excuses and declined. 'Then I was hauled off to the cop shop and busted.'

News quickly reached the BBC top brass and Chris Peers, along with his client, was ordered to go and see them. 'I felt like a naughty schoolboy,' recalls Chris. 'The upshot of it was that David was made to sign a piece of paper that he'd never smoke another joint. He said, "I don't think I want to do this." I said, "David, don't be a fucking idiot. Sign the fucking thing. Just sign it!" He was a real character.'

David knew they were going to make an example of him, but by far the worst aspect of the whole scenario was having to tell his father – he was deputy director-general of MI5.

5

As Radio 1, due to lack of funding, had to share a significant portion of its programming with Radio 2, it became almost impossible for the station to establish a separate identity. The result of all this was anomalies like Jimmy Young, very much a remnant of the old Light Programme and a controversial choice for Radio 1's mid-morning show. Considerably older than his peers, he was manifestly unsuited to the slick new pirate-like sound. 'Having people like Jimmy Young on Radio 1 just felt uncomfortable,' believes Tim Blackmore. 'It meant that the content of his show couldn't be wholeheartedly Radio 1, it had to take account of the rump of the Light Programme because it was also being broadcast on Radio 2.'

Robin Scott, however, took great store in Jimmy, and, although he came from the old school, he was quick to adapt to the ways of self-op, becoming one of its best exponents. There, however, an unfortunate incident the day Bobby Kennedy was assassinated. Jimmy was on air when Scott came into the studio with the news that the American politician had died of his injuries. The message was to play some appropriate music, Elgar perhaps, and to stay with that until they heard from him again. All was fine: after a short announcement was given by the newsreader, sombre classical music came on. Unfortunately, when Young came back on the air, he punched up, by force of habit, his own jingle, the *Jimmy Young Show* jingle – cue a fair amount of dismay and Scott's telephone ringing off its cradle. John

Peel was among the first to ring Scott up and say he thought it was a disgrace. As for Young himself, he was desperately upset after realising what he'd done, but by then it was too late.

Jimmy's producer was the formidable Doreen Davies. A straight talker, with a strong South London accent, Doreen had come up through the ranks of the BBC and was one of the very few women with any sort of power on the network. Doreen had a very clear idea of what the format of Jimmy's show should be and the kind of music to be played: easy-going songs, nothing too heavy. Indeed, Young was quite open about the fact that he didn't choose the music himself. As far as he was concerned, this was a personality-type show and his main job was to establish contact with the people at home.

Doreen visualised the typical listener as a housewife with two young children carrying out the housework, or girls working at a fish finger factory. 'If you've seen shoals of fish fingers hurtling down chutes and all the girls listening and bopping to the radio, you wouldn't play Jimi Hendrix,' Doreen explained. 'That would be too much.'

This kind of thinking inevitably led to Doreen's idea for a recipe slot, despite the fact that Jimmy himself knew next to nothing about cooking. The feature started with a speeded-up chipmunk voice asking, 'What's the recipe today, Jim?' These recipes were sent in by listeners and Doreen often tried them out first on her long-suffering husband, Derek. Her edict was that they had to be made from available ingredients and not too difficult to prepare. Young knew that the recipe slot was working after just one week when bus drivers and taxi drivers rolled down their windows and shouted out to him in the street, 'What's the recipe today, Jim?' Such was its success that there were even several best-selling books featuring the most popular recipes.

Bizarrely, Jimmy also took to singing during his show, having been a popular crooner in the 1950s; he had a recording contract with Decca and scored a number one hit with his version of 'Unchained Melody'. By 1972, though, he was ordered to stop after BBC officials felt that his 'sweet music' songs were out of keeping with a pop service. In truth, Jimmy's singing, along with those recipes, which had no place on a pop station, was all filler really, saving precious needle-time. And yet they endeared Jimmy to the nation and, within a year, he not only had seven million listeners but was the only DJ at the BBC who had his own post room and staff to sieve through the 400-plus letters and postcards that came in for him every day.

Someone who did very much fit in with the ethos of Radio 1 was Alan Freeman, affectionately known as 'Fluff'. Freeman started his career in his native Australia as an announcer on Melbourne local radio before settling in England in 1957. He vividly recalled the first time he listened to the BBC. A Frank Sinatra song was playing and when it finished a voice came on and said, 'And that was Frank Sinatra on a gramophone record.' Alan fell about laughing. Here was the BBC sounding so quiet and dainty, so far removed from the brash qualities of commercial radio that he'd been used to in Australia. 'My God,' he thought, 'they need a bit of livening up, don't they?' Alan joined the Light Programme in 1961 and his chart show *Pick of the Pops*, which he continued to present on Radio 1 until 1972, became a national institution.

Someone who came to be a huge admirer of Alan Freeman was Paul Gambaccini, especially in the way he used his voice. 'Alan had a musical sense of his own voice,' Paul says. 'I subsequently found out that he'd wanted to be a musical performer, opera, hence his love of classics and insertion of classical bits into his rock show. When Kate Bush's "Wuthering Heights" had fallen from the number one position, his introduction was simply: "And the wuthering has withered." His sense of words and his sense of sound – this is what radio is about.'

Alan's homosexuality was widely known amongst his colleagues, but no one made a fuss about it and it made no difference. 'He was a lovely person. We all loved him,' says Dave Cash. 'He was great fun.' Freeman was always available to help the new incumbents and share his years of experience. One of his mottos was: 'Remember, brain in gear before mouth in motion.' Tim Blackmore, who later became Freeman's manager, recalls that people would always go to him for advice. 'And he was very good to them. On some occasions he'd have four or five people in the studio while he was doing a programme.

They'd just be people who had written to him wanting advice or invited to pop in to get an autograph and watch his show.'

Along with Jimmy Young and *Pick of the Pops*, another programme to broadcast simultaneously on Radio 1 and 2 was *Junior Choice*, which from February 1968 was hosted by Ed Stewart. Despite his background on the pirate ships, nobody at Radio 1 really knew what to do with Ed. He was first tried out on a show called *Happening Sunday*, which didn't really happen at all and was taken off before the end of the first year. Jeff Griffin, *Happening Sunday*'s producer, recalls Ed storming into his office one day, asking why the show had been taken off. This was the first Jeff had heard about it. 'What do you mean we've been taken off?' he asked the DJ.

"I've just read it in the *Evening Standard*,' Ed replied.

'That was very typical BBC,' says Jeff today. 'You tended to find out what was going on by reading the papers rather than anybody telling you within the building.'

Jeff was just as disappointed as Ed was to lose the programme, his first on the new network. Jeff had joined the BBC as an engineer straight from school in 1959 and became one of its youngest producers, at the age of just 23, working in the popular music department. While for Jeff the end of *Happening Sunday* merely meant that he was posted to another assignment, for Ed it was the start of a whole new career direction. And it was all thanks to the show's theme tune, co-written by Jeff and featuring a school choir, with Ed playfully talking and joking around with the kids. Hearing this, producer Derek Chinnery liked the way Ed interacted with the children and thought that he'd be ideal to take over from Leslie Crowther as the new host of *Junior Choice*. Chinnery had been looking to replace Crowther for some time.

Junior Choice mixed pop favourites with novelty records and, at its peak, attracted 15 million listeners. The Queen Mother even confided to Ed that she never missed a show while taking her Sunday morning bath. Managing to popularise novelty songs like Max Bygraves' 'Pink Toothbrush', Terry Scott's 'My Brother' and Clive Dunn's 'Granddad', for which the nation can be grateful for or not, *Junior*

Choice made a household name out of Ed Stewart, and he remained its host for more than a decade. He also gravitated to television, hosting *Top of the Pops* and the children's favourite *Crackerjack*.

Another ex-pirate who had to wait a few months before getting his break was Dave Lee Travis. Hailing from Buxton in Derbyshire, Travis was a club DJ in the Manchester area before embarking on a self-promoted UK tour of ballrooms and theatres, presenting his own shows. Consequently, he was asked by Herman's Hermits to become manager and warm-up DJ on their 1964 tour of the United States. Back in England, he joined Radio Caroline before getting his first Radio 1 gig as the host of *Pop North*, which came live from Manchester every Thursday lunchtime. But it was in the seventies that Travis's public image was seared into the nation's consciousness as the 'Hairy Monster', later the 'Hairy Cornflake'. It was a nickname coined during an outside broadcast in London when Travis was interviewing the Norwegian actress Julie Ege and fellow DJ David Hamilton referred to them as beauty and the beast: 'The beautiful Miss Ege and the hairy monster from 2,000 miles up the M1 motorway.'

Also hoping to make an instant impact was Mike Raven, whose weekly R&B show on Sunday night was essential listening for every blues fan in the country. Mike stayed on until 1971, when he left Radio 1 to enjoy a successful career as an actor in several horror pictures. And then there was a certain Terry Wogan, at the time virtually unknown outside Ireland. The son of a Limerick grocer, Wogan was a Dublin bank clerk before becoming a presenter on RTE, Ireland's national television and radio broadcaster. It was a senior producer at the BBC, Mark White, who happened to hear a tape Wogan had sent in, who put him on *Midday Spin*, a half-hour selection of records on the Light Programme. This was 1966, and Wogan was still working from Ireland, his voice coming down the line from an RTE studio in Dublin. When Radio 1 started, Wogan was amongst several presenters, including Bob Holness and Mike Lennox, to host *Late Night Extra*, which featured news and music, mostly from various BBC house orchestras, and was simultaneously broadcast on Radio 2. It was a job that necessitated a weekly commute by plane from Dublin to London, much to the annoyance of his main employers RTE, who told him to concentrate on his work for them – or else. It wasn't long before Wogan found the decision made for him.

It was a strange set-up at Radio 1: while the studios themselves were situated within Broadcasting House, the production offices were based at Egton House, just across the way in Langham Street. Both buildings were connected by a small pedestrian tunnel under the road that led into the main foyer of Broadcasting House. That little bit of detachment meant that by and large BBC management let Radio 1 get on with it, 'probably through ignorance rather than anything else,' says producer Chris Lycett. 'We were always slightly at arm's length, we weren't part of the BBC. They could always say, "It's the rowdy lot in the house next door."'

Egton House wasn't a very attractive building. Noel Edmonds referred to it as 'a very low-grade civil service-type building'. It had four floors and a small basement. The Radio 1 offices occupied the third and fourth floors as well as a bit of the basement. The BBC's gramophone library was housed on the ground and first floors. By 1992, this library was reported to contain more than a million records. Reception was the domain of a stalwart BBC commissionaire. 'Firm and fair,' DJ Mike Smith remembered, 'and militarily upright.' Another well-known character who ruled reception for years was Clare, a tough cockney, always on the ball; no one got past her without good reason. Once, during the first Gulf War, Alan Yentob arrived but forgot his ID. Clare was adamant: he wasn't getting in. 'I don't know you from Adam,' she stoically announced. 'For all I know you could be a Shi'ite separatist.'

At Egton House, the third floor housed all the evening and weekend programmes, with the DJs having to share a series of poky offices with their producers. The fourth floor was the domain of the main weekday output, along with the offices of senior executives. Again, office space was cramped with DJs sharing with their producer.

The massive typing pool was open plan and referred to in derogatory terms as 'the play pen'. Indeed, calling it a typing pool was to denigrate the amazing work the secretaries did. They ran the show, really, due to the inordinate amount of paperwork involved in the operation. Every individual show's running order was methodically typed out. Every record or tape played had its details recorded for copyright payment purposes, with reporting sheets going to the Performing Rights Society and the Musicians' Union. The secretaries also fielded phone calls and visits from record pluggers, collected post and dealt with their producer's requirements.

Today music stations are completely digitised. It was a different story when Radio 1 started, especially in the way the programmes were constructed. Producers used devices which rather looked like washboards and were portrait A4-sized with plastic frames. The names of the records to be played were put on long strips of paper, which were then inserted into the frame, along with other information, such as what oldies were going to be played, features, news items and so on. Once finished, it was photocopied multiple times. A two-hour show might fill up as much as a ten-page script. This is why the programmes on Radio 1 were always referred to as strip shows. Amazingly, this was still the practice as late as 1990.

Another case of BBC bureaucracy was that if a DJ wanted an oldie, he would have to trawl through hundreds of filing cards to find a reference number, fill in a requisition set of forms, and then have to wait to have the records delivered to him. It was a production line. And while Radio 1 wasn't a 24-hour service in the early days, it did make big demands on people's time for what was a relatively small renumeration. 'The pay structure in the BBC was very much civil service-structured level pay grades,' recalls Chris Lycett. 'You worked your way up and kept your nose clean. And you never negotiated a salary, you accepted what they gave you. I never negotiated from the day I first walked into the BBC.'

While it's true to say that no show was broadcast from Egton House, there was a small studio which was used mainly for editing purposes or for making promos and jingles. Located in the bowels of the building, and close to one of the Underground tunnels, when a train came thundering past all work would have to stop until the room stopped shaking and the noise had abated. This studio was predominantly the domain of Kenny Everett, where he created all the wonderful and weird sounds for his show.

Starting in July of 1968, Kenny could be heard daily on an hour-long evening slot. *Foreverett,* as the new show was called, went ahead without the stewardship of Angela Bond. She believed it to be a mistake moving to a daily slot, that the high standards Kenny had managed to achieve would be difficult to maintain over such a gruelling schedule. While much of Kenny's show was unscripted and off the cuff, it still took two or three days of preparation and at the end of each broadcast he would be emotionally and physically drained. Angela was worried that he was taking on too much and that her replacements didn't know how best to handle his talent. Kenny waved her concerns away and forged ahead regardless.

Within a few weeks, cracks began to appear. Kenny started turning up unannounced in Angela's office complaining that his new producers were trying 'to get inside my whole body and work it themselves'. He was exhausted, unable to churn out conveyor-belt genius. Angela Bond agreed to come to the rescue – but on one condition. She told her bosses that she would only do it if Kenny was given a Saturday morning show. They agreed.

Along with Doreen Davies, Angela Bond was the only female producer of a pop radio show at the BBC and operating in what was very much a male-dominated environment. It was something that Johnnie Walker picked up on when he arrived a year later. 'It used to annoy me that the BBC was so sexist. At Egton House they had an entire team of secretaries working for all the producers, but they were never thought of as producer material. There was hardly any promotion, they were just girls who did the typing. I remember one girl there who was a really on-the-ball secretary and she eventually left to become a producer on a commercial station, before later coming back to the BBC as a producer. She had to leave to be thought of as a producer.'

There seemed also to be a paucity of young producers eager to push the envelope or buck the system. One of them was Tim Blackmore, who joined Radio 1 from the World Service and worked as a production assistant on the breakfast show before taking over full responsibility. Although Tim and Tony Blackburn were around the same age, Blackburn was vastly more experienced about the mechanics of running a pop service. It was Blackburn who explained to Tim the format of how each half hour used to work on Radio London. 'And I embraced the idea,' says Tim, 'and introduced it to the breakfast show, which it hadn't had before, which is where every half hour is identical. The first record played was from 1 to 10 of the playlist, the second record played was from 11 to 40, the third is a brand new one, the fourth is probably an oldie, then you have a 1 to 10 again, then an 11 to 40, so there's a consistent dynamic.'

Tim liked Blackburn, calling him, 'the archetypal DJ', but the two men never developed a close association. One of the problems was politics. Tim was from a Liberal left background, while Blackburn was public-school educated and a staunch Tory. 'On more than one occasion we had to apologise when Tony would have a go at trade unions. It took some time for him to realise, given the impartiality of the BBC, that there were limits beyond which you couldn't go.'

Personal politics was always a no-no on Radio 1. Blackburn went one step too far in 1973 when he was performing in a pantomime during the tense backdrop of a national miners' strike. When the lights suddenly went out on stage, he improvised a bit of comedy business that it was the miners' fault and they all ought to get back to work. It made the press and he was reprimanded and taken off the air. Douglas Muggeridge, then controller of Radio 1, suggested that he go on holiday, but Blackburn decided to stay at home. It wasn't long before a reporter showed up at the door, wanting to know why he wasn't at work. Blackburn feigned a sore throat but knew that it wouldn't fool anyone for long. When more of the press showed up the following day, he called the office. 'Oh, for God's sake,' cried Muggeridge. 'Come back, then!'

Dave Lee Travis also came a cropper during his stint on the breakfast show in the late seventies when he encouraged his listeners to complete a protest form against seal clubbing that was in the morning newspapers.

These were heady days for young producers like Tim Blackmore, still in his early twenties and finding himself suddenly thrust into a different world – one 'of sheer excitement', as he called it. Everyone seemed to want a piece of him, and there were invites galore to media functions. One of the first he recalls going to was a record launch for a band called Grapefruit. 'I walked in and standing by a pillar to my left were all four Beatles. And I remember thinking, "Jesus Christ, I'm in a room with the Beatles." I was in a privileged position at Radio 1 and I never forgot it. I was choosing what the nation listened to, with no expertise whatsoever other than a love of music. As it happened, it turned out I was good at it.'

Then there were the lunches with music executives and pluggers hoping to bend his ear into playing their records. One of his very first experiences of pluggers, who were very much a breed apart, was with Dave Margereson, later the manager of Supertramp. They'd gone to a steak restaurant near Broadcasting House. 'Dave said, "As you're my guest, would you like to choose our wine?" I look at this wine list. I had never seen a wine list in my life.' Coming from a poor background, and with a father who was a teetotal Methodist clergyman, Tim's experience of fancy restaurants bordered on zero. He decided to own up. 'Dave, I have never seen a wine list in my life. I'm afraid I can be no use to you.' Margereson looked at him from across the table. 'This is the first time I've taken someone out to lunch, so I don't know what to do, either.'

In the days of the Light Programme, Derek Chinnery devised a show called *Pop Inn*, which took place every Tuesday at the Paris studio on Lower Regent Street, a converted cinema that the BBC had taken over. It was an hour of music for which tickets were available for the public to 'pop in' and see popular artists of the day interviewed on stage. Johnny Beerling suggested to Chinnery they modify that show and call it the *Radio 1 Club*. Entrance would be free: listeners were merely required to send in their details to receive a membership card. And they did in huge numbers: by the end of the first week they had 15,000 applications.

Launched that October, the *Radio 1 Club* turned out to be an instant success, going out every lunchtime on weekdays from the Paris studio, featuring live music and requests. Keen to avoid any accusation of being too London-centric, Beerling quickly broadened its scope, taking the show to places like Birmingham, Manchester, Glasgow, Belfast and Swansea. 'We were always looking for different locations,' said Beerling. 'Also places that identified with the image of the DJ, so Rosko would do it at discos and ballrooms, Alan Freeman at youth clubs and Ed Stewart in schools.' Going around the country also presented the opportunity to lend exposure to up-and-coming local musical artists.

Because of union rules, regular studio engineers, trained in the delicate process of balancing live music to acquire the best sound, were not allowed to work on the programme. This meant that local outside broadcast engineers came in, most of whom were only really used to covering things like football matches. 'Some of them were very good and did their best,' wrote Beerling in his memoirs, 'others were grumpy old buggers who hated pop music and you were lucky if they managed to get the vocal microphone opened up when the lead singer started to sing.'

During its run, the *Radio 1 Club* courted a fair bit of controversy. There was a report of fans attacking a BBC commissionaire at one event, while in 1970 a bomb scare prompted Dave Lee Travis and 200 people to be evacuated. In 1971, another bomb scare hit the *Radio 1 Club* in Shrewsbury civic hall. This time DJ Stuart Henry refused to leave and continued broadcasting.

If anything, the *Radio 1 Club*, now with 280,000 members, proved too popular. Beerling recalls the BBC receiving numerous complaints of kids skipping school in order to attend. A group of students in

Falkirk even threatened strike action because their headmaster refused permission for them to attend the show at the local town hall. Something had to be done, and the *Radio 1 Club* was taken off the air for almost a year, returning late in 1972 at the new time of 5 p.m. to avoid any truancy issues.

Beerling was now carving out a path as one of the most important producers at the station. Indicative of some of the new blood coming into the BBC, Beerling did not come from a privileged background or an Oxbridge education. Born in 1937, he was raised in a small village in Kent with no mains electricity; a battery-powered radio was the sole source of entertainment. During National Service, he worked as a radio fitter, then, posted to Aden, he did a bit of broadcasting on the forces network. Demobbed, his dad took him to a radio show that the BBC used to hold annually at Earl's Court. At the recruitment desk, he managed to secure an interview which led to a job as an engineer. He walked into Broadcasting House for the very first time in October 1957, hardly realising it would be his home for the next thirty-six years.

While the technical side of the job did appeal to him, what Beerling really wanted to do was on a more creative level: to put programmes together. The problem was that all the producers and studio managers seemed to have been to university and had degrees like sociology. Undeterred, Beerling applied anyway. 'Somebody took a brave decision and said, "We mustn't be classist about this, we'll take this working-class oik and let him train as a studio manager and see if he has any artistic bent."'

Beerling went to the BBC training school for studio managers at Wood Norton in Evesham, where for three months he learned about tape editing, sound balance and all manner of technical business. After some initial work in the Overseas Service, he was transferred to the Home Service and began working on shows like *Housewives' Choice* and *Pick of the Pops*, before graduating to the gramophone department.

Arriving at the BBC in the early sixties, Tony Wilson also trained at Wood Norton. Having applied straight after he left school, Tony was the youngest person ever to be accepted on a studio manager's course and, like Beerling, was one of a very select few who didn't come from university. As a sound engineer, Tony worked for the World Service but quickly gravitated to pop and light entertainment programmes. Such was his reputation that he was seen as a natural to work at Radio 1.

Owing to the needle-time regulations, a great deal of live music was being recorded and played on Radio 1. Tony worked as an engineer on a lot of these sessions which were taking place day in, day out. There were so many of them that more than half a dozen studios in London, including at Maida Vale and the Aeolian Hall on New Bond Street, were booked pretty much flat out to service all the different programmes on Radios 1 and 2 with music content.

With so many sessions going on, this inevitably led to mountains of reel-to-reel tape and not very much space to store all of it. A decision was made that after a tape's contractual use, which normally was two broadcasts, it was to be wiped and recycled, the view at the time being that it wasn't of any value. 'One or two producers and engineers would keep the odd session that they thought was particularly memorable,' says Tony. 'As far as management was concerned, it was seen as just part of the fodder.'

For Tony, the biggest gripe was the equipment being used by the BBC, a lot of which – including hulking great mixing desks with rotary faders and quarter-inch mono or stereo tape recorders – dated back to the war. Bernie Andrews once compared the equipment he had to work on as 'out of the Ark'. Musicians who came in for sessions couldn't believe how out of date it was compared to commercial studios. Indeed, The Who refused to be recorded by the BBC. In the end, Bernie got special permission to hire a commercial studio for the afternoon so that the session could take place. The Who even recorded a special jingle for Radio 1.

Another sound engineer, Chris Lycett, recalls working on an early seventies Bowie session at the Maida Vale studio. 'Bowie walked into the studio and there was this archaic equipment. The casing was painted battleship grey and the desk was built by Mulliner Park Ward, who used to build Rolls-Royce bodies, so it was built to last. Bowie took one look at it. "Fuck me," he said. "It looks like the flight deck of a Lancaster bomber." I knew exactly what he meant.'

The norms for recording sessions in those days was to record pretty much everything as live. There was not a lot of stopping and starting. And getting something like four songs recorded and mixed in a relatively short period of time wasn't easy. 'Inevitably sessions got extended,' says Tony Wilson, 'and it became normal practice to record on one day and then mix on another day. Even so, the amount of work meant that it was sensible and economic to have really good equipment to be able to get things done in that time.'

Unfortunately, the BBC never quite saw things the same way and for years their studios lagged woefully behind the commercial sector. Just think, all that great music of the late sixties and early to mid-seventies was recorded on inadequate equipment. But thanks to great engineers, stuff like the *Peel Sessions* came out remarkably well and are today treasured recordings.

For years, people like Jeff Griffin, Tony Wilson and Chris Lycett were vocal advocates for better studio facilities. 'It did take the BBC quite a long time to find the will and the money to move into multi-track working,' says Tony. 'But once it got its act together, it poured money in, got the latest top-end equipment, turned the studios into proper studios and was at the forefront of technology rather than lagging sadly behind.'

It wasn't just the equipment that caused problems. Even during live session work in studios, the unions held sway. Tony Brandon recalls one particularly militant shop steward. 'There was an agreement with the Musicians' Union that their members would not perform in a humidity level above a certain point. And in the middle of this recording session suddenly the orchestra ground to a halt. This fella had a temperature gauge hanging from a music stand and saw that the needle had gone past the allocated point and he just stopped the session. There's a musician with heart.'

★

Pete Brady's afternoon show was going well, despite the occasional misstep, such as the time he interviewed the English matador Henry Higgins. 'My producer and I discovered after the interview that we shouldn't have done that because bullfighting was banned on the BBC. There was a bit of a kerfuffle over that when people wrote in and complained.'

Then there was the time Pete was away in Europe and heard a record being played constantly on the radio called 'Je t'aime… moi non plus' by Serge Gainsbourg and the English actress Jane Birkin, complete with suggestive sound effects of very heavy breathing. 'I thought, "Oh, that's cool," bought a copy, brought it back and slammed it on the air,' remembers Pete. 'And I got in real trouble because it was banned here. I didn't know that.'

Trading on his client's popularity, Pete's agent managed to find him television work on *Magpie*, a new children's show that was ITV's answer to *Blue Peter*. Pete had never done television before but was keen to give it a try. 'I really enjoyed doing *Magpie*. I was twenty-six and it was every young guy's dream. I played around with planes and racing cars. I was the John Noakes of *Magpie*. But it soon became apparent I couldn't do both jobs.' And it was Radio 1 that got the push.

His replacement was Dave Cash, who'd been with the station since the beginning but thus far used only sparingly. 'I think I was chosen because both Pete and I had a Canadian twang.' Born in Bushey in Hertfordshire, Dave emigrated to Canada with his family in the late 1940s but returned to the UK in 1964, drawn by the romance of pirate radio. It was on Radio London that Dave made a name for himself, thanks to an engaging broadcasting style. 'Red Robinson, the famous Canadian disc jockey, said to me, "If you want to be good at this, talk to people, not at them." And I've always kept to that.' Working at Radio 1, however, was a whole new level of different. 'Radio 1 was the thing. There was still no commercial radio in this country, so if you wanted to hear pop music, it was Radio 1. Your audience was counted in millions.'

With such huge audiences, it was no surprise that the DJs on Radio 1 became national figures. Crowds regularly turned up outside Broadcasting House hoping for their autographs. 'They were as big as the pop stars,' says Tim Blackmore. 'You couldn't walk down the street with Tony Blackburn any more than you could walk down the street with the Beatles. I've driven cars with a DJ inside and young girls hanging onto the boot. Scary stuff.'

As host of the biggest show on air, Blackburn was really the face of Radio 1 and got the lion's share of publicity. He was also the most in-demand personality, working almost non-stop beyond his duties on the station with television appearances, supermarket openings, promotional events and discos. 'There was one week when I only slept for about eight hours and I had a couple of blackouts,' he told the *Guardian* in 2007. 'Whenever I opened up a shop, I had to have police there. I did one supermarket opening in Norwich where there were so many people that the windows caved in.' Blackburn did a lot of supermarket openings. He once joked that he was booked by the same supermarket he'd opened twenty years before, only this time they wanted him to go back and close it down.

Sometimes the attention was unwanted. Tony Brandon recalls a woman turning up at his home with a suitcase and telling his wife that she had come to stay. 'People listen to DJs every day and so they become part of their lives,' he says. 'And because of the informality of the job, they do feel as if they know you.'

The fame affected people in different ways, negatively in the case of Emperor Rosko, as he freely admits. 'I dealt with it very badly. I was probably a king-sized prick. I had absolutely no time for any answer that didn't please me.'

It didn't take long for the DJs to exploit their fame by showing up to perform at dance halls, pubs and night clubs. 'That's how a DJ worth his salt made any money back in those days,' claims Rosko. A DJ could earn far more in just a single night spinning records in a club than his entire weekly wage packet from the BBC. Dave Cash played a lot of the Mecca halls around the country and got so busy he had to hire a driver. 'I might be up in Leeds or Manchester and be through at eleven o'clock and be on Radio 1 noon the next day, so I'd have to sleep on the way back. That's what we all did.'

It was Rosko who took all this to the next level when Dave Lee Travis showed him a mobile disco that he'd knocked together to tour the clubs. Thinking big, Rosko brought in some professional help and built up a system that was at the time the world's largest mobile discotheque, the Rosko International Roadshow. It was a huge success. Rosko's jive-talking style did, however, present a problem when he showed up at a reggae club one night. When he arrived in his van, the man on the door refused to let him in. 'You're not Rosko, man! You're white!' This happened quite often. 'They all thought I was a black guy – and I couldn't get in!' To prove his identity, Rosko would invariably have to go into his DJ patter. 'Have mercy!' he'd begin and a look of instant recognition would flash across the face of the club owner. 'You're him!' they'd say.

Playing the clubs up and down the UK, Rosko picked up on what was popular on the dance floor and incorporated it into his show; he certainly helped to popularise soul and reggae music. He did sometimes criticise his fellow DJs for playing overly 'poppy' music. He was also renowned for re-editing some of the songs that he played on air. 'If a record was good but not great, I picked bits out of them and chopped them down and just played a one-minute version of it. It got a lot of artists very crazy when I did that.'

One DJ who made a habit of travelling all over the country was Jimmy Savile. His show *Savile's Travels* went out on a Sunday and saw him going around the UK with a reel-to-reel tape recorder, talking to members of the public. Savile was already a recognisable personality, familiar from Radio Luxembourg and the first presenter on BBC TV's *Top of the Pops* in 1964, and he was shrewd enough to see how Radio 1 fared before agreeing to join up in 1968.

When he arrived, no one at Radio 1 was quite sure what to make of him. 'Jimmy was something of an enigma,' wrote Beerling. 'In all the time I knew him he never stopped being "Jimmy Savile". Yet I always thought there was a different Jimmy underneath the part he played, but no matter how hard I looked I never found it.' Not many did, but it was clear that he was hiding in plain sight from the start of his Radio 1 career.

It was during his time on *Savile's Travels* that one of the most infamous Savile stories was meant to have occurred. Viewed by some as an urban myth, it did the rounds of Egton House for years, and in hindsight, following the revelations of Savile's sexual crimes, is even more disturbing. Because of the immense amount of travelling required, Savile brought along with him a caravan. At the end of one personal appearance, a young member of the audience was invited inside by Savile. A member of the production team was sitting close by when a little old lady arrived.

'Where's Jimmy?' she asked.

'Er, he's gone already, I'm afraid,' the man lied. By this time the movement of the caravan indicated that some kind of physical activity was going on inside.

'Oh dear,' said the old lady. 'Well, please will you give him this from me?' She reached into her bag and handed over a jar of marmalade. 'I made it myself. It's for Jimmy. To thank him for everything he's doing for the young people.'

6

Towards the end of 1968, Robin Scott was invited to lunch by David Attenborough. During the meal, Attenborough revealed his intention to leave his post as controller of BBC 2 to become director of programmes, making him responsible for the output of both BBC television channels. Scott was asked to be his replacement. Obviously, Scott was attracted by the thought of going back to television and following in Attenborough's trailblazing footsteps, but at the same time he was enjoying himself immensely at Radio 1. In the end, the pull of BBC 2 was too much and he left Broadcasting House to go to Television Centre in White City. He was to look back on his time at Radio 1 as one of the highlights of his broadcasting career, having managed to create something that was to endure for years in the form he'd put together.

Scott's replacement as controller of Radio 1 and 2 was Douglas Muggeridge. 'It was an extraordinary choice,' says David Symonds. 'He was a complete enigma.' Yes, Muggeridge was very much a BBC man, but he didn't really have much time for pop music. Public-school educated, Muggeridge started his career as a reporter on the *Liverpool Daily Post* and joined the BBC as a producer in 1956. Johnny Beerling came to regard him as 'a bit out of his depth', while producer Jeff Griffin didn't think it was a very bright appointment. 'It was a case of people like me shrugging their shoulders and going, "Well, OK, let's see how we can work around this because he doesn't know what he's doing.'" Muggeridge quickly acquired the nickname 'Doug the mug'.

Radio 1 was still very much ruled by the old brigade, people who had little sympathy or knowledge about pop music. 'They were completely misplaced,' said Bernie Andrews. 'These were the people that were making quite important decisions and you had to work with them. The management of the networks and the departments involving pop music were completely out of touch.' Ian Trethowan, for example, the managing director of BBC Radio, once threatened not to have any pop guests in the building because there was too much noise and cacophony in the streets from screaming fans when David Cassidy came in.

And there was Mark White, head of Radio 1 programmes. Tony Brandon recalls him as 'a military gent in his fifties with this wax moustache, not someone you would immediately associate with The Doors. He was a bit of an anachronism. But he was a very nice man.' White was a lover of vintage cars. Tim Blackmore remembers a music function where White was accompanied by his wife. 'At one point, Aidan Day asked Mark's wife what Mark liked doing in his spare time. And she said, quite innocently, "Most of all he likes judging Bristols." If you know your rhyming slang, you'll understand why at that point the table collapsed. Mark was, in fact, a renowned expert on Bristol motor cars.'

To be fair, White knew his talent. One day White came into Blackmore's office with a cassette tape that he wanted to play him. 'This chap has got a very unusual broadcasting style,' White said. 'Tell me what you think of it because I'm wondering whether we should employ him.' White played the tape. It was Bob Harris and he was subsequently hired.

For the DJs there wasn't much interaction with management. It was the producers who kept them in line. 'There were layers of bureaucracy,' says Dave Cash. 'It was junior, medium and high. A junior couldn't go and speak to a high, he had to go through a medium. And at that time, it was all Oxbridge.'

55

Nor was there much feedback from management. DJs might get a word from the producer about audience figures, but that was about it. There was very little on what the hierarchy thought about a show or an individual DJ's performance. Here was an organisation in the business of communication, dedicated to sending its message out to the millions, and yet they didn't communicate that well with their own employees. 'You never found out who it was that made the decisions,' states Tony Brandon. 'The chain of command was quite obscure.'

There was a uniquely BBC thing called a 'programme review board'. At this, various senior people from different departments met up once a month to listen to specific programmes and give their verdict on what they'd heard. God forbid if any of this filtered down to the DJs. Tony Brandon recalls bumping into one of these people in the corridor and asking, 'How did the review board go?' The casual answer was, 'Oh, they seem to like you.'

This lack of feedback hardly instilled confidence, especially since most of the jocks were on short-term contracts. In the pre-commercial radio days, the BBC rather had the field of play to themselves and could call the shots. This policy extended for years. Noel Edmonds confirms that during his fourteen years at Radio 1, he never had longer than a thirteen-week contract. 'The management were gods because I knew they could destroy this whole thing for me just by deciding that actually "he doesn't fit any more". There was a culture of fear. It was in their interest to keep everybody rather nervous about whether or not they were going to change things.'

For someone like Pete Drummond, this just reeked of internal politics. For him, joining the BBC was rather like joining the civil service, while at the same time there was always a feeling that DJs didn't fully belong, that because of the contract situation they felt they were always freelancers. 'I remember coming towards the end of one contract and a producer at Egton House looked at me and said, "What are you doing in here? I thought your contract had ended." I said, "No. Not yet." So, there was this feeling of not being appreciated.'

★

One of the more high-profile pirate DJs who didn't come to work for Radio 1 at the start was Johnnie Walker. Following the pirate shutdown, Radio Caroline was the only station to carry on broadcasting, by moving its entire operation to Dutch waters. Walker and the others who stayed on with him continued to work in full knowledge of the legal implications. 'We were going into exile. You couldn't come back into the UK because you might be arrested. It was tough.'

Johnnie Walker owes his passion for music to his elder brother who loved rock'n'roll and that's when he first heard Elvis and Chuck Berry. Living in Birmingham, it was difficult to pick up the pirate frequencies when they first arrived on the scene. 'I used to have to string a long piece of wire out of my bedroom window all along the roof, which enabled me to pick up Radio London and occasionally Caroline.' Working as a car mechanic and salesman, Johnnie spent most of his spare cash buying records and landed a job as a DJ in his local Locarno ballroom. 'What I loved about discotheques was that you could play the music loud and there were no parents around to tell you to turn it down.' That exposure led to other jobs. Soon Johnnie was gigging up to four nights a week. Coming into work tired and late led to an ultimatum from his garage manager. Remembers Johnnie: '"One man cannot serve two masters," the garage manager said to me. "You've got to decide between the motor trade, where you've got a good future, or being a disc jockey. I'll give you two weeks to think about it."'

'I don't need two weeks,' said Johnnie. 'I'll tell you now, I'll be a disc jockey.'

When Johnnie got home his dad was furious. 'What are you going to do now?' Johnnie said he might travel round the world or work on the pirate ships. Which he did.

The end finally came for Radio Caroline in March 1968, when the boat was towed back to Amsterdam due to mounting unpaid bills. It was then that Johnnie discovered he'd been blacklisted by the BBC; every producer at Radio 1 had been sent a memo that read: 'On no account must you employ the services of Johnnie Walker until at least a year has gone by and the taint of criminality has subsided.' And that's pretty much what happened.

By the spring of 1969, all was apparently forgiven and Johnnie was given a Saturday afternoon show. At the time, this was seen as something of a try-out slot, as it competed with a plethora of sports coverage on other channels. Johnnie recalls that his debut happened to fall on Cup Final day and, as a consequence, hardly anybody was listening. But that didn't stop the nerves. 'You knew that there were seven floors above you, with a lot of executives, and they all were able to tune in to every BBC network in their offices. So, you knew that a lot of people were listening in and with that comes a lot of pressure.'

Like his pirate predecessors, Johnnie found it difficult at first adapting to having a producer, one of whom used to come into the studio and sit next to him at the desk with his stopwatch and clipboard. 'I told him he should be on the other side of the glass, with the studio engineer, so he did eventually move. On Radio 1 it was very difficult to be the same spontaneous DJ that you had been on the pirates. Eventually I got used to it and found the balance. If I got a bollocking once every two weeks, I thought, "I'm just doing about right here."'

Another surprise was the way Broadcasting House still appeared to operate in the manner it had done in the old days. 'If you wanted a drink, your producer used to ring the canteen and then someone used to come down, mostly women in their waitress uniform, with a tray with a silver pot of coffee. Very BBC.'

Helping him to find his feet was Teddy Warwick, who became something of a mentor. One of the senior producers, Warwick was able to explain the BBC structure to Johnnie, 'because I found it quite odd. It still had a bureaucratic way of doing things and Teddy was very good at calming me down at times.'

Johnnie wasn't the only one who warmed to Warwick; he was much loved around the BBC. 'First and foremost, Teddy loved music,' says Tim Blackmore. 'And he loved music makers. He also had a great sense of humour. And he was worldly-wise.' A great lover of jazz, having been a jazz producer, he embraced the concept of Radio 1, and his contribution in helping launch the station has been much overlooked. While it was Robin Scott who oversaw things at the start, it was people like Teddy, along with Beerling and Chinnery, who selflessly worked at the coalface.

As for his fellow DJs, Johnnie got along pretty well with them while at the same time being acutely aware that, if the rota was changed or he fell out of favour with the management, any one of them could get his show. 'Radio 1 was a highly competitive situation.'

Even if a programme was doing well, it didn't mean a DJ was safe. Dave Cash's afternoon show was very popular with listeners until one day he was told, 'We want to try this new chap from Ireland, his name's Terry Wogan, and he'll be taking over for the afternoons.' Wogan had impressed Radio 1 executives covering for *The Jimmy Young Show* while the veteran was on holiday. Having previously commuted from Dublin to London, it was this regular slot in the afternoons that led Wogan to move his family to England.

As for Cash, he was shifted to Sundays and a *Parkinson*-style chat show. While he managed to attract a guestlist that included the likes of Peter Sellers, Spike Milligan, John Cleese and Antonia Fraser – fascinating people whom Cash enjoyed meeting – the format didn't suit him. 'My agent said I was foolish because the BBC wanted to groom me for television. "It's not me," I said. "I'm a disc jockey and that's where I want to stay."'

It wasn't just the DJs who faced being moved around, producers, too, could find themselves working on different shows, whether they liked it or not. One producer who felt particularly hard done by was Bernie Andrews, who had built up a formidable partnership with John Peel. Always ready to back his man, when management complained that Peel's vocal delivery made him sound as if he was on drugs and that he should be dropped, Bernie argued his case. 'Bernie believed desperately in Peel,' says Chris Lycett, 'and in what he played and what he was doing. But Bernie wasn't very good at handling the management. He was quite bolshie and confrontational.' According to Pete Drummond, who landed a job with Radio 1 thanks to Bernie, the producer was a maverick. 'He definitely liked to stir things up.'

Bernie cared nothing for the nuances of BBC protocol and thought nothing of lighting up the odd jazz cigarette at work, smoked surreptitiously under his desk, with the windows wide open. Once he put on a pair of frogman's flippers and walked into the office of the department head to complain about the damp in his office.

By the spring of 1969, management came to the conclusion that Bernie and Peel were too much of a handful and needed to be split up. Bernie was devastated and felt even more persecuted when he was assigned to what he deemed to be formulaic daytime flotsam and jetsam. He did, however, remain a significant figure. Late in 1972, he heard a tape by a new band that couldn't get a record deal. He fixed them their first ever radio session, with Peel hosting and Bernie producing, that offered the band an ideal opportunity to showcase themselves nationally. The band were called Queen.

Bernie's replacement on the Peel show was John Walters, an ex-art teacher who'd been a trumpet player in the Alan Price Set, before drifting into broadcasting and joining Radio 1 in 1967 as a staff producer. 'John was a huge talent,' says fellow producer Tony Wilson. 'He had such acute observational powers and ways of analysing the world and stripping it down to its bare bones. He was mercilessly unkind to Peel, always taking the piss out of him, because Peel was very much a head in the clouds kind of guy.'

According to Chris Lycett, Bernie never forgave Walters for taking over what he considered to be his gig. But perhaps for Peel it was a change for the better. 'Walters managed Peel much better because Bernie just got up management's nose,' says Lycett. 'There's little doubt that Peel wouldn't have lasted as long as he did if he'd been left with Bernie.'

Someone else on the move was David Symonds, who lost his drivetime show and went over to Sundays. That he saw it coming didn't make the decision any easier to swallow. When he first started on Radio 1, Robin Scott decided to pair him with Ron Belchier, his old producer from the Light Programme's *Easy Beat*. 'I don't think that's a very good idea,' David had told Scott. 'I've taken this thing about as far as I can go with Ron. I think to try and go any further with it would be pushing it.' While they'd worked well together on *Easy Beat*, David found Ron heavy maintenance. 'Let's say he was changeable,' David says. 'But they didn't listen. I was paired with Ron on that drive show and eventually it all fell apart.'

The truth was that Belchier had started to drink heavily. 'He was not a good bet in the afternoon,' confirms David. 'If you wanted to see him about something you needed to do it in the mornings.' As things carried on, David began to become increasingly concerned. Finally, he approached Donald MacLean, assistant head of department at Aeolian Hall, and told him about Belchier's drink problem, suggesting that he and Belchier cease working together. But David didn't get the response he was hoping for. MacLean thanked him for going to see him. 'And then overnight I was removed from the show,' David remembers. What made matters worse was that his replacement was Tony Brandon, who happened to be David's best friend, 'so that was deeply hurtful'.

Just a couple of weeks later Ron Belchier was diagnosed with a stomach ulcer and taken to hospital. Still, it annoys David that his bosses at the BBC saw fit to throw him to the wolves while remaining loyal to a producer who was clearly unable to properly function.

7

By the close of the sixties and the start of a new decade, Radio 1 was in pretty decent shape. It still had its detractors; Labour MP Gwilym Roberts even went so far as to argue for a general ban on the continuous broadcasting of pop music because many of his constituents were complaining of headaches.

Although the Musicians' Union had turned down a new bid by the BBC for an increase in needle-time, the station was gradually gaining more of a musical identity, helped considerably by a reduction in programme sharing with Radio 2. Much of the specialist music, such as jazz, country and folk, had also been shifted across to Radio 2, leaving more space for the rock and progressive bands that were starting to become popular.

Things were beginning to change in other areas, too, notably when Annie Nightingale became the first female DJ on Radio 1, although she had to fight prejudice from the get-go. An only child, Annie was born in London and studied at the Regent Street Polytechnic, now the University of Westminster, before going into music journalism. Such was her passion for music that she always wanted to play it rather than write about it, but it never crossed her mind that she might work for the BBC. It seemed so remote a possibility, especially when she was told in no uncertain fashion by a senior executive that female presenters came over on the radio as 'too fishwifey'. These views were fairly common. In the opening weeks of Radio 1, weather presenter

Rosie O'Day had received twelve complaints merely due to the fact that she was a woman. 'Please, please spare us from Rosie O'Day reading the weather forecast,' wrote one listener. 'It sounds more like a children's fairy story. I'm sure she is a charming girl, but let us stick to a man for the weather news!'

While Annie did eventually begin working sporadically on the Light Programme in the mid-sixties, including contributions to *Woman's Hour*, trying to get a job on Radio 1 when it launched proved problematic. Despite her experience as a music journalist and presenter, she was rejected because of the assumption that DJs had to be male. Doreen Davies talked about the Radio 1 jocks as 'her boys'. To Doreen they were surrogate husbands for listeners. While the real husbands went out to work, the DJ came into the house during the day via the radio and entertained the housewives. 'That's why Doreen didn't want women on,' claims David Hamilton. 'It was all men.'

With her own music column in *Cosmopolitan*, Annie became the most vocal critic of the station's refusal to sign any female DJs. Eventually public opinion changed; they had to take on someone and, because she had been circling the most persistently, Annie was the ideal choice. She was handed her own Sunday evening show. But after managing to get her foot in the door, Annie was dismayed when Derek Chinnery told her that the only reason Radio 1 took her on was because of her journalistic credentials and that she wasn't regarded as a real DJ.

Moving from the few presenting jobs she'd done in the past to a DJ was a huge leap in the dark for Annie. 'It was like taking over from an airline pilot in mid-flight, with no training manual,' she explained in a *Daily Telegraph* interview in 2017. 'It was absolutely terrifying. I had to learn on live radio. In the middle of my first show I pressed the wrong button and brought the national broadcaster to a shuddering halt.'

Luckily, Annie was given Bernie Andrews as her producer. He helped enormously to build up her confidence and abilities, but it was still tough going at the beginning. Feeling very much the token woman, Annie found Egton House a 'boys-only roost' full of 'locker-room humour'. At the first Radio 1 meeting she attended, the wife of the station's head told her to use her femininity in order to get ahead. For months Annie was never able to shake off the impression that the powers that be were waiting for her to make mistakes and she expected to only last a year at best.

Outside the Radio 1 bubble, it wasn't any better. Like her fellow jocks, Annie did her fair share of gigs around the country, as she explained to the *Radio Times* in 2013. 'I'd turn up and they'd give me a mic and say, "Just talk into that, love." I'd say, "Hang on, I'm on Radio 1 and I've brought my records with me." But they'd say, "We'll play the records." And there'd be a Miss Wet T-Shirt contest going on.'

Having managed to kick open the door for her sex, Annie thought it would only be a matter of time before there was an influx of other female DJs following her in, but there was nothing. In an internal BBC report in 1973, the head of light entertainment wrote that women didn't have the aptitude or the interest to present sport, politics or music. It would be another twelve years before Radio 1 hired another female jock.

Another important early development in 1970 was *In Concert*, the brainchild of producer Jeff Griffin. Ever since he'd worked on early jazz and R&B shows for the Light Programme, where he recorded sessions with the likes of Georgie Fame and Humphrey Lyttelton, Jeff had envisaged doing something much more expansive, a full-blown concert rather than just running through a few numbers. His chance came during a live session with Led Zeppelin for the John Peel show at the Maida Vale studio. The session went well and everyone went to the pub, which one normally did after a session in those days. Chatting away, Jimmy Page turned to Jeff and said, 'We liked the session, but really it still doesn't actually allow us to do what we want to do. We like to really get our teeth into the numbers, which is why we like doing live gigs.'

This was music to Jeff's ears. 'That's really interesting,' he said to Page, 'because I've been trying to get Radio 1 to accept something like that for some time. If I did a pilot programme, would you be prepared to do it, because with the success you're now enjoying, something might come of it?' The band agreed and Jeff began to make plans.

The one-hour show took place at the Playhouse Theatre, just off Trafalgar Square, and was generally seen as a success, although Jeff had to wait several months to be given the green light for a series. Going out on Sunday night, hosted by John Peel and recorded at the Paris studio in Regent Street, Jeff's aim for *In Concert* was to give an outlet to bands who were doing interesting work and came over well as a live act. The first band he booked for the opening programme was the progressive rock group Family. 'The trouble was, when we came to record it, their singer Roger Chapman had lost his voice. We struggled through one of the songs but it was obvious he couldn't carry on and so we went on to record a couple of instrumentals. Then Peely said, "Why don't I give Marc a call?" I said, "Marc?" He said, "Yes, Tyrannosaurus Rex." At the time John had a flat near Regent's Park and Bolan lived fairly close. Peel gave him a call and Marc came down with a mate, and so the first programme was Family and Tyrannosaurus Rex.'

One of the artists Jeff was keen to feature on the show was David Bowie. One morning Jeff received a call from his chief assistant, whose job it was to cast a critical eye over the calibre and suitability of the guests. 'This chap Bowie,' he asked. 'You've booked him for a whole hour! What's that all about?' By 1970 the 'Space Oddity' single had been a hit, but it didn't really do Bowie much good and he was still trying to find his way in the business. 'I'd seen him do a fantastic concert at the Purcell Room at the Southbank Centre in November of '69,' recalls Jeff. 'Once I knew I was going to do this series I was out all the time catching gigs and watching artists. My wife said I was hardly ever home because I was out seeing bands. But having seen Bowie, I knew that he had the talent and that show went down quite well.'

Other artists appearing that first year included Elton John, Pink Floyd and Black Sabbath. Led Zeppelin returned in 1971, and, in March 1972, Deep Purple performed 'Smoke on the Water' live for the first time. Each band received only the standard Musicians' Union rate of pay.

Jeff's favourite *In Concert* took place in that first year, when he managed to entice Joni Mitchell to do an acoustic set. Jeff was a big fan. 'The atmosphere in the studio was just so wonderful,' he remembers. 'At least half the songs she did were new ones, because she'd spent the summer on the Greek Islands and this was the stuff that later came out on her *Blue* album the following year. Afterwards my wife and I went out to dinner with Joni and James Taylor. It was a magical evening.'

While Radio 1 listeners continued to love Kenny Everett's irreverent style, Angela Bond was conscious that he could sometimes go too far. Yes, this unpredictability was an integral part of his appeal, but it could lead to the occasional lapse into bad taste or excessive mockery and he would be hauled in front of management. In addition, Kenny didn't feel obliged to stay quiet on what he saw as the failings of Radio 1, especially the bureaucratic nature that infested Broadcasting House and the fact that the place was run by people who didn't know anything about pop radio. 'Pinstripe prunes in offices miles away,' said Kenny.

In an interview with *Melody Maker*, he condemned Radio 1 as 'awful – really revolting'. The suits went mad. He was summoned in front of the executive elite and made to sign a document in which he pledged to stop making adverse comments in the press. Of course, the minute he was approached by a journalist he said, 'I'm terribly sorry, but I've signed a piece of paper which says that I won't speak to the press about how awful Radio 1 is.' The next day's headline ran: BEEB GAGS CUDDLY KEN. Another reprimand followed.

Kenny wasn't alone in his criticism of those who paid his salary. John Peel was another malcontent, and felt not the slightest guilt in airing his views, even on the BBC's documentary strand *Man Alive* when they interviewed him in 1970 for a programme about Radio 1. He didn't mince his words. 'If you listen to Radio 1 for an entire week or a year even, you won't hear anything at all that relates to anything that's going on. It's incredibly predictable sort of porridge, just meaningless stuff.'

By this time, resentful of her attempts to rein in some of his excesses, Kenny had fallen out with Angela Bond, and to err on the side of caution, two producers were chosen to replace her: Teddy Warwick and Derek Chinnery. However fine a pair of producers Chinnery and Warwick were, they lacked Angela's restraining influence and Kenny continued to sail pretty close to the wind until finally, almost inevitably, he went too far.

On 18 July 1970, the final news item on Kenny's show concerned Mary Peyton, wife of Conservative Minister of Transport John Peyton, passing her driving test. Kenny couldn't resist chipping in: 'Probably crammed a fiver into the examiner's hand.' It was a relatively innocuous throwaway line; Teddy Warwick was standing behind Kenny when he said it, after which Kenny shut the mic, turned round and said, 'They can't make anything out of that, can they?' History was to prove otherwise: it was all that management required and within forty-eight hours Kenny had been sacked on the orders of the BBC's Managing Director of Radio Ian Trethowan. Chinnery did his best to calm things down, suggesting Kenny vanish for a bit of gardening leave until the controversy subsided, but Trethowan was adamant: 'He goes.'

The reaction to Everett's dismissal was immediate. 'We were outraged about it,' remembers Johnnie Walker. 'How ridiculous and stupid to get rid of somebody so talented. But it was very typical of the BBC. They like to hire somebody who's a bit zany and is going to get lots of people listening, but when it gets a little bit close to the edge, they don't back them.' Others like Tony Brandon weren't shocked, indeed he was more surprised that Kenny had lasted as long as he did. 'There were people at the BBC who would have had him removed from the premises even earlier.'

Angela Bond and other producers voiced their strong disapproval over the decision and asked for his immediate reinstatement. Johnny Beerling was furious about the sacking. 'It was disgraceful and certainly diminished the BBC in the eyes of the public.' Beerling made his feelings known in a letter to Trethowan but it didn't do any good.

Incredibly, the most creative and one of the most popular DJs on air was out of work.

Kenny's cheeky remark about the transport minister's wife was not the only reason for his dismissal. There was also a political purpose behind it due to his strong stance against the Musicians' Union and what he deemed to be the idiocy of needle-time. As early as November 1967, Kenny was referring to 'grotty musicians' being behind the needle-time agreement. This kind of statement did little to foster good relations between the BBC and the Union, and in April 1968 the Musicians' Union General Secretary Hardie Ratcliffe wrote to the BBC complaining that Radio 1 DJs, especially Kenny Everett, were continuing to make disparaging remarks about needle-time. 'I hope that we shall never reach a point where we can no longer talk to each other,' Ratcliffe wrote, 'but circumstances are driving us close to it.' He even raised the issue of Kenny's continued presence within the BBC. 'Just how does Mr Everett get away with it?' This was a reference to another public jibe by Everett against the Union. 'But he is still around,' Ratcliffe's letter went on. 'He is no doubt regarded by the public as of much greater importance than your Governors or Director-General. You have created a position for him in which he can attack the Union with impunity. This is simply not good enough.'

This letter was undoubtedly meant to put pressure on the BBC and it did result in various memos being issued highlighting the need to rein Everett in. However, it was becoming increasingly clear that many in the BBC shared similar reservations about the ways in which the Musicians' Union worked in regard to needle-time, not least the DJs themselves, particularly those who had come from the pirates. Despite this, Kenny was seen as a nuisance in the BBC's ongoing and delicate dialogue with the Musicians' Union to increase its needle-time. 'It was getting to the situation where he was seriously upsetting negotiations,' confirmed Teddy Warwick. And so, he had to go.

The real beneficiary of Kenny's sacking was an up-and-coming DJ called Noel Edmonds, who ended up with Kenny's slot, becoming, at 21, the youngest jock at the station – a record that stood until 1999.

A kid from Ilford, East London, of lower-middle-class parents who'd made sacrifices to send him to public school – which he despised – Noel's radio career was motivated by the pirates and the music explosion of the sixties. He would have done anything to get on the ships; instead he had to make do with a small studio in his bedroom and doing local hospital radio. Leaving school, Noel did a year of student teaching, all the time yearning to somehow catch a break as a DJ. 'I remember listening to Blackburn start Radio 1 and thinking, "Oh, my God, that's the place I want to be."'

Out of the blue, Noel was asked to audition for Radio Luxembourg and was offered a job as a newsreader – all because of a letter and an audition tape that he'd sent to Radio London years earlier. These had been kept, along with his phone number, by one of the DJs from the ship, Tony Windsor, who had been tasked with recruiting new talent for Luxembourg. It was an incredible stroke of good fortune.

By the summer of 1969, aged 20, Noel was at Radio 1 and taken under the wing of James Fisher, who ran the on-air trailer and promotions department. 'He had a very nice studio set-up at Broadcasting House and sometimes I'd be there till one or two o'clock in the morning, recording bits and pieces, editing stuff, practising my craft,' Noel says. 'The day that man walked on the moon was the day that my first voice-over went out on the breakfast show on Radio 1.'

Noel's persistence and work ethic got him noticed and he started filling in for holidaying DJs. In April 1970, he was offered a series on Saturday afternoons. And then the big opportunity arrived. Noel was in Weymouth with producer Johnny Beerling preparing for an outside broadcast when news broke of Kenny's firing. The two men sat backstage trying to soak it in. Pity the poor bugger who's got to follow Kenny, was the general feeling. Noel went on and did his show, then, just before the end, Beerling lent over and, handing him a bit of paper, said, 'Remember we were talking about that poor bugger. Douglas Muggeridge wants you to call him.' Noel got on the phone. 'He was very, very BBC, old Douglas, and he said, "You probably know why I'm calling you, Noel. We'd like you to take over from Kenny." Now, I imagined that there'd been a massive walkout and I was the last person they'd asked. I said, "Can I have some time to think about it." He said, "By all means think about it. Would you call me back in ten minutes?"'

It was the chance of a lifetime, but also a terrifying prospect replacing such a hugely popular figure. Noel turned to Beerling. 'What shall I do? How can I hope to fill Everett's shoes?' All Beerling could say to the young DJ was to be himself and the listeners would be won over. Noel called Muggeridge back, accepted the offer and walked into the firestorm. 'And the firestorm lasted for about nine months before I made that show my own.'

The press didn't help. On his first day in the job, the *Evening Standard* wrote: 'Heaven help poor Noel Edmonds, who, from today onwards, has been given the unenviable job of governing in the ten-till-twelve spot in the wake of the deposed enfant terrible of Broadcasting House.' And for the first few weeks, it looked as if they were going to be right. Installed as the show's producer, Tim Blackmore didn't think Noel was getting his personality across and wondered how to change things. 'Noel at this point had not developed into the sophisticated creative animal he later became.' Then fortune stepped in.

An executive decision was made to move Noel to Sundays. It was the opportunity Tim needed to deal with Edmonds' identity problem by doing something different. He identified a change in the music scene, the rise of singer-songwriters like Neil Diamond, Cat Stevens, Elton John and Gordon Lightfoot. Why couldn't the Sunday morning show be a vehicle to embrace the singer-songwriter? Teddy Warwick liked the idea and gave Tim the go-ahead. Others weren't so keen about giving over a prominent part of the show to obscure artists and album tracks. At one departmental meeting an executive producer told Tim, 'You're not going with my philosophy.'

'And what's that?' Tim asked.

'Two thirty and bright. That is to say, nothing longer than two minutes and thirty seconds and bright tempo.' And there they were playing four-and-a-half-minute album tracks.

But it worked. And later on, the show began to feature groups like Crosby, Stills and Nash, Bread and The Eagles. 'Cat Stevens used to invite Noel and me to go and listen to his new recordings and decide which was the single,' claims Tim. 'Our relationship was that strong with some of these artists. We single-handedly got The Strawbs into the chart and have best-selling albums because we championed Dave Cousins as a singer-songwriter. That Sunday morning show became incredibly important in terms of what it did.'

Tim's insistence on going in this direction suited Noel down to the ground, since it was quite clear from the beginning that Noel was not pretending to be a music jock. 'There were two sorts of DJs on Radio 1,' he says. 'One was the personality jocks, then there were the music jocks, clearly people like Peel and Johnnie Walker. I never made any secret of the fact that I couldn't wait for the record to end so I could talk again.'

What singled Noel out from many of his colleagues was his utter mastery of the equipment at his disposal. 'Noel was a brilliant technical operator,' says Andy Peebles. No one loved those continuity studios more than Noel. 'I could get a tune out of them. When I was really on form, three cartridge machines, three record decks, three open reel tape machines, I could do a link and use every single one of those machines. I loved all that.'

At the same time as working with Noel, with whom Tim Blackmore developed a good, long-lasting relationship, Tim was also the producer on a Saturday morning show presented by Stuart Henry. Hailing from Scotland, Henry was at the station from its earliest days and built up a great rapport with his audience. He was also immensely popular with his colleagues. Tim remembers him as 'a man of conviction, someone who wanted to see social justice and championed care for the environment before anyone thought of the word green'. Every week, Henry tried to raise awareness on an issue that he felt people should be concerned about. One in particular was about the increase of chemicals in detergents that were being dumped into rivers and acting as a fertiliser to plankton, thus blocking up waterways. The backlash resulted in both Henry and Tim being forced to publicly apologise to the detergent industry.

But Henry's real radio legacy was a slot on his show called 'She's Leaving Home', which raised awareness of teenage runaways and tried to put missing youngsters back in touch with their families. 'It was phenomenally successful,' says Tim. 'And lots of families were reunited. No one else was doing that at the time.' For Henry, radio was always more than just playing pop music: 'It's awful nice if the disc jockey can have some effect, some relevance to people's lives.'

Sadly, Henry was battling with the early signs of multiple sclerosis which sometimes caused a slight impediment in his speech. BBC management put this down to a consumption of drink and drugs. 'People thought he was stoned,' says Johnny Beerling, 'because he did like to smoke the odd joint now and again.' It was largely due to this misconception that he was sacked from Radio 1 in 1974.

Henry lost his long battle with multiple sclerosis in 1995. Tim Blackmore read the tribute at his funeral. 'He was a natural personality and a very warm person,' remembers Johnny Beerling. 'I loved him dearly.'

Another 'personality' Tim came into contact with was Jimmy Savile, when he was assistant producer on *Speakeasy*, a discussion programme that the DJ fronted between 1969 and 1973. Going out on Sunday afternoons, *Speakeasy* was Radio 1's first talk show and involved a studio audience of young people, largely drawn from schools and clubs (and often accompanied by teachers and leaders), for an open discussion, with invited guests, on moral and ethical topics of interest to teenagers. It was produced by Reverend Roy Trevivian, who worked in the BBC's religious department. From almost the word go, Tim realised Savile was far from your average person. 'He would bring his mother to the recordings and we all had to call her the Duchess. How mad is that!' Here was a man who seemed to be 'performing' all the time, with the silly outfits, the cigar and the catchphrases. 'I did two series with Jimmy,' says Tim, 'something like twenty-six programmes, and I don't think I ever had a conversation with the real Jimmy Savile.'

It was also extremely rare for Savile to turn up at any of the Radio 1 events. One year, the gramophone department asked Tim to lean on Savile to attend the Christmas party as all the other jocks were going to be there. After much persuasion, Savile agreed to pop in. Tim was already at the party when the commissionaire rang him to say that Savile had arrived and could he come and get him.

> I went down to the foyer and, taking him back up in the lift, said, "When we get in, there's three or four people that really want to meet you. I'll take you to them, introduce you and you can just have a brief chat. Then you can go…" He interrupted me: "No, no, no. No, no, no." I said, "What do you mean, no, no, no?" He said, "We will go and sit down in a corner somewhere and they will come to us." And they did. He held court. Weird as he was, he had this aura of power.

In Concert's Jeff Griffin had brought in Tony Wilson as his engineer, due to a mutual passion for rock music, but by the summer Wilson had left the show to become a producer. As his replacement, Griffin turned to a young engineer working on the show called Chris Lycett. For Chris, the BBC represented something of a family business; his father worked for the corporation in outside broadcasting and his elder brother was currently employed by them. As for Chris, he had rather hankered for life as a civil engineer until his brother took him to the BBC stand at the annual radio show at Earl's Court. It's where he caught the broadcasting bug and, after leaving school, he applied to be a studio manager. This was 1966 and the BBC were only taking graduates in that position. Instead he applied to be a technical operator, which didn't require a degree, and he was hired. Chris then spent three months at the Evesham training school. 'That was my version of university,' he says.

After eighteen months in the job, Chris caught a lucky break. 'The BBC realised they hadn't got enough studio managers because half of them had buggered off to television, so they amalgamated technical operators and studio managers, which meant I was doing the job they originally turned me down for.' By 1969 Chris was working as a sound mixer for John Peel, which was always an experience. 'There was this one Sunday. It was a lovely summer day and we were all a bit grumpy being inside the studio when it was nice and sunny outside and Peel signed off with, "That's all there is for this week. I think I'll just go into the park and watch the clouds write poems in the sky."'

With *In Concert*, the production team found out on the Monday who was booked to play on the Thursday, the day of the recording. Fairly nervous about his first time as *In Concert*'s engineer, Chris rang Jeff Griffin to find out who his first week's artists were.

'It's Pink Floyd,' said Jeff.

'Oh,' Chris replied.

'Yes, and actually it's worse than that,' Jeff said, because he had a wry sense of humour. 'They've got a twelve-piece brass section and twenty-piece choir.' The band were to perform the twenty-four-minute 'Atom Heart Mother Suite'.

On the Thursday, Chris, by then 'bricking it', made his way to the Paris studio on Lower Regent Street. The usual thing was to go in before lunch and set the studio up, have a beer and then come back and do a soundcheck in the afternoon ready to begin the recording around 7 p.m. By the evening, Chris's nerves had not lessened. Floyd sounded magnificent live in the hall but how was he going to capture it all working on the BBC's archaic equipment? In the end, it came out quite well. 'I was very proud of that,' he says, 'although I don't think Floyd liked it as much as they might have done.'

Chris went on to work on a whole host of *In Concert* performances, including sessions with David Bowie and with Queen that are now highly regarded. 'In a funny kind of way, yes, of course you were chuffed to bits that you were a part of it,' Chris says, 'but it was just a job, and you didn't think of it as anything special.'

Another show that focused on what it called 'adventurous contemporary sounds' was *Sounds of the 70s*, playing the best in soul, rock and folk music from the USA and UK, such as Yes, Simon & Garfunkel, Genesis, Roxy Music, Bowie, Led Zeppelin and Santana. Such was the seriousness designated to this programme that there was a minimum of chat or jingles. The entirety of the track was played with no talking over the intro or fade out.

Sounds of the 70s went out every weekday evening with a different presenter each night, including a newcomer to the station: Bob Harris. In his native Northampton, Harris used to listen avidly to Peel's *Perfumed Garden* on the pirates and moved to London in 1966 with the express desire to follow his hero onto the radio. The chosen route was journalism and Harris became one of the founding editors of *Time Out* magazine. After setting up an interview with Peel, the pair became friends, with Peel acting something of a champion for Bob, understanding his desire to get into broadcasting. Peel introduced Bob to Jeff Griffin who likewise recognised a kindred spirit and suggested that they do a pilot show, and, if it sounded good, he'd pass it on to Radio 1 management. The pilot was recorded at Broadcasting House. 'I literally shivered with the thrill of walking into the place,' Bob wrote in his memoirs.

Nothing much happened for several months then Bob got a call. Peel was off on holiday for a month and would he take over his Wednesday *Sounds of the 70s* slot? 'I found myself, absolutely from nowhere, I'd done no radio before, sitting in for my great hero.' Due to needle-time restrictions, Bob had to rely a lot on live sessions, which was fine by him. There was also an emphasis on going out and finding new bands. Bob recalled being knocked out by a group called Wishbone Ash that he saw play at the Marquee and brought them in to perform for the very first time on radio. Elton John had recently released his second album and so he was brought in, too, to record a session that comprised of four songs, all for the princely sum of £25.

After Peel returned and nothing else was forthcoming, Bob thought he'd lost his chance at Radio 1. Meanwhile things weren't going well for David Symonds, at the time one of the hosts of *Sounds of the 70s*. Ever since the departure of Robin Scott, David had grown disillusioned with the station and its direction of travel. For him the men in suits were in the driving seat, but 'they didn't know anything and it got worse'. There always seemed to be a battle to get things the way he wanted. One of the features on his show was 'Record of the

Week', which was played every day. 'I felt I had a stake in that because it had my name on it, but in effect the record was usually chosen by my producer,' he says. 'I can remember almost having a fistfight with him over one song. I'd heard Judy Collins's "Both Sides, Now" and thought it was so beautiful and that it was sure to be a hit, but he said, "No, we're not playing it." I think I eventually talked him into it, but everything was really hard.'

The final straw came when a new jingle package arrived. 'It said Radio 1 was wonderful – well, it wasn't. I just felt that it wasn't true. And therefore, if it wasn't true, I wasn't being true to myself.' David resigned.

He popped up again as the first voice on air when Capital Radio launched in October 1973. By 1978, he was back at the Beeb as a Radio 4 announcer before once again having his own afternoon music show, this time on Radio 2 presenting *Much More Music*, a programme of easy listening. By 1981 he'd been doing the show for three years and enjoying himself; it was all going very well. The head of Radio 2 at that time was David Hatch, whom David admits he never much cared for.

> Hatch called me into his office one Friday, before going on air, which is something you should never do. If you've got some heavy news for someone, never do it before they go on air. But this is the BBC, they do what they like. So, I went in, and without looking up from his desk, he said, "Well, thank you very much indeed, David, but that will be all." And I said, "Pardon?" He said, "This afternoon is going to be your last one. But thanks for everything. It's been terrific." I was stunned. I couldn't think of anything to say. But I finally drew myself up to my full height, and standing over him I said, "Can I say something?" He said, "Certainly." I said, "Of all the most revolting little men I've ever met in my life, you are quite the most revolting." He said, "I beg your pardon?" and got up from his desk, but by then I was gone.

In a state of some shock, David walked to the studios to start setting up his show. David Hamilton was in the neighbouring studio live on air. He took one look at Symonds and knew something was wrong. 'I've been fired,' David said through the glass.

'Why?' asked Hamilton.

'I don't know. I've no idea.' David later found out that one of the DJs at the station had used his influence to bring in a friend of his, and David was the one who had to make room for them.

'What are you going to do?' asked Hamilton.

'I'm going to take off my clothes and drink wine,' said David, not unreasonably. 'And I'm going to present and I'm going to enunciate like a true English gentleman, like you would never know that this guy is sitting there in the altogether.' And that's exactly what he did.

Bob Harris was seen as the ideal replacement for Symonds and was encouraged by Jeff Griffin. Bob was told to just bring in his favourite records and Jeff would show him how to put that together into a show. These were lessons Harris were to value and use for the rest of his career.

Bob wanted his new show to reflect the growing significance of singer-songwriters like Carole King, Van Morrison and Joni Mitchell, along with oldies (Bob had a real penchant for rock'n'roll), so a really eclectic mix. Over the course of the next year there were live sessions from the likes of Syd Barrett, Lindisfarne, Cat Stevens and the Faces.

Jeff Griffin recorded a number of these live sessions for *Sounds of the 70s*. It always puzzled him why the powers that be nearly always scheduled them early in the morning, again demonstrating absolutely no understanding of the music business. 'Morning is not the best time of day to record any sort of rock'n'roll artist as anyone who knows anything about them would know. You'd be lucky to see them, never mind hear them.'

Such was the popularity of *Sounds of the 70s* that in the 1972 *Melody Maker* readers' poll it was voted the country's number one radio show. It was also one of the very few shows on Radio 1 that had the added benefit of improved sound quality of the Radio 2 VHF frequency.

★

While some DJs were flying at Radio 1, others were finding it that much harder to connect with the audience, for a variety of reasons. In the case of Tony Brandon, it was decided that he was more suited to the calmer sounds of Radio 2, especially given the fact that he was already in his thirties by the time Radio 1 started, when most of his colleagues were in their twenties. 'I said my goodbyes to the audience on Radio 1 on the Friday and on Monday I was up and running with a daily show on Radio 2.'

There were no worries when it came to Emperor Rosko, whose show was one of the highest rated on the network. With massive listening figures, Rosko was able to break songs and break bands. 'We'd play a new record on a Saturday and it would be top ten on the Monday – and that's power.' Rosko was also asked to host a new show called *Roundtable*, where the latest record releases were reviewed by a panel of DJs. Over the years, musicians were invited to voice their opinions, the likes of Paul McCartney, Kate Bush, Joe Strummer, David Bowie, Kylie Minogue, Elvis Costello, Morrissey and Paul Weller. Rosko recalls Little Richard turning up once. 'He was quite mad and it was very hard to shut him up. The one guest I hated the most was Don McLean – all he wanted to do was talk about Vietnam. I had to sling him out.'

Rosko was also highly respected amongst his peers. Tim Blackmore calls him 'the Phil Spector of disc jockeys' in the way he created his own unique soundscapes. David Atkey was also a big fan and vividly remembers his very first gig as a producer on Radio 1 because it was on the Rosko show. David joined Radio 1 in 1968. Prior to that he'd tried his luck as a musician in a band, but, when they never made the big time, working on Radio 1 seemed like the perfect way to remain involved in the business that he loved – music. Working initially as a technical operator, David also tried his luck as a DJ and sent in tapes. Alas, the panel evaluating these efforts concluded that his voice wasn't right for broadcasting. Instead they put him to work on voicing promotion trails. Then his big opportunity arrived, or so he thought. A DJ hadn't turned up for a show. 'It came to about five minutes to go and a producer called Ted Beston said to me, "I hear you've been doing some tapes. You're going to have to go in and do it." I said, "Oh, right." I go in, get all ready and, about a minute to go, in walks the DJ. I was so disappointed because I thought it would just have given me a chance to have a go. But it wasn't to be.' Instead David went round to the other side of the glass and became a producer. 'And my first job was to produce this guy that was an absolute idol of mine – Emperor Rosko.'

On the first day, David walked into the studio as Rosko was busy recording something. Playing it back, Rosko turned to face David. 'What do you think?' A thought flashed through David's mind: how could he possibly say anything to this man, especially since he'd only just become a producer and had never done anything like this before? Finally, he managed to scramble out the words, 'It's good.'

Rosko looked at him inquisitively. 'Are you sure it's all right?' he pressed.

'Well, maybe it was a bit long,' said David, feeling a bit more emboldened. 'If you cut that little bit out there…'

'Great, that's what I thought,' said Rosko. 'You edit it up and do it.'

That was the start of a long friendship. 'He was a lovely man,' says David. 'You'd think he would be Mr Know It All, because he was a larger than life personality on air, but when you met him, he wasn't like that at all. In private, he was much quieter. I liked him a lot.'

Now a producer working on a daytime show, David was required to attend the playlist meeting. This was where the week's new releases were discussed. It took place on Tuesdays at 1 p.m. in the office of Doreen Davies, who also acted as chair.

It was very democratic. Each producer arrived with his own selection of records, Doreen would put them on a turntable and play each of them, and then there followed a discussion, sometimes heated, about which of them went on the playlist. The playlist was divided into three sections: there was an A-list, that was songs designated for maximum rotation, a B-list for minimum rotation and a C-list, which was songs that got the odd play. These records were to be played across the whole daytime schedule, Monday to Friday, 7 a.m. to 7 p.m., and were generally Top 40 records. Once all that was decided, matters turned towards the previous week's playlist and which records were going to be demoted or upgraded, and which records were going to be removed altogether.

These meetings could last up to three hours, after which the playlist was typed up by a secretary and placed in the reception of Egton House so that the pluggers could take a look. 'It was like a secret society going away to deliberate on careers in the music industry,' Johnny Beerling says of those meetings, 'because fortunes could be made or lost by the music we played on the radio.'

There seemed to be no stopping Johnnie Walker as he moved to a prestigious weekday lunchtime slot in 1971. The excitement of his new prominence on the station was somewhat diluted by the fact that he'd been given a producer famous for drinking too much at lunchtime and being something of a bastard in the afternoon. 'He had an awful reputation and it was really difficult. I said to Teddy Warwick, "It's fantastic, you give me a two-hour show and two hours of needle-time and this really difficult producer, so what's your advice?" And he said, "Do everything in the morning. Don't attempt to have any meetings or anything in the afternoon." What an admission.'

That wasn't the only dilemma facing Johnnie. Moving from the weekend, he was now operating in a mainstream slot which meant that he was expected to toe the line. On Radio Caroline, Ronan O'Rahilly had had one clear philosophy: he didn't hire DJs and then tell them what to play and what not to play. He hired them because they knew what to put on the turntable. 'The BBC didn't give you that freedom at all,' says Johnnie.

This had been a constant frustration for a lot of the ex-pirate jocks on Radio 1. 'You never picked the music,' states Dave Cash. 'You could suggest, but you couldn't have control.' While some producers were more laid-back and easy going – 'Yeah, put that in' – others were more BBC types and inflexible. 'I had one producer,' recalls Pete Drummond, 'where we were doing a programme and I wanted to play this record by Dr. John and he said, "I can't put it in. It's just too way out. I'll get into trouble." Because if we did anything wrong, it was down to the producer for not keeping us under control. Anyway, he almost started crying about this record. I said, "For God's sake, don't put it in then."'

The problem at Radio 1 was the way in which it polarised the music that it was playing. During daytime, it was mostly Top 40 pop, while in the evening and at weekends it was much more album/progressive-type music. This is true of most radio stations even today: 7 a.m. to 7 p.m. is when station management want a consistent mainstream sound, so if you are tuning in you know, 'Ah, this is Radio 1.' For Johnnie there had to be something in-between. 'There was a mid-way, which is where I was. That was the problem. I didn't fit into the slot that the BBC imagined I would.'

Johnnie prided himself in having his ear to the ground, reading the music press, going to gigs, listening to the latest releases, and so it infuriated him when he asked to play a record only to be told that he couldn't. 'It became very frustrating. Instead of them being appreciative of somebody who was so keen on music, I was a nuisance to them.' It was even worse when he tried featuring the occasional album track on his show. 'The execs really freaked out when I played an album track. They thought an album was something for John Peel at night-time, but I said: "A lot of these tracks are going to be singles anyway." Which they were.' One of the best examples was the first time Johnnie heard the debut album from The Eagles. 'I thought, "I've got to play 'Take it Easy', what a fantastic track that is." It just happened to be going around on a big record at 33 r.p.m. Later, of course, it was a massive hit single.' It was the same with an album called *Layla And Other Assorted Love Songs* by Derek and the Dominos, which featured Eric Clapton. Johnnie loved the title track, 'Layla', but was stopped from playing it on the air. Radio 1 was only too happy to put it on the playlist when it was later released as a single and hit the charts.

For Johnnie, part of the joy of being a DJ was connecting with people, and part of that was sharing his love of music with them, finding a new record and being the first to play it. 'My listeners really appreciated it. People still come up to me now and say, "You helped form my music taste, you introduced me to so many bands."' That was the power of radio and the importance that these DJs played in the life of the nation. With that came great responsibility, of course. 'I understood the power,' says Noel Edmonds. 'And I always treated it with the utmost respect and gratitude.'

Johnnie was to discover that the influence he and his colleagues exerted extended far beyond the music. One day he came across a speech that was given in 1854 by Chief Seattle of the Suquamish tribe. The speech was a response to the US government's land treaty to buy the native lands off the Native American tribes. It is regarded as a powerful plea for respect of Native American rights and one of the first truly environmental statements. Unexpectedly moved by the chief's words, Johnnie decided to read the speech out on his show. The response was extraordinary. Arriving at the studio the next day, his producer said that he'd been inundated with phone calls from listeners asking where they could get a copy. Johnnie announced that if anyone wanted a copy of the speech to send a stamped addressed envelope to the BBC. Over the next two weeks sacks of mail came in and Derek Chinnery called Johnnie into his office to give him a horrendous telling off: 'What the hell is this all about?!'

'It was your producer who suggested I ask people to send in a SAE,' answered Johnnie. 'I thought it would be all right.'

Derek stared hard at him. 'It's not all right. What is this rubbish anyway? I've got to hire people now to fill these envelopes.'

'I thought you'd be pleased to get such a reaction,' Johnnie carried on. 'I've touched the audience with something that they've really responded to. It can't all be, "What's the recipe today, Jim?" and "Fight the flab". Occasionally it's maybe something a bit deeper than that.'

Chinnery was not amused.

By early 1972, Chinnery had taken over from Mark White to become head of Radio 1, putting him in pole position for the controller's job when it became available again. Teddy Warwick was made his chief assistant. Johnny Beerling also moved up the ranks, with control over several shows, and Doreen Davies become an executive producer overseeing the daytime schedule. Doreen was the only woman with any real power at Radio 1. 'And she was very much in power,' says Tony Wilson. 'Her focus, like most of management, was on the daytime chaps and she kept us in order with an almost motherly interest.'

Doreen was seen as a headmistress type. 'She was matron,' recalls Tim Blackmore, someone who very much looked after the scruples of the place. 'We used to dub her the head of morals,' says Johnnie Walker. 'She used to say things like, "Marvin Gaye's 'Sexual Healing', well, we're not going to ban the record. You can play it, boys, but please refer to it on air as 'Marvin Gaye and the healing'." She didn't want that word "sexual" mentioned.'

When Johnnie Walker started playing Lou Reed's 'Walk on the Wild Side', Chris Lycett was ambling down the corridor and was asked to pop inside Doreen's office. 'Chris,' she began. 'There's a lot of fuss about this record. The *Daily Mail* are ringing up asking why we're playing Lou Reed on the *Johnnie Walker Show*. I've listened to it and I can't really think what's wrong with it.' Most people had a pretty good idea of what the song was about, given lyrics like 'shaved her legs and then he was a she!' That was pretty risqué for Radio 1, but patently the management hadn't a clue. Then Doreen asked, 'Chris, what does "giving head" mean?'

A few years later, when the record was reissued, in view of changing public opinion, Derek Chinnery opted to listen to the song again before deciding whether or not to ban it. In order for him to hear the words more clearly, he played it at a slower speed. When it came around to the line about 'giving head', Chinnery said, according to Teddy Warwick, '"Giving head", umm, obviously a reference to buggery.' All Warwick could say to that was, 'Well, he's been talking through his arse for years.'

Another cherished Doreen story involved a request by three secretaries at Egton House to use the men's toilet to fill their kettle, since it was nearer to where they worked than the ladies'. They felt, to save them an awfully long walk, that if they banged hard on the door, made sure there was nobody in, they could quickly go in and use the facilities.

'I don't know about that,' mused Doreen. 'I'll have to think about it over the weekend. I'll let you know on Monday.'

Monday arrived. 'Doreen, what do you think?' the three secretaries asked.

Doreen gave her verdict. 'Sue and Jill, you can, but Sarah can't.'

'Why can't Sarah?'

'Because she's not married,' said Doreen.

One of the nuisances for Doreen and other members of management were the record pluggers. Their job was to get the record they were plugging played on the radio, by hook or by crook. Pluggers would leave their vinyl offerings in the DJs' pigeonholes at Egton House. Emperor Rosko recalls that in the early seventies he'd receive about 150 new records every week, 'of which only a few were playable'.

Pluggers weren't supposed to go beyond reception unless they were signed in by a BBC staff member. Their persistence, though, could sometimes make them a menace. There's a story of a plugger asking to see a producer only to be told that he was in the toilet. Minutes later, the producer was sitting quietly in the gents' when a record was pushed under the cubicle door.

Usually it was the producers who fielded most of the pluggers, not the DJs. 'And if they were clever, the plugger would look after the secretaries,' says Johnnie Walker, 'occasionally invite them to a reception or give them tickets to a gig, because it was the secretary that gave them access to the producer.'

One particular producer had no time whatsoever for pluggers. Ron Belchier could be difficult and a bit crabby at times. 'He should have been in the army really,' reveals Chris Lycett. 'If the pluggers were girls, he'd bawl them out, "What are you bringing me this crap for?" and they'd leave the building in tears.' At a house party, Belchier confronted a plugger, calling him a 'fucking parasite', before the producer was forcibly removed from the room by Dave Lee Travis and Paul Burnett. The next day Derek Chinnery had to ring the plugger up to apologise.

Judd Lander was a plugger at the time for Epic. He was also a harmonica player and years later provided the opening for Culture Club's 'Karma Chameleon'. Lander became so frustrated at not being able to get inside Egton House that he managed to apprehend a window cleaner's cradle that hung down the side of the building. 'One afternoon, Ron was sorting out the schedules in his office on the fourth floor,' relates Chris Lycett, 'when suddenly he looked behind him and there was Judd waving outside and trying to push this record through the window.'

For the re-release of David Bowie's single 'Space Oddity', a couple of pluggers contacted NASA and hired space suits which they dressed up in and stood outside Egton House trying to catch the eye of any DJ. Pluggers became such a nuisance that Chinnery once banned all of them for a week. In the end, an appointments system was introduced where pluggers were given five minutes each with a producer.

With so much at stake, some pluggers resorted to bribery. 'A few of them tried to buy us,' claims Dave Cash. 'I just cut them off when they did that. I'd tell them: "You can't pay me enough." One guy offered me £100 if I played this record and I said, "You've got your noughts wrong."' Even Ed Stewart revealed that he was once asked to play a certain record with the promise of an encounter with a local beauty queen. He declined.

For Emperor Rosko, the pluggers were vital because they brought all the songs that the DJs wanted, and as a result, he was able to build up a 'hell of a record collection. You could also go to a record company building and open their cupboards and just take what you wanted, because they were so happy to get a record played on Radio 1,' he says. Rosko used to fill the boot of his car with piles of vinyl. And pluggers would do anything to get a song on his show. 'You can use your imagination on how they would go about doing that. I don't think I paid for a meal for ten years in London.'

Such inducements were all part of the game, but the BBC operated strict guidelines about just how much a DJ could accept and where to draw the line. 'You were very tightly controlled,' reveals Noel Edmonds. 'You had to choose your invitations from record companies very carefully. There was a code of conduct about how many lunches you could take and what gifts were acceptable.' Obviously, DJs could take records home because they needed to hear them. They could be wined and dined because that's where most of the pluggers did their pitch and told DJs about their new record or band. And they could be taken to concerts because it was important to see the artists perform live. What DJs couldn't take were holidays or cash. There was a story about a BBC producer in the Light Programme days who was found to have taken a holiday in Malta in return for playing a Dorothy Squires record. He was put on gardening leave and never came back.

It's true to say that some of the producers were seduced by this lifestyle of endless record industry lunches. One producer turned up to a playback of a new album and asked where he'd be sitting for the meal. He was told that it was just a playing of the record, along with a drink and a few cocktail nibbles. 'What!' said the producer. 'My invite clearly said "Album Lunch".'

'No, read it again, it says "Album Launch".' The producer walked out.

Inevitably, like anywhere else, there was always talk about bribery and corruption, regardless of whether it was actually taking place. The press was often digging away for any skeletons and it was in this climate that the *News of the World* sniffed a potential story that might uncover rabid corruption at Radio 1. Putting together a sting operation, several of their reporters posed as record executives forming a new label and invited DJs and producers from Radio 1 to a party at a central London flat to talk about this new venture. Tim Blackmore recalls attending this party but leaving early. Then a few weeks later he received a phone call asking him to go to Scotland Yard. No sooner had he arrived than he was taken into an interview room by an inspector and his sergeant. 'We're going to read you two statements,' said the inspector. 'After we've finished, we'll invite you to make a statement in response.'

The first statement was from a record promotions man whom Tim recalled briefly meeting. He claimed that he and his wife and Tim and his wife were great friends, that they regularly socialised at each other's homes, that for Christmas he'd given Tim a television set, and later a case of whisky. All of this was total fiction.

'I'm sitting there thinking, "My God, what is this all about?"' remembers Tim. 'So, I make a statement saying, "Yes, I do know this man, but he's never been to my house, I've never been to his, and I've certainly never had a television set from him or anybody else!"'

The inspector moved on to read the second statement, which was from a woman called Camila who claimed to have seen Tim in his office at Aeolian Hall when he was producing the breakfast show. The purpose of her visit was to get him to play a record she was promoting, and in order to encourage him to do so she handed over an envelope with money inside. The allegation was that Tim told her it was not enough, so she returned to his office a week later with twice the figure. 'That's better,' was his supposed comment, before taking the money out, passing some of it to a colleague and keeping the rest. Subsequently the same woman was promoting another record and Tim had agreed to make it 'Record of the Week', provided she spend the weekend with him at his flat in Cadogan Square. 'By this time, I'm in abject panic,' recalls Tim. 'I'm in Scotland Yard with two policemen. I'm almost trembling. I made statements rebutting it all. And then on the way out the inspector said to me, "I wouldn't worry too much, sir, if I was you. We've checked it out and we know you haven't an office in Aeolian Hall and the address in Cadogan Square doesn't exist." It was frightening because had any of that got out everybody would have said, no smoke without fire. As it was, nothing was printed about me.'

That didn't stop the paper printing other stories, all unsubstantiated, that had the effect of turning people's lives upside down. For the sake of a few cheap headlines, a cloud of suspicion fell over the entire radio station. For the record, in his entire time with Radio 1, Tim says he was never offered any backhander or bribe.

The classic line-up: Radio 1 DJs pose for the press outside All Saints Church, 4 September 1967.
Chris Barham/Daily Mail/Shutterstock

ABOVE: Tony Blackburn presents the first Radio 1 breakfast show, overseen by controller Robin Scott, 30 September 1967. *Evening Standard/Hulton Archive/Getty*

RIGHT: The launch of Radio 1, 'The Swinging New Radio Service', made the cover of that week's *Radio Times*. *Radio Times/Immediate Media*

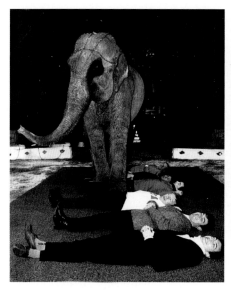

LEFT: The fun of being a Radio 1 DJ, at Billy Smart's Circus for a BBC Christmas special. *Mirrorpix*

RIGHT: Stuart Henry, one of the first DJs to use his platform to raise awareness about social issues, such as the environment and teenage runaways. *Chris Ware/Keystone Features/Hulton Archive/Getty*

Emperor Rosko hailed from Hollywood and with his cool look and Harley-Davidson motorbike was everyone's idea of a rock DJ. *Reg Lancaster/Express/Hulton Archive/Getty*

LEFT: John Peel survived numerous controversies and attempts to sack him to become the longest-serving of the original Radio 1 DJs, and the most respected. *Mirrorpix*

RIGHT: On 7 January 1970, Annie Nightingale became the station's first female presenter, in a largely male dominated environment, and is currently its longest-serving DJ. *Chris Barham/ANL/Shutterstock*

Johnnie Walker championed the progressive album music of the seventies and railed against the station's prevailing Top 40 pop sound, which ultimately led to him walking out. *Paul Popper/Popperfoto/Getty*

ABOVE: Pictured here outside Broadcasting House in 1971, Kenny Everett was master of the airwaves, a unique talent the BBC were unable to control and he was sacked for one misdemeanour too many. *Jack Kay/Daily Express/Getty*

RIGHT: When it started, Radio 1 was an odd mix of young guns and veteran broadcasters: (L–R) Jimmy Young, Tony Blackburn, Pete Murray, Terry Wogan and Ed Stewart. *Mirrorpix*

The Who's Keith Moon stood in for a holidaying John Peel in 1973. The shows were pre-recorded in the mornings when the drummer was most likely to not be incapacitated. *Jack Kay/Daily Express/Hulton Archive/Getty*

ABOVE: Abba visit the Radio 1 studio and record a jingle for the station to the tune of 'Waterloo'. *BBC Photo Library*

LEFT: Good friends in real life, Tony Blackburn and David Hamilton concocted a phoney rivalry where they insulted each other on the air. It all made for good publicity. *Mirrorpix*

In 1973, Noel Edmonds took over the breakfast show, attracting 12 million listeners a week. The DJs were now as popular as the pop stars whose records they played. *ANL/Shutterstock*

LEFT: Pop stars sometimes dropped in to spin a few discs. Elton John spun the platters in 1975 and 1976 with his shows 'EJ the DJ'. *Mirrorpix*

RIGHT: 'Greetings, pop pickers.' Alan Freeman, affectionately known as 'Fluff', was one of the most loved and admired of all DJs, but deeply insecure beneath the showbiz bravado. *Don Smith/Radio Times via Getty*

A Radio 1 'Funday' in May 1975 at Mallory Park racetrack near Leicester descends into chaos when thousands of Bay City Roller fans run riot to get close to their idols. *Mirrorpix*

Radio 1 celebrates its tenth anniversary with (L–R) Alan Freeman, Dave Lee Travis, Paul Gambaccini, Paul Burnett, Kid Jensen and Tony Blackburn. *Mirrorpix*

A special edition of the record review show *Roundtable* in February 1979 saw Michael Jackson, incredulously wearing a pith helmet throughout, joining George Harrison and host David 'Kid' Jensen. *Dave Pickthorn/BBC Photo Library*

British daredevil Eddie Kidd jumps ten Radio 1 DJs with his motorcycle at Brands Hatch racing circuit and sets a world record, 4 September 1978. *Ted Blackbrow/ANL/Shutterstock*

8

Even after all its success, Radio 1 was still perceived by the rest of the BBC as something of an anomaly, something certain factions continued to look down on. That perception wasn't helped when in 1972 journalist and broadcaster Ludovic Kennedy made a speech in which he described all Radio 1 DJs and their audience as moronic and that the presenters had no respect for the English language. This was seized upon by the press; the *Daily Mirror* went so far as to run a poll to find the most moronic DJ of all.

Derek Chinnery wanted to change all that: he decided the network should embark upon some more 'serious' programming. It began that summer with an exhaustive fourteen-part documentary on the Beatles produced by Johnny Beerling. The BBC had bought a radio documentary on Elvis from an American company and heard rumours that their next project was about the Fab Four. Beerling was told that if anyone ought to be doing a Beatles documentary, it really ought to be Radio 1 and he was assigned to the task.

The research was exhaustive and took Beerling to Liverpool, Hamburg and the United States, where he interviewed, amongst others, Ed Sullivan. The Beatles themselves refused to be involved but authorised the co-operation of the Apple office. Narrated by Brian Matthew, who had worked and travelled with the group, *The Beatles Story* was a big success. 'They sold that programme all over the world,' says Beerling. It certainly set the style for home-produced popular music documentaries on Radio 1 for years to come.

Next up was a prestigious twenty-six-part series exploring the development of popular music from the birth of rock'n'roll to the new heavier sound of the 1970s. It was to be called *The Story of Pop* and was the brainchild of Derek Chinnery. The enormous task of putting it all together fell to Tim Blackmore, with Johnny Beerling acting as executive producer.

More than 240 interviews were recorded by the production team and Tim found himself flying round the world meeting music industry giants as well as artists such as Paul McCartney, Elton John and Carly Simon. Beerling meanwhile jetted off to the States again where he pulled off the coup of interviewing John Lennon.

By far Tim's most memorable encounter was with Phil Spector, the producer best known for his 'Wall of Sound' technique. Spector was then living as a virtual recluse in an enormous mansion in Los Angeles surrounded by electrified wire fences. Through intermediaries, Tim managed to fix a meeting. It was an illuminating interview. Tim's sense of unease was not helped when Spector explained to him that every one of his rooms was equipped with voice-activated tape machines and that there were armed bodyguards around the house. 'You could be here for twenty-six days and no one would know where you were,' Spector rather ominously announced. 'You can only leave when I say I'm ready for you to leave.'

At one point, Spector asked, 'Are you guys scared of guns?' Then, standing up, he left the room. It was several minutes before he returned wearing a baggy boiler suit adorned with security guard badges and a yellow straw hat. The reason for the costume change, he explained, was so that they wouldn't be able to spot the gun he was wearing. After that, he sat at the piano and played and sang some of his most memorable songs.

By the time Spector had finished talking and showing his guests round the house, it was about four in the morning. Tim made his excuses and left, heading, as he says, 'back into the real world'.

With everything recorded and edited, attention turned to who should narrate the series. 'We thought of quite a few names,' recalls Tim. 'But in the end, I decided that Alan Freeman was the only person who would have the credibility because it would sound like he was talking about things he knew.'

The Story of Pop was a groundbreaking documentary and a huge success, sold to almost eighty countries and repeated several times. It also spawned books and a partwork magazine series. Tim recalls being summoned to Chinnery's office and receiving a hearty well done. 'But I fear, Tim, you have rather given yourself a millstone.'

'What's that?' he asked.

'You've peaked too soon.'

In March 1973, Kenny Everett was invited back to Radio 1. However, there were to be conditions. For a start he wasn't allowed to appear live on the station under any circumstances. He would pre-record his shows at his home in the country and send the two reels of tape in by courier. They lasted an hour and went out every Saturday morning. Teddy Warwick was once again producing and grew exasperated that the tapes were never precisely the same length: sometimes fifty-seven minutes, another time fifty-nine or sixty-one minutes. In the end Teddy sent him a letter: 'Kenny, I'll get a collection going for your local village church clock because that's obviously the one you use to time your programme.'

Sadly, Kenny was only under contract for six months and by the summer he was gone again, this time never to return.

Still going strong was *In Concert* and 1973 was to be a memorable year with an early performance from Queen and a rare appearance from Bob Marley and the Wailers. Pete Drummond was the host for the show. 'They were actually the second group and people had come to see the other band,' he remembers. 'After I'd managed to beat my way through the exotic tobacco smoke in the dressing room, I said to Bob, "Listen, if the audience are a bit lukewarm, it's because they've never heard of you. Don't worry about that, this is for the audience on the radio." In the end I think they went down all right.'

That June, Noel Edmonds took over the coveted breakfast show slot from Tony Blackburn. The BBC had come to regard Noel as a very safe pair of hands, and with his long hair and penchant for wearing fur coats and platform shoes, his was the perfect look for the time.

Blackburn wasn't just disappointed at losing the breakfast show, he was furious. 'Tony hated me for taking over from him,' says Noel. 'Literally hated me.' Worse, Blackburn was pushed to mid-mornings and had to follow Noel. 'There is a tape of a handover between Noel and Tony that is so frosty you can almost see the icicles in the studio,' reveals David Hamilton. Blackburn remained at Radio 1 for another decade, but one feels he never truly got over losing the breakfast show. 'The loss of it left a deep scar,' he told the *Daily Telegraph* in 2010, 'and I was eaten up with anger and resentment.'

At the time, Noel lived in North London and drove to the studios every morning with a collapsible bike in the boot of his car, just in case he broke down. In six years, he never missed a show. Arriving at Broadcasting House, he'd walk into the continuity studio where the tech operator was finishing a 12-hour shift; sometimes Noel had to wake him up. 'So, there I was, 23 years old, and I'm talking to 14 million people. I mean, the power and influence. I don't think it went completely to my head. It's incomprehensible today that so much responsibility was on my shoulders.'

One major obstacle was the man Noel was facing across the airwaves on Radio 2's breakfast show, Terry Wogan. 'Terry and I were rivals, not bitter, but we were huge rivals.' Wogan had recently left Radio 1 to take over the breakfast show at Radio 2, staying put for the next twelve years, during which time he became both a cult figure and something of a national institution.

Noel had only to look up to see Wogan through the glass connecting the two studios. One morning he formulated a little playful prank. 'I got all these empty polystyrene cups and put them on a tray and waited for Terry to open his microphone. I pushed my way in through the airlock doors and he obviously sensed somebody, but carried on talking and turned around to look at me. He smiled and I mouthed, tea or coffee? He carried on talking, nodding, and then I did a prank trip and shot the polystyrene cups all over the control desk. He couldn't talk for two links.'

Noel lent the breakfast slot his trademark creativity and penchant for comedy, most famously with his prank phone calls. It was a deliberate move to involve the listeners more and tap into the enormous creative resource that was out there – the public – by getting them to participate and engage with the show. He was arguably the first person to do *Candid Camera*-style wind-ups on the phone, much copied since, and the whole idea came about rather innocuously. 'We used to get about 3,000 letters a week. During a show I was looking through some of them and noticed one letter had a phone number. I asked the engineer if we could record on the phone. He said we could, so during the next record I phoned this person up.'

Noel wasn't trying to do anything other than just say, 'Hello, thanks very much for writing,' but when the man came on the phone it was, 'No, it's not you. It can't be.'

'Yes, it is,' asserted Noel.

'Noooooo.'

'Yes, and you're on the breakfast show. Hang on a minute, the record's coming to an end.' By the time Noel got back on the phone the man was going, 'Oh, my God, it really is Noel Edmonds.'

It was the realisation that something could be made out of this that led Noel to start doing a series of telephone pranks. 'They were cripplingly funny to do. I was almost sick on one occasion I was laughing so much.' It was all good-natured because people would nominate a friend or family member to be pranked. One daughter said her mum had been having trouble with her phone line, so Noel called, pretending to be an engineer from BT. 'Hello, Mrs Watson,' he said. 'I'm at the exchange now and we're trying to sort things out, but please don't use your phone, madam, for the next ten minutes or so because if it rings I'll get an electric shock.' It was drummed into this woman not to use the phone. Of course, the joke was that Noel phoned back after three minutes, she picks the receiver up and there's an almighty 'Arghhhh' from the other end of the line, at which point she throws the phone down. Noel phones back, she picks it up and there's a quiet little voice: 'Are you all right?' Cue Noel saying how lucky it was that he was wearing rubber boots.

While Noel enjoyed allowing his inclination for comedy free rein, he was less enthused with the music he was having to play, much of which was playlist fodder. 'Quite often I'd turn off the speakers in the studio because I couldn't stand something. I'd also take my headphones off so I could vaguely hear when the song was about to end. Of course, in the days of vinyl you could see when it was going to end. You were obliged to play the popular music of the day and sound enthusiastic about it because you're a salesperson. Light entertainment presenters on radio and television are salespeople. You are selling a good time. Every time you open a microphone, you're performing.'

The Breakfast Show brought Noel enormous fame, as did regular appearances as a presenter on *Top of the Pops*. 'You didn't have to do *Top of the Pops*, but it was the one you wanted. And if you got the Christmas Day edition, that was huge.' Noel was originally drafted in as a replacement for Ed Stewart who was making too many mistakes and the production team couldn't afford to keep stopping and starting.

For a lot of DJs, making the transition over to *Top of the Pops* was a doddle. People like Tony Blackburn were complete naturals. Blackburn hosted the show pretty much from the start of his Radio 1 career. One memorable show had him presenting alongside Alan Freeman. Blackburn had been suffering from flu and during the recording of one of the links he fainted into Freeman's arms. After Blackburn came round, Fluff was heard to say, 'That was a wonderful moment for me.'

For other DJs, doing *Top of the Pops* was much more of a wrench, while for a few it was a complete no-no. Johnnie Walker only hosted the show once, in January 1974. 'I was chucked in at the deep end when somebody couldn't make it. I had no rehearsal, no nothing, they just said stand there and do ten seconds. I looked as scared as I felt. I wasn't very good and wasn't asked again.' Another malcontent was

Andy Peebles. 'I hated doing *Top of the Pops*. You didn't have to do it but you were pretty unpopular if you refused. It was all part of the Radio 1 system.'

Like Blackburn, Noel was another natural and stayed a regular host on the show for the next seven years. It certainly increased his fame. 'I've been mobbed,' he says. 'I've had my car smashed outside Television Centre by 200 Bay City Roller fans who couldn't find their favourite Roller, so picked on me.'

The fame game was something Noel wasn't entirely comfortable with. 'Initially it was overwhelming for me because I wasn't a natural extrovert.' Called upon to do shop openings, his mere presence would have the same effect as if a pop star was there. 'Opening a record shop in Bury St Edmonds once, the whole window collapsed in, thankfully in one sheet of glass so no one was hurt. I can remember being in situations where the police came and said to the owner of the store, "Get him out of here. We'll give you ten minutes of police cover and after that we're taking him out, if you don't. He's causing a bloody riot out here."'

Johnnie Walker was someone else who was never at ease with the showbiz element of the job. He was never one to open supermarkets. 'It was very enjoyable to go to a club or a disco and do a personal appearance, which we all used to do quite a lot, I enjoyed that. But I never really thought of myself as famous.'

Noel quickly realised that the best way to get through these public appearances was to approach the whole thing as if it were a performance. He also did a lot of preparatory work, something that many of his colleagues never bothered with. 'But I did. If we were going to open a new Sainsburys in Grimsby or a new shopping centre in Birmingham, I would know all about it, so when I met the MD, I knew his name, I knew where he'd worked previously, and I got rebooked. And the word spread around. I used to do a lot of corporates because of that diligence.'

The most obvious indication of the sheer pulling power of Radio 1 came when Noel took his breakfast show up to the north-east, occupying over a whole floor of the local Holiday Inn. Out of the window in the near distance he could see cars tearing down a dual carriageway and a thought dropped into his mind: 'I wonder how many of those people driving are actually listening to me right now?' In the next link, Noel opened the mic and asked if those currently approaching such and such a junction could turn their head lamps on. 'Almost every single car put their head lamps on at that moment. Everybody in the studio went, "Fuck me! That is unreal."'

It helped, of course, that Radio 1 enjoyed a monopoly of the airwaves when it came to pop music. But all that was about to change with the imminent arrival of commercial radio. In anticipation, the BBC had already begun to freshen up the schedules by moving Noel to breakfast time and getting rid of people like Jimmy Young, who went to Radio 2, where he stayed for almost thirty years.

There was new blood as well in the shape of David Hamilton. Or rather old blood since David had worked on the Light Programme since the early sixties and was amongst Radio 1's first intake of DJs. He wasn't, however, given very much to do. 'Even though I was only in my late twenties, I guess I was associated with the old style of scripted broadcast.' He did the occasional *Pop Inn* and *Radio 1 Club*, as well as stand-in spots for Jimmy Young and Terry Wogan, but it wasn't until 1973 that he got his own daily show. As he put it: 'Hardly an overnight success, eleven years since my first broadcast on the BBC.'

From a childhood spent partly in a damp Putney flat and partly on his grandparents' Sussex farm, the radio was David's window on the world, and he would entertain his family with impersonations of the stars from *It's That Man Again* (ITMA) and *Take It from Here*. Later, as a teenager obsessed with rock'n'roll, he regularly tuned in to Radio Luxembourg where his idol was Pete Murray. One day he saw a photograph of Murray in a teen magazine glamorously astride a horse and thought, what a great job – horse riding and answering his fan mail by day and playing records at night. Determined to become a DJ, the young David hired a Grundig tape recorder and read into it articles from newspapers in a bid to tone down the rough edges in his voice.

During his National Service in Germany, he worked for the British Forces Network before landing a job on the Light Programme. So, yes, it had been a long hard slog. But his delight at being given his own three-hour afternoon show was somewhat diluted when Derek Chinnery informed him that a third of his programme had to be non-needle-time.

Despite more backdoor negotiations, the problem of needle-time persisted and while the station had managed to gain a few more hours, it was not enough to satisfy anyone very much. David knew that if listeners rumbled the fact that his wasn't a record show, they'd desert in droves, so he indulged in a bit of subterfuge. At that time, artists and bands would come in to record a live version of a song or their current release and this was played instead of the vinyl, thus saving on needle-time. 'What I used to do was this,' reveals David. 'If we had a band that did a live session, if it sounded vaguely like the record, I played it, and if we said, "Oh God, that sounds awful," then we dumped it and played the record. What did it matter? The group had been paid, and that was the point. So, we got around it like that. Who was to know?'

This, of course, made a mockery of the whole thing. And it wasn't just the DJs indulging in this kind of subterfuge, but the record industry itself. Producer David Atkey worked on a few of these sessions at Maida Vale and recalls one band that really didn't sound very good. As he was telling them to do it again, a record company promotions man came over. 'You do know, don't you, that at the end of this I'm going to give you a tape?'

'What do you mean "a tape"?' asked David.

'I'm going to give you a tape with a different mix of the single, so this session doesn't really matter. We're just doing it to fulfil the Musicians' Union rules.'

David admits that at the beginning he was somewhat naive about these kinds of arrangements. 'That's the trouble – you don't get a management book about being a producer at Radio 1 and nobody tells you these little tricks of the trade. You learnt them as you went along.'

Sometimes Hamilton simply ran out of being able to play records, so would just have to talk. That's why he always had to read out endless requests. The one thing he couldn't disguise was the awful house orchestras. David was lumbered with the Johnny Arthey Orchestra and his singers, who performed a daily six-minute medley of current songs at three o'clock. Not surprisingly, when the commercial stations began, this kind of programming was the first to be targeted. For example, at three o'clock on Capital they went straight in with three blockbuster records, while David was stuck with Johnny Arthey's Orchestra. 'In many ways it was an unfair battle. But the ratings held up.'

Finally achieving his ambition of his own show, David almost came a cropper early on when he played the Rolling Stones track 'Star Star'. The song was almost halfway through when the technical operator banged on the glass to ask David, who was setting up the next record, if he'd heard the lyrics. David hadn't. 'I think you better listen to them,' he said. 'I threw the switch and I could hear Mick Jagger singing "You're a star fucker, star fucker, star fucker, star fucker." This was on the housewives' favourite spot in the afternoon. I immediately faded it out and went to the other record.' The track was off the Stones' newly released *Goats Head Soup* LP. David glanced at the vinyl and noticed a bright sticker in the middle of the label which said: 'Under no circumstances must track five be played due to offensive language.' David had mistakenly played the wrong track. Apart from a few irate letters, he just about got away with it.

David wasn't the only one prone to the odd unintentional gaffe. James Alexander Gordon, who later went on to read the football results on BBC Radio 5 Live, was a newsreader at Radio 1 and David recalls one incident that took place around the time of the infamous Jeremy Thorpe trial. This concerned the accusation that Thorpe, a married Liberal Party MP and former leader of the party, had had a homosexual relationship with a young man called Norman Scott and that Thorpe had bungled a planned conspiracy to murder Scott when he'd threatened to expose their affair. 'I was about to open my programme and James read this news bulletin. Without a crack in his voice, he said, "When Jeremy Thorpe and Norman Scott met in court at Minehead today, it was the first time that they'd come face to face for four years." I couldn't actually speak, pressed the talkback and I said, "James, do you realise what you've just said?" He came back to me: "I don't think about the fucking news. I just read it." I said, "You'd better think again about the first item you read." He came back and said, "Oh my God, did I say that?"'

During his Radio 1 career, David was good friends with Tony Blackburn and the pair of them hatched an act where they insulted each other on the air. 'He was rude about me, and I was rude about him,' says David. 'Tony actually did a whole edition of *Top of the Pops* wearing a T-shirt reading: "I hate David Hamilton." And I came on later with one reading: "And I hate Tony Blackburn." I regarded it all as good publicity.'

Like Blackburn, David was known to litter his show with jokes. One night a comedian told him what was a fairly risqué joke, but it was so funny David decided to tell it on air anyway. The following day Derek Chinnery came into the studio when David was in the middle of his show. 'What was that joke you told yesterday?'

'Which one?' asked David.

Chinnery mentioned this risqué joke. 'I can listen to the tape of your show back but tell me exactly what you said.'

Hamilton told him the joke.

'Well, I've had a lot of complaints about that,' stated Chinnery.

'How many is that, Derek?'

It was seven.

'We've got fifteen million listeners and you've had seven complaints,' said David.

'You may think it's funny,' declared Chinnery. 'But I've got to answer them all.'

David's executive producer was Doreen Davies, whose motherly influence on the show resulted in a daily feature called 'Keep Young and Beautiful', where listeners sent in their own beauty tips and David read them out on air. It began with the jingle: 'Keep young and beautiful, it's your duty to be beautiful, keep young and beautiful, if you want to be loved.' It's hard to conceive anything like this being broadcast today. Indeed, at the time it provoked a furious backlash from the women's liberation movement. Nevertheless, the item proved so successful that it spawned a paperback book: *David Hamilton's Beauty Tips for Women*, which no doubt annoyed the feminists even more.

Another feature that ran along similar lines was *Make Ends Meet*. These were tips about how to save money, something particularly prominent in people's minds in the economising early to mid-seventies. Again, these were sent in by listeners. One gem went: 'Turn off the lights when you leave a room, that is unless there is somebody still in it, of course.' And, again, these items only really came about to negate the effects of needle-time.

Like most of his fellow DJs, a lot of the fun for David was discovering new acts and he was particularly drawn to the Philadelphia sound, a genre of soul music characterised by funk influences and lush instrumental arrangements. Throughout his career, David had always done a lot of presenting work on television and at the time was an announcer for the ITV variety show *Sunday Night at the London Palladium*. 'One afternoon I was sitting in the wings watching rehearsals and three black girls came out and sang a song called "Year of Decision". Diana Ross had recently left the Supremes, and I thought these could be the new Supremes. It was The Three Degrees.' Back at Radio 1 on the Monday morning, David made 'Year of Decision' his 'Record of the Week', or, as he called it, his Hamilton hotshot, and it peaked at number thirteen in the charts. But it was the follow-up single, 'When Will I See You Again', another Hamilton hotshot, that made the top spot and launched the girls' career.

When Terry Wogan moved across to Radio 2's breakfast show, his daytime slot was filled by Alan Freeman. But there was one slight problem. 'Alan kind of hated pop music,' says his producer Tony Wilson. 'His real love was rock music and together we started slipping bits of rock into the show until Douglas Muggeridge got a bit fed up with it and called us into his office. "If you want to play all this rock stuff," he told us, "I'm going to take you off afternoons and you can have your own show on Saturday." And that's what we did. That was the first *Rock Show*.'

Starting in June 1973, the *Saturday Rock Show* was to feature music from the progressive, hard rock and heavy metal genres. Right from the start, Freeman was deeply sceptical that he would be taken seriously by rock fans. After all, this was the man best known for *Pick of the Pops* and doing soap powder ads on the telly. 'But the response we got from listeners was so positive,' confirms Wilson. 'We'd get large volumes of mail. Everyone loved it.'

Wilson liked Fluff very much. 'He was great,' he said, 'but ever so neurotic.' But prior to working with Freeman, Wilson had seriously thought about quitting the BBC after being stuck largely doing what he considered to be lightweight pap. He still believed that his move from engineering to producing was the right choice, especially now that he was able to promote his own love of rock music, first with Freeman, and then later even more successfully with Tommy Vance.

Even better was the fact that he was left largely to his own devices. The management at Radio 1 had the good sense to understand the need for some rock output, but none of them knew anything about it or were particularly interested. 'Consequently, I had almost no communication at all with management. Nobody really questioned what I was doing.' This was in stark contrast to producers of the high-profile daytime shows. 'The management were constantly on their backs,' confirms Wilson, 'interfering all day long.'

Wilson saw his producing role as basically running the show. Since the DJs were hardly ever around, thanks to their hectic lives beyond Radio 1, it was the producer who kept the show ticking along. This did depend, of course, on the personality of the DJ, or those with the time or inclination to put the effort in. 'For example, John Peel,' says Wilson. 'Everything in Peel's show was Peel. Everything. He did have this rather indefinable ability to sniff out the right thing. He would just decide that he really liked something that was quite left-field, play a bit and people would pick up on it, and not just because he'd played it, but because he had sensed something that was right and for the time.'

Working with Fluff and Tommy Vance was different. Once a week they met up for maybe half a day in order to put the show together. 'I would have a pretty firm idea of what we should play and they'd

101

have their own suggestions.' It was also the producer's role to book and record sessions, along with listening to new releases, sometimes eighty new singles and between thirty and forty albums a week, attending playlist meetings, planning future broadcasts and, of course, dealing with a DJ's ego and personal problems.

Johnny Beerling always thought that to be a disc jockey 'you've got to have an ego the size of a mountain to imagine that anybody wants to sit and listen to you five days a week'. Some took to it more naturally than others, of course, and it was often the producer's job to facilitate the varying moods and conditions of his presenter.

While millions of people were out there listening to them, DJs never really thought of it in those terms. Beerling recalls an instance backstage at a concert organised by Radio 1 at Wembley Stadium. Steve Wright was about to go on and introduce an act when he suddenly went into a panic. 'I can't go out there in front of all those people,' he said. Beerling took him to one side. 'You talk to that many every day, Steve. You just don't think about it.' As Steve adds: 'Radio is a one-to-one medium. I always imagine myself talking to one person. But if you're going out at Wembley and you can actually see how many thousands are in the crowd, that does make me nervous. I'm occasionally nervous on the air even today but I just think of the one person and I speak just to them.'

9

When Johnny Beerling looks back on his time with Radio 1, one of his proudest achievements was undoubtedly the summer Roadshow, which ran for twenty-seven years. The Roadshow replaced the Radio 1 Club, which was seen as past its sell-by date, and was another opportunity to get out of Broadcasting House, tour the country and meet listeners. In the days before social media, it was one of the few ways that the audience could interact with their favourite DJs. In effect, the Roadshow was just someone spinning records in a booth on a beach, usually in the rain, except by this time their fame was such that thousands of people flocked to see them. 'If Tony Blackburn or Noel Edmonds turned up, we needed a police escort to get them in and out of the show,' says Beerling. But the success of the Roadshow took everyone by surprise.

The idea came to Beerling while he was on a camping holiday with his family in the south of France. Relaxing one day outside his tent, he saw a large crowd of people walking past and wondered where they were all going. He followed them to a field where a variety show with audience participation was taking place on a mobile stage that had been towed in on the back of a lorry. 'I thought, "That ought to work in the UK. And it would be the perfect way of promoting the station in the summer holidays."'

The first hurdle Beerling encountered was that the BBC didn't have the type of vehicle required to make it work. Putting out some feelers,

Beerling heard back from a producer in Bristol who knew of a chap called John Miles, the manager of a folk band from Somerset called The Wurzels. Miles owned an old furniture truck that he'd transformed into a mobile stage that he used to take The Wurzels around on to perform at local fairs. Beerling got in touch to see if it was available for hire, but there was one slight problem. 'I'd scrapped it a couple of weeks before because it kept breaking down,' Miles explains, 'but I said I'd build a new one if they gave us an agreement that they'd take it for the summer.'

Beerling went down to Somerset to see Miles. He'd built a scale model out of Weetabix boxes of the kind of trailer that he thought might work. Beerling liked it and gave the go-ahead to build it. Today, of course, this would be a multi-million-pound endeavour, along with all kinds of restrictions, regulations and health and safety checks. Instead, Miles found a chassis he thought was big enough, took it to a local coachbuilder, along with a drawing of what he wanted, and left them to it. The finished rig included panels for a portable stage and the whole thing was towed by a Range Rover driven by Miles's brother, Tony.

The inaugural Roadshow, hosted by Alan Freeman, took place in Newquay that July. Things almost got off to a disastrous start when the engineer announced that he didn't have a long enough mains cable. Beerling suggested he find the nearest electrical shop and buy some more. 'Oh no, me dear,' the engineer said, 'you can't buy no cable unless you've got a BBC-headed notepaper order form.' Luckily the show's secretary had some and quickly rustled up an order for another 100 yards of cable. 'That's how we got on the air,' says Beerling. And far from bringing along their own power generator, the team resorted to sticking their plug into the mains socket of a local café.

That first year, Beerling undertook a backbreaking route round the entire UK coastline in six weeks. It was such a ridiculous schedule that sometimes the vehicles didn't get to the next location until three in the morning. With everyone pitching in, the Roadshow immediately caught on with the public. 'It never pretended to be anything other than what it was,' says Chris Lycett. 'End-of-the-pier stuff. Very English.'

Buoyed by its success, Beerling asked the Miles brothers if he could use the same vehicle again next summer. They agreed, provided that they were given a licence to produce merchandise for the Roadshow. At the time, Radio 1 didn't take merchandise all that seriously. John Miles recalls going to meet the man in charge of it all and being surprised to see that the operation consisted of just him and one secretary. An agreement was reached for the brothers to produce official Roadshow merchandising and they built what became known as the goody mobile which sold stickers, T-shirts, posters, mugs and pens. Over the next few years, such was the demand that three sales units had to be built and they ended up offering about eighty-five different items.

Beginning with just a few trinkets at the early Roadshows, the Miles brothers effectively became the merchandising arm of Radio 1, selling items through mail order all year round, such as calendars which sold in quantities of 50,000 to 60,000. The brothers also expanded into BBC TV shows like *Seaside Special*, *Crackerjack* and *It's a Knockout*. Their BBC operation grew so big that they opened a shop in Bristol. John Miles also went on to represent a total of nine Radio 1 jocks.

The Miles brothers worked as a partnership. John mainly stayed in the office, looking after the financial side of things, while Tony was happy to go out on the road, responsible for getting the vehicles to a different location each day. To everyone's surprise, not least his own, Tony became something of an unlikely star, earning the nickname of Smiley Miley when he came up with the mileage game where members of the audience had to guess how many miles the Roadshow truck had travelled from the previous venue.

In the early days, the biggest problem with the transport was the lack of toilet facilities – rather difficult as the DJ was unable to leave during the live broadcast. 'The sight of Stuart Henry peeing into an empty milk bottle in the back corridor was not the most attractive one,' reported Beerling. One day Stuart was in full flow when the producer ran up the steps calling out, 'Oh, Stuart, I'd like you to meet Miss Scotland.' There was a mad scramble as Stuart quickly finished what he was doing and zipped up his pants, only to discover that he'd been pranked.

With its potential for raising the profile of Radio 1 across the nation, the arrival of the Roadshow couldn't have been better timed, because the network's monopoly was about to end. Commercial radio was on its way.

Ask any of the DJs who worked at Radio 1 during those first years and they'll tell you that it was a golden age. 'That was the time when they had no competition at all,' says David Hamilton. 'When everyone who wanted to listen to pop music listened to Radio 1.' That was all about to change.

The election of 1970 saw the Conservative Party led by Ted Heath come into office. The Tories were staunch advocates of commercial radio. Indeed, there is even a theory that Labour were booted out of power partly due to younger voters displaying a residue of contempt over their decision to close the pirates. In any case, there had been mounting pressure over many years for the establishment of commercial radio, supported by advertising. In 1972, Heath's government passed a bill for the introduction of commercial radio and in October 1973 LBC (London Broadcasting Company) went on the air, quickly followed by Capital Radio. The first voice on Capital just happened to be former Radio 1 jock David Symonds. Over the next few years, commercial stations mushroomed all over the country and the audience for Radio 1 was slowly eroded.

At first, there was an element of complacency at Radio 1 about this new development. 'We lived in a cocoon in Egton House,' says Tim Blackmore. 'We were Radio 1. We were the kings. We did feel that we were something rather special. And there was a sense of "Who are these upstarts?"'

David Hamilton recalls how complacent someone like Derek Chinnery was, who at one meeting announced, 'I'm not worried about the commercial stations because we have the stars, we have the household names.' He got a bit of a shock during another staff meeting when someone said, 'Have you seen all these cars in London with Capital Radio stickers on them?' It did suggest that an awful lot of people were listening to this new station. 'It was then that the BBC realised that they had a fight on their hands,' confirms Hamilton.

Because LBC and Capital were run by businessmen who knew what they were doing, it brought a highly competitive edge to the radio market. And they were quick to exploit the fact that a commercial station could do things that the BBC, as effectively a state-owned broadcaster, weren't allowed to do, such as give cash away as a competition prize. In the early days of Capital, people were hired to travel around London looking for cars with a Capital sticker in the window, take down their license plate number and, if it was read out on air, the owner won a full tank of petrol. There were other advantages, too, for those in the commercial sector, such as the fact that they tended to be localised and could focus their travel bulletins accordingly, which for drivers, especially during rush hours, was a real advantage. This was a problem for a national station like Radio 1, because if you were talking about problems in Sauchiehall Street in Glasgow, that was of no interest to people listening in England. Equally a hold-up on the Old Kent Road was of no interest to people in Scotland.

The BBC's cosy monopoly was gone for good and the realisation that they had proper competition came as a nasty shock. It was a them-and-us situation. To the BBC, they were nasty commercial animals who were only concerned about money, while the BBC were concerned about art and the quality of their output. That was the rationale. When Tim Blackmore later joined Capital, he came to realise that they weren't 'them' at all. 'They were a bit like us. They were people who just happened to be earning their living a different way, but they still cared every bit as passionately about the music.'

Tim was one of many Radio 1 employees who was to cross over to the competition. Dave Cash quickly jumped ship to be amongst the original line-up at Capital. It wasn't too hard a decision to leave Radio 1. 'I went up to Derek Chinnery's office and told him I'd been offered a job at "the new commercial radio station" and that I'd like to take it. He said, "Oh yes, would you like some more coffee?" They didn't give a fuck that I was leaving.'

Cash loved it at Capital. For one thing there was no needle-time; it was all records. 'If you wanted to do live music, you did it through choice, not because you had to.'

Faced with this new competitor, the BBC was forced to raise its game. 'Although the BBC typically always thought that they were superior,' says Paul Hollingdale, 'the reality of it was that radio was changing and I think Radio 1 got better when commercial radio got going.'

One of the first things Radio 1 realised needed improving was how it provided its news, given that LBC was an all-news/talk station and Capital had its own fully equipped and staffed newsroom. Radio 1 had always carried a short news bulletin on the half hour, every hour, but that two-minute bulletin no longer cut the mustard. It was decided to expand the news service with a fifteen-minute news and current affairs show called *Newsbeat*, heard twice daily at 12.30 p.m. and 5.30 p.m. The idea was to create a different sort of radio news, fast-paced and informal. However, not all the DJs were enthusiastic, notably Johnnie Walker, since it was his show that lost out. 'I used to get a vibe going from twelve o'clock and then *Newsbeat* would come on at half past and I'd have to sit in the studio with my feet up on the desk waiting to go back on at 12.45.' Regardless of Johnnie's grumblings, *Newsbeat* quickly established itself as an accepted and authoritative news source, and it continues to this day.

One of the earliest members of the *Newsbeat* team was a young presenter from Radio Solent, Richard Skinner. The BBC sent a couple of producers round the country to recruit people to work on the new show and heard Richard reading the news. Stopping their car, they turned around and drove straight to the station to urge him to audition. Their hunch was right and Skinner came on board, provisionally as showbiz editor. Along with interviewing countless pop stars, Richard also enjoyed trips to America covering popular shows like *Kojak*, *Charlie's Angels* and *Starsky & Hutch*.

Richard's most vivid memories revolve around some of the news stories that he covered. During the fall of Saigon, he was interviewing a BBC foreign correspondent who was speaking from a public telephone in the Vietnamese city. Midway through their conversation the line seemed to go dead, then the reporter was heard to say, 'Sorry, I've got to go, there are tanks coming around the corner.' After that, all that came over the line was the roar of tank engines and gunfire.

There was also the time Richard was kidnapped by the IRA in Belfast. 'I spent all day riding around in a taxi with a gun in my back,' he told the BBC. 'They took all of my money and delivered me back to my hotel at the end.'

By the time of the Falklands War in 1982, Richard had left his presenting duties on *Newsbeat* to become one of its producers, forced to navigate the dark waters of government censorship. For the duration of the conflict, the *Newsbeat* team were fed raw material from the frontline, much of it distressing. 'We had a Ministry of Defence censor in the studio with us telling us what we could broadcast and putting lines through our scripts,' Richard later recalled. 'At one point a report came in and this guy took so much out of it that I threw it across the studio at him, because there was nothing left; we were broadcasting nonsense.'

Despite the advent of commercial radio stations, Radio 1 continued to pull in huge audiences and was now a fixed landmark in the cultural life of millions of people. It managed to do that because the music it played through the daytime appealed to grandparents and grandchildren alike. 'It was a family station,' says DJ Paul Burnett. 'You'd play Engelbert Humperdinck next to Slade. It was that kind of station. It was accepted that was how it was. In the evenings with John Peel it became more for students and a younger crowd, with much more experimental music.'

Also, people didn't just listen at home, but while they drove the kids to school and on their drive to work, where invariably the factory radio or the one in the office was tuned to Radio 1. 'While people were at work, I think it was a great companion,' says David Hamilton.

This was also the age of the transistor, so people took their 'tranny' with them to the park, to the beach, or relaxing in the garden. 'Back then Radio 1 was huge,' says Tim Blackmore. 'It was a key part of the cultural life of anybody who enjoyed pop music, and that was the majority of the population at that time.'

If anything, this meant that the DJs were even more popular. 'I sold my life story three times to different newspapers,' claims David Hamilton. 'We used to joke that if we farted it would make headlines.' Every year a Radio 1 calendar was issued and sold in its thousands. 'The funny thing was nobody wanted to be Mr January,' says David Hamilton. 'If you were Mr December, then you knew you were going to be there for the year, but if you were Mr January, you weren't so sure.'

As 1973 became 1974 two more DJs were added to the roster. Paul Burnett arrived, having worked on the pirate ships, followed by a long stint on Radio Luxembourg. Before Radio 1 came calling, he was convinced that he'd missed the boat. He'd already turned 30 and was sending in audition tapes to Radio 2. It was his former colleague from Radio Luxembourg, Noel Edmonds, who played a pivotal role in his recruitment after inviting him to a Radio 1 outside broadcast. 'There I was as a Radio Luxembourg DJ and didn't realise that what Noel was doing was introducing me to some of the big guns like Johnny Beerling, and that directly led to the Radio 1 job.'

Paul had had something of a nomadic childhood. His parents were entertainers who regularly toured the country and Paul spent his formative years living with them in a caravan, going from town to town and to a succession of schools. In such an environment the radio played a vital role, an escape route for the young boy's imagination. 'You had all these stations like Hilversum, Berlin and Radio Luxembourg, and you'd tune in, and I just imagined it as this dial running across Europe picking up these stations.' In his early teens, Paul came across American Forces Network and was exposed to the exotic sound of rock'n'roll and pop music.

But his love for broadcasting began when he joined the RAF in the early sixties and was sent to Aden, where he worked at the same radio station Johnny Beerling had left just a few years earlier. 'It was a proper radio station, on medium wave and heard throughout the desert areas where all these units were based. I forgot about being in the RAF, I just lived for the evenings when I could go down there and do all these programmes.' Paul loved it so much that when he left, he thought it was the end of the world. 'I actually cried in the studio, thinking, "I'll never get this chance again."'

Back in England, the pirate ships were in full force and he was encouraged to try out for Radio Scarborough, which had just started broadcasting on the choppy North Sea. 'I was seasick every day. After my show, I just went straight back to bed. I'd do the whole show in pyjamas; God knows what I smelt like!' Radio Scarborough was by far the smallest of the pirate ships, about half the size of Caroline and London. 'We all lived in one room with little bunks that were curtained off either side of a big table where we all ate. There were some nice days when the weather was calm and you went up on deck in the sunshine and then it seemed like the best job in the world. But most days I was desperately ill.'

Paul must have been relieved when the government chop came and he enjoyed a brief stint on Manx Radio on the Isle of Man, before being headhunted by Radio Luxembourg. It was Derek Chinnery's idea to ease Paul into the Radio 1 schedules and he tried him out first on Sunday mornings following Ed Stewart's *Junior Choice*. Ed had a reputation for meanness, something he enjoyed playing up to. Just starting his first show, Paul saw the door to his studio opening and Ed popping his head round. 'Just to say, welcome to Radio 1.' Paul thought that was a nice gesture. 'By the way,' said Ed, not quite finished. 'Have you got ten bob on you because I've got a taxi outside!' Paul never got it back. They became very good friends after that. And Paul says that Stewart was 'always the most generous of people'.

Paul quickly got to know some of his other colleagues. He liked Alan Freeman and always enjoyed bumping into John Peel for a chat, while Emperor Rosko was something of a hero. 'With his Harley-Davidson, long hair flowing and leather jackets, he was everybody's idea of a rock DJ.' Paul also admired the professionalism of Tony Blackburn. 'Tony is a one-off. He's so focused. People used to make fun of him for that, but he was a very shrewd and clever guy. He tells those stupid jokes, but he knows exactly what he's doing and he knows exactly who he's broadcasting to.'

Paul liked Terry Wogan, too, another consummate professional and calm under pressure. A good example of this was when Paul popped into Radio 2's studio one morning for a chat when Wogan was on air. He was running a tape of Douglas Bader (the famous Battle of Britain fighter ace who lost his leg in a flying accident) making an appeal on behalf of Remembrance Sunday. As Paul recalls:

> We were chatting away and Terry was lining up the next record. He saw that the tape was coming to an end and at that point looked at the label of the record and realised he couldn't possibly play it. He tore the vinyl off the turntable and threw it across the studio. It just missed me actually. Now he's live on air: "That was Douglas Bader there," he says, "telling us why we should all buy a poppy. What a great hero he was…" And he's desperately trying to find another record to put on. It wasn't easy back then. We didn't have computers where you could just press a few buttons. He finally gets this record on and collapses back in his chair.

In the meantime, Paul had picked up the discarded record. It was Andy Fairweather Low's 'Wide Eyed and Legless', which was a big hit at the time. 'Can you imagine if Terry had played that after Douglas Bader? Nobody would have believed that it wasn't deliberate.'

The second new DJ arrived complete with an American accent that was to make him one of the most instantly identifiable broadcasters on the radio. Paul Gambaccini grew up in the Bronx, New York City, and vividly recalls the first time he heard Elvis Presley on the radio singing '(Let Me Be Your) Teddy Bear'. His father suddenly came running down the stairs and appeared at the kitchen door. 'He cried: "How can you listen to such damn music?" And with a balletic leap that would have dignified Nureyev he jumped across the room and switched off the dial in one motion.' All that was going through the young Paul's mind at that moment was, 'Well, if this gets a rise out of my dad, there must be something to it.' From then on, Paul religiously tuned into music stations and experienced the heyday of rock'n'roll coming through the wireless.

In the late sixties, Paul studied at Dartmouth College, an Ivy League university in New Hampshire, and managed to get a job on the campus radio station. Obtaining a degree in history, Paul came to study in England at Oxford University on a scholarship, while at the same time pursuing a journalistic career. After sending a few record reviews on spec to *Rolling Stone* magazine, Paul was taken on as a freelancer. One afternoon he took the train to London to pay a visit to the magazine's UK office and there on reception was a woman, braless and rolling a joint. 'I just thought to myself, "I might as well give up now, I can't compete with these people, they're too hip."' Over the next few years, however, Paul increased his output for *Rolling Stone*, getting his first cover stories in 1973 interviewing Elton John and Paul McCartney.

By this time, Paul was friendly with John Peel and his producer John Walters. Over lunch one day, Walters announced that he was starting a weekly magazine programme on Radio 1 called *Rockspeak* and wanted a ten-minute American look at the scene. Then turning to Paul, he said, 'Would you like to do it?' Since arriving in England, Paul had listened to Radio 1 and found much to be admired. 'I recognised immediately the greatness of Alan Freeman, and I loved the tightness of Tony Blackburn on the breakfast show, and the fact that he played a lot of Motown.' There was also an undeniable feeling that with his experience and musical knowledge, he could do just as good a job. He went in and did a demo. 'I was expecting like any scared kid to be laughed out of court, but when I was finished the producer said, "OK, that's fine," and it was broadcast as I'd done it.' John Walters liked what Paul was doing and quickly extended his slot to fifteen minutes, as well as asking if he could do a few interviews as well.

Paul worked in Walters' office at Egton House which he shared with Peel. It was already a small office but with all the *Peel Sessions* on reel-to-reel tapes stacked up, along with piles of unheard records brought in by pluggers, there was hardly space for anything else. 'There were times when you had to sit on an upturned bin because there was no room,' recalls Paul. 'The room was truly wall-to-wall music and we would as human beings just fit in.'

Paul spent his first two years at Radio 1 in that room and learnt a great deal from Walters, but especially Peel. So much in fact that Paul unhesitatingly describes himself as son of Peel. 'I call him mentor, hero and friend, and I'm not exaggerating.'

Paul quickly discovered that there was a clear divide between those who worked on the third floor, which housed the evening and weekend show production staff, and the fourth floor, occupied by the more mainstream pop-orientated daytime shows. Paul certainly knew that he belonged on the third floor. And there was also the moment when he realised that he was different from anyone else in Egton House. He hadn't been at the station that long when he bumped into Tony Blackburn in a corridor. Blackburn was trying to find out a fact about a record. 'I thought, "That's pretty poor. Everybody knows that." Then I thought, "Actually, everybody does not know that. As a matter of fact, I'm the only one who knows that. I'm the freak." I realised that was what made me different. I was the one who had all of this knowledge because to me it had just been automatic. It had never occurred to me that's what made me different.' For years to come, Paul became the go-to guy at Radio 1 about music history.

Some wags used to say that the third floor was the intellectuals and musos and the fourth floor was the people who opened supermarkets. 'The idea was basically that you never met,' recalls producer Trevor Dann. 'We looked down on them and they looked down on us.' That separation existed for years. Staff were either third floor or fourth floor and there wasn't much cross-fertilisation. 'There was always this internal strife between the two,' recalls Johnny Beerling. 'I think it was Roger Lewis, when he came in as head of Radio 1, who said, "Ratings by day and reputation by night," and there was some logic to that.'

For DJs like Pete Drummond, an alumnus of the third floor, the division was almost an existential one. 'I thought there were people there who were not interested in music at all, and just didn't care.

When I said to them, "The music's important," they kind of looked at me like, "Are you mad?" What? That kind of rock music? Your Pink Floyd and your Grateful Dead? Because I'm damn sure the daytime jocks didn't bother to question anything, they just played the rubbish. You could take one of the guys on the daytime and put a parrot on instead of him and you'd still get an audience; might even get more people listening.'

Gambaccini saw it as nothing less than the battle for the soul of Radio 1. 'At that time, people thought that one philosophy was going to predominate, either it was going to be music-based, as personified by Peel, or personality-based Top 40, as personified by the likes of Blackburn. And so, there was this occasional sniping between the two floors.'

The most striking example of this was the relationship between Peel and Blackburn, DJs who in personality and broadcasting style couldn't have been more different. 'They didn't like each other,' claims David Hamilton. 'Most of all, they didn't like what each of them stood for. Tony thought that Peel had a minuscule student audience in the evening, which in a way was true, and I think Peel thought Tony was a commercial creature who did pantos, opened supermarkets and wasn't really interested in the music.' Peel even went on record as saying he thought that Blackburn was 'the anti-Christ' and that he represented everything he found disagreeable about broadcasting. 'Kenny Everett and I,' he said, 'used to get together to try and plot his downfall.'

How much of this backbiting was played out for the benefit of the press is hard to say with any certainty. According to producer Trevor Dann, Peel was later to re-evaluate his opinion on Blackburn. 'He changed his mind totally about Tony as he got older. He told me once, "We all used to take the piss out of Tony on the pirate ships, but as I've grown up, I've realised he was right all along. He was playing these great records from Tamala Motown and we were playing this terrible progressive rock."'

In spite of all the politics and internal strife, both the third and fourth floors realised that each of them had just as important a role to

115

play. It was a question of blending the radio station together in terms of its output. 'Of course,' says Paul Gambacini, 'by the time the late seventies came around, and we had these astonishing listening figures, everybody suddenly realised, "There is no war. It's already happened and both sides won." There's room for both.'

10

There has long been a fascination for some DJs with motor sport and fast cars – owning them and racing them – and never more so than during Radio 1's heyday of the 1970s. Noel Edmonds was a big petrolhead, as was Johnnie Walker. Shortly after joining, Johnnie took part in a stock car racing night at Wimbledon Stadium that went out on the air. Bunched together with forty other cars, Johnnie was doing well until he spun off and crashed. 'I was frantically waving and pointing down to the door because my leg was trapped and I was in real pain. I kept blacking out. I was left by the stewards for quite a long time. Apparently, the commentator said, "Look at that Johnnie Walker, he's still waving to the crowd, who does he think he is?"' In the end the stewards got him out and took him to hospital where it was discovered he had a compound fracture. 'I had an operation where they put a plate in my leg. I was feeling a bit woozy and they called me up to go on the breakfast show. And there's Tony Blackburn, "How are you, Johnnie?" That was very weird. I wasn't in any condition to go on the radio at that time.'

While Walker was incapacitated, Pete Brady was brought back to the station to cover for him. 'I was on for about two or three weeks and then all hell broke loose because I shouldn't have been doing it. As far as the BBC was concerned, I worked for ITV. "How dare you!" But my agent had a contract signed really quick.'

Johnny Beerling also loved his motor racing and, following the success of the Roadshow, came up with the idea of the Radio 1 'Funday', which combined personal appearances by DJs and pop stars along with motor sport activities. The first event took place at Brands Hatch in the summer of 1974. Along with a full programme of racing, the DJs themselves needed little encouragement to compete in their own race, driving Ford Escorts around the track. The event was broadcast live and ticket proceeds went to charity.

These Fundays proved another massive success. One memorable event took place when Beerling persuaded stunt rider Eddie Kidd to drive his motorcycle off a ramp and leap over nine prone DJs. Radio 1 took out £1 million insurance in case anything went wrong. Poor Tony Blackburn drew the short straw and was positioned at the end. Dave Lee Travis was situated somewhere in the middle and had the task of doing a live commentary as Kidd's bike flew overhead.

By far the most memorable Funday took place in May 1975 in front of 47,000 people at Mallory Park racetrack near Leicester. Nobody had anticipated such a crowd turning up. A month before the event, Beerling and producer Dave Atkey paid a visit to the venue and spoke with the organisers. 'We're going to have the Bay City Rollers here, The Three Degrees and the Wombles, so we have to be careful about security.'

'Yeah, don't worry,' reassured the organisers. 'We've got security. We pay the police and they come in and police it all.'

The night before, the production team stayed in a local hotel and at seven o'clock in the morning Dave Atkey climbed into his car to drive to the event. 'The roads were totally blocked,' he recalls. 'The police had to get me to go on the wrong side of the road so I could get there in time.' Dave couldn't believe the size of the crowd when he arrived, while thousands more were trying to get in.

Anticipating problems, Dave found the police commander to ask how many policemen he had under his charge. The answer was thirty. 'We're stuffed, aren't we?' said Dave. 'What are we going to do?' The police were of a mind to shut the whole thing down. 'If we do that, you're going to have a riot,' Dave warned. It was agreed to go ahead with the event and a bulletin was put out on air appealing that anyone on their way should turn back.

One of the striking features of Mallory Park was a large lake situated close to the racetrack with a manmade island in the middle where the Radio 1 mobile studio was set up. The idea was for the Bay City Rollers to land by helicopter on the island and then come over to the studio for a chat. But the sight of the helicopter in the sky prompted a mass exodus from the stands of screaming teenage girls. 'There was a Formula 2 race ripping round the circuit at 140-odd mph,' recalls Paul Burnett, who was on air at the time, 'and these kids, they couldn't care less. They were running across the track with the race going on and wading through the lake to get to the tent where the Bay City Rollers were going to be.' The police and race stewards managed to intercept most of them, while the more determined had to be rescued by members of the BBC Sub Aqua club.

Standing next to Paul in the studio was the chief constable of the area who now wanted to pull the plug if nothing was done. 'It was just pandemonium,' Paul recalls. 'How nobody got killed or anything I don't know.' In the end, it was decided that the Rollers couldn't land and their appearance at the event was cancelled.

While all this was going on, Tony Blackburn was zooming around on the lagoon in a speedboat driven by a Womble. 'If I live to be 200 years old,' John Peel commented afterwards, 'I'm never going to experience anything like that again in my life.'

Despite the huge success of Radio 1, the network was still looked down upon by the top echelons of the BBC. It was popular culture and therefore somehow inferior to the rest of the output. 'It was almost like Radio 1 was tolerated within this massive edifice that was the BBC,' says Noel Edmonds. 'We were the drunken yob at the dinner party. We were the loudmouth at the end of the Downton table. We were tolerated. And, of course, they had to tolerate us because we were the most successful in terms of justifying the licence fee.'

Beerling recalls going to a big management meeting where the opening of more BBC local radio stations was under discussion. Beerling made the suggestion to Ian Trethowan, the managing director of radio, that what people really wanted to hear was an improved Radio 1 service in the evening, especially more hours. At the time Radio 1 shut down at midnight. 'There is little point in doing this,' argued Trethowan, 'as the reception isn't good enough and, in any case, Radio 1 is not exciting. BBC local radio is!'

If further proof were needed, when, in the final months of 1974, the BBC found itself in financial straits, £10 million in the red and the government refusing to increase the licence fee, the corporation announced plans to make stringent cuts in both radio and television. Radio 1, along with Radio 2, bore most of the brunt, having to share even more programming. Local radio and Radio 3 were spared. One of the big casualties was the decision to axe *Sounds of the 70s*. While the show had its supporters, such as Teddy Warwick, others in management, notably Derek Chinnery, were much less enthusiastic about the whole idea of showcasing ten-minute progressive rock tracks. So out it went, along with Bob Harris's career at Radio 1. Fortunately for Bob, he had already made the transition to television as host of BBC 2's *The Old Grey Whistle Test* and was well on his way to becoming a broadcasting national institution.

The strange thing was, at the same time that the BBC were heavily cutting back, it was the complete reverse in the music industry. The mid-seventies was the height of profligacy. With so much money spilling around, hospitality was viewed as a tax write-off and there were wild record receptions and expensive press junkets galore. Paul Gambaccini recalls being flown with Alan Freeman to Piz Gloria, a revolving restaurant on the Schilthorn in the Bernese Alps of Switzerland, made famous in the James Bond movie *On Her Majesty's Secret Service*. Joined by journalists from across Europe, they were there to report on the launch of Uriah Heep's latest album. Arriving by cable car, everyone was advised not to have more than one drink due to the high altitude. 'So,' says Paul, 'what does Alan Freeman do? He has two drinks and collapses face down into his plate of food.' During the subsequent photo-shoot, Paul is fairly certain he saved the life of one of the band members. 'The photographers kept saying, "Move this way, that way, back up a bit," and I realised, "Wait a minute, the guy's actually going to walk backwards off the edge of an alp. Stop!"'

Back at the good old BBC, it really was a case of scrambling around in the coffers, trying to make savings. Even when the BBC later managed to get the licence fee raised, there was no money for Radio 1 or 2 to restore the earlier cuts. All this, in spite of Radio 1 having a daily audience of 10.6 million. It wouldn't be until 1977 that most of the cuts were restored. And it was as late as 1978 before there was no longer an overlap of programmes on both networks and Radio 1 became truly independent.

As it was, the DJs whose programmes featured on both networks just had to make do, especially the peculiar challenge of having to compromise the music selection to appease both sets of listeners. This happened to David Hamilton when, early in 1975, Radio 2 axed its afternoon show and David's show went out on both Radio 1 and 2. 'In a way that was fantastic because Radio 2 had a phenomenal signal and could be heard from Ireland to Paris, so it gave us a tremendous audience. For a while the British Forces station in Germany was taking the programme as well.' As a result, the reported audience he was getting was something like 18 million.

Naturally such exposure led to other work, not least a presenting role on *Top of the Pops*. Like his job as a DJ, the *Top of the Pops* gig never paid well. 'I don't think my fee ever ran to three figures,' he says. But it was another great shop window and led to a string of personal appearances and gigs – one night it might be Aberdeen, the next Plymouth. After a while David found it easier to plan a weekend of gigs in roughly the same area and so cut down on the travelling. 'I totted up recently that I did over 1,000 discos and dance halls and over 1,000 shop openings.'

These gigs always paid more than the BBC did. David thought it odd that here he was broadcasting to millions and yet he was getting sometimes as much as three times more money playing in a club in front of 200 people.

He recalls that his first club gig was in Taunton. 'I got there and thought, "What the bloody hell do I do?" And all these people were coming towards me, looking at me, expecting some sort of an act.' In the end, he made the resident DJ spin the records while he just did the links. Coming away from the experience with the feeling that he had short-changed his audience, David asked his Radio 1 colleagues what kind of things they did during their club dates. 'Rosko had this fantastic show he took to clubs. He had lighting, he had go-go dancers, he was terrific. And then some of the other guys told me that sometimes they played these little games, and so one or two of these I picked up for myself.' One game went by the name of 'Two in a T-shirt'. David would announce to the audience, 'I want to give away a Radio 1 T-shirt and do we have a young lady who would like to come on stage and model it?' The girl would come up and put the T-shirt on. 'Now we need a male model,' and up would come some obliging chap. Then came the twist, as David turned to his assistant to ask for another T-shirt, and the answer came back, 'We've only got one.' As David faced the audience bemoaning, 'What are we going to do?', they'd all shout out, 'Share it!' 'Then the guy would get into the T-shirt with the girl, usually from the back, his arms down her arms, and they'd be there locked in the T-shirt and I would pronounce them man and wife.'

Then there was the beer-drinking contest. Four men volunteered to come up on stage. 'I'd say, "We now need four assistants," and four girls would sit on their laps. Then I'd say, "Can we have the beer, please?" And this beer would come out in baby bottles. What I didn't realise when we first started doing it was that people get much more inebriated drinking beer through baby bottles – one night this bloke threw up all over the stage.'

It would not be unusual after a gig for David or any other DJ to be approached by young women. Going up and down the country, it was quite possible for a DJ to arrive at a situation where they had a girl in every city. Many of these DJs had become sex symbols, their posters adorning the walls of admiring teenage girls, and groupies did throw themselves at them, just as they did rock stars. David Hamilton recalls being propositioned outside Broadcasting House. 'I was in a car and this girl tapped on the window and said, "Are you David Hamilton?" I said, "Yes." She said, "Would you like to go with me?" I replied, "I'm just going to the BBC at the moment," and made my excuses.'

On another occasion a woman turned up with her suitcase at Hamilton's front door, saying she had left her husband and children to live with him. As politely as he could, David informed her he was already living with someone, thank you very much and goodbye.

Of course, most of the DJs were single, red-blooded young males and a busy sex life was hardly a crime. However, consensual sex between adults was different to the predatory behaviour that was also going on, whether this was opportunistic attacks or the grooming of the young and vulnerable. The name of Jimmy Savile now casts a large ominous shadow over what was happening back then. Many people working in television and radio knew the rumours about Savile, and about other people, but it's of little surprise that the full extent of Savile's monstrous crimes didn't come to light at the time. To a large extent this was due to the culture back then, when certain behaviour was tolerated in the workplace, where women were often the target of lewd remarks, or of sexual assault. This was a male-dominated landscape and you just had to put up with it. It was rare for women to come forward to report such behaviour, given fears that nobody would believe them, especially when it was going to be their word against a public figure of Savile's standing and connections. Those women who were brave enough to make a complaint were let down by institutions such as the BBC and the police.

While Savile very much hid in plain sight, he was always careful to reveal very little about himself and hardly, if ever, socialised with his colleagues at Radio 1. 'You didn't mix with Savile because he wouldn't let you,' remembers Dave Cash. Any offer to meet up and share a few drinks was always rebuffed. '"I've got to go up to Leeds to work in the infirmary for nowt," he'd say. We used to think he was a hero,' says Cash. 'Little did we know what he was really up to. He had us all fooled.'

Occasionally, he might show up at a BBC function, a director-general's drink thing. 'We would be suited and booted and all holding our glass of sherry,' recalls Noel Edmonds. 'And in would swan Savile wearing a gold lamé tracksuit. He'd arrive late, walk around making no sense at all, and then wander off again.'

When David Chinnery held a party at his home for all the DJs, Savile was the last one to arrive. 'He must have been waiting in a car around the corner to see that everybody was in,' says Hamilton. 'And he came in dripping with jewellery. He went straight to Chinnery, who was with his wife Doreen, kissed Doreen all up her arm, gave Chinnery about twenty minutes of his time, and then departed. I think it was David Jensen who said, "Now royalty has left, we can have a party."' Hamilton also recalls Savile turning up in a T-shirt once bearing the sport brand logo 'Speedo', only his jacket was covering up the 's'.

Paul Gambaccini sums up the feeling of many when he says that Savile was simply 'not one of us. He entered Radio 1 as the Jimmy Savile industry already established. I didn't like him. He didn't run his own board. He never bothered to learn the equipment. He would just go into the studio, where his producer Ted Beston decided the music, and just do some links, and then it was left to the engineers to edit the programme together. I thought: "Why would anyone want to do this, if you are not in a relationship with the music you play?"'

Noel Edmonds agrees. 'I just thought he was a shit broadcaster, and that was my only judgement. Everything about him was low grade.'

Paul Gambaccini was still working on *Rockspeak* for John Walters and another show called *All American Heroes*, which showcased US talent, when he got a phone call from executive producer Stuart Grundy about hosting a programme solely devoted to American hits. Paul had had no clue that management was gearing up to give him a big new show, a show that he ended up fronting for the next eleven years.

At the time, Paul was temporarily working for a radio station in Boston, USA, but still sending in tapes to Radio 1 for broadcast. But a series of disturbing incidents told him to leave the city fast. His apartment was broken into, one of his assistants was stabbed with an ice pick in a laundromat, a woman was murdered on his street corner and, at one point, he had to take cover during a shoot-out in the local chemist. 'I thought, "The karma here is not good."' He returned to London.

Paul's new show highlighting the week's US chart music got underway in September. 'I was really annoyed because the number one song my first week was John Denver's "I'm Sorry", which I thought was a pitiful sentiment with which to begin. But the second week it was "Fame" by David Bowie.' Paul began his first programme with the Bruce Springsteen anthem 'Born to Run', which had just come out. From his college radio days, Paul always had an instinct for a hit record and knew that the Springsteen track was going to be a giant. In 1998, when he joined Radio 2 and resurrected his *America's Greatest Hits* show, he opened once again with 'Born to Run'.

Towards the end of 1975, it was announced that Douglas Muggeridge was stepping down as controller of Radio 1 and 2. His replacement was a surprise to many, especially Derek Chinnery, who expected to get the job. The new man chosen, Charles McLelland, had been head of the BBC Arabic service from 1971 to 1975. Tim Blackmore summed up what many people were thinking. 'We all said, "What the hell's going on here?"' Jeff Griffin found McLelland a pleasant enough guy. 'He certainly knew a bit more about music than Douglas Muggeridge did, which would not have been difficult,' he recalls. 'But again, probably not the right appointment.'

With McLelland's appointment, the general perception that decisions were being made at Radio 1 by people who knew very little about the station and how it worked was given even greater credence. There were other examples, too. Howard Newby, who had taken over from Ian Trethowan as managing director of radio, informed Teddy Warwick that *Melody Maker* was carrying a full-page advertisement for the new Mike Oldfield album, announcing that it could be heard exclusively on John Peel's show. Around Egton House this was seen as something of a coup – getting one over on their commercial rivals, plus free promotion for the station. Newby, however, didn't see it that way, as the advert contravened BBC policy on advertising and Warwick was reprimanded. Beerling for one was incensed, writing in his diary: 'This is so much bollocks. It's fucking impossible to run Radio 1 competitively with shit like this holding us back at every turn.'

There were other restrictions, too, in what exactly a DJ could and could not say on air. There were three definite areas they could not stray into – religion, the Royal family and sex. Bad language was also a no-no. After all, a DJ was a guest in people's homes and so such rules did have their place. But some of the other rules and regulations simply baffled people. In 1968, Pink Floyd's song 'It Would Be So Nice' was banned from Radio 1 for breaching the BBC's strict no-advertising policy due to a reference to the *Evening Standard* newspaper in the opening verse. Beerling was constantly seeking clarification of what could and couldn't be done around the draconian laws that the BBC operated under. For example, he could have offset many of the costs of the Roadshows by having sponsorship, but, of course, this wasn't allowed because the BBC was a public service.

The Roadshow itself was now something of a national institution, attracting enormous crowds of day-trippers wherever they landed. It was even the subject of a short film, directed by Roy Lovejoy, the acclaimed editor of films like *2001: A Space Odyssey*. Called *Radio 1 on the Road*, it went out as the support feature to the Australian film *Picnic at Hanging Rock*.

The Roadshow was as much an outing for the DJs and staff as it was for the public. Some of the DJs brought their wives and family with them and their own motorhomes to stay in. 'You learnt very early on not to stay in a hotel in town because you wouldn't get a night's sleep,' says Noel Edmonds. After some of the shows, Tony Miles would organise a barbecue for the staff on the beach or they'd have get-togethers in the hotel restaurant and play games of forfeit, with the victim invariably asked to do something silly like remove goldfish from a tank with their mouth, drink beer through a sock, or change clothes with the person next to them. For Beerling, all this larking around created a real bond which was reflected in how the shows came across to the public.

Taking the Roadshow to places like Cornwall or Wales was always a big deal for the local population. Living hundreds of miles away from Broadcasting House, suddenly people felt in touch with what they listened to every day. 'It was a major phenomenon,' says Tim Blackmore. 'It always amazed me to see the Roadshow vehicles driving through the town and people lining the streets. It was like the circus coming to town.'

It might be hard to understand now, but 20,000 people would turn up in, say, Newquay just to see a DJ play records on a stage. 'The amazing thing was,' says Beerling, 'Radio 1 had attracted such a big audience that you would get whole families planning their holiday around the Roadshow timetable and following us everywhere for that whole week.' Some were even more adventurous and would follow the Roadshow across the country for the entire summer, turning up every day.

The Roadshow visited forty-five venues each year and at the time the BBC were probably the only organisation able to mount such a large-scale operation. 'It stopped all life in that town for that particular day,' recalled DJ Peter Powell. The typical Roadshow summer season started in July and ran for eight weeks, broadcasting live from 11 a.m. to 12.30 p.m. each weekday. And it wasn't just about spinning records, there was the occasional star guest and competitions, the big two being Smiley Miley's Mileage Game and Bits and Pieces, where audience members had to name as many pop hits as they could listening to brief excerpts.

Being offered the Roadshow was a good measure of the popularity of individual DJs, as was where exactly in the country they sent you. Noel Edmonds recalls being asked to do the West Country, where the Roadshow picked up most of its biggest crowds. 'You didn't want to get the north-west. You didn't want to get Morecombe in the rain, or the North Sea; Skegness would blow the arm off the records. I can remember doing Newquay and a policeman said, "Our estimate is 24,000 people on the beach. I've never seen a crowd like it." I asked how many men he had under his command. He said, "I've got Frank with me, he's out the back checking everyone's all right." So, there were only two policemen controlling a crowd of 24,000. And you really felt the power of walking out on a stage in front of that number of people, but also broadcasting to millions at the same time.'

After three years, the decision was made to build a proper vehicle to replace the now rather ramshackle original, which by today's standards would almost certainly never have been allowed on the road. 'In Scotland, we were stopped once by the police,' relates John Miles. 'They said, "This is illegal," something about the weight ratio on the back wheel to the front wheel, and we thought, "Oh God, they're going to stop us using it." In the end, they let us off. But we didn't realise all those things.'

Another time a wheel came off the trailer and a breakdown truck was hurriedly called so that they could carry on to the next town. 'We got it there just in time,' recalls John Miles. 'I mean, you've got 13 million listeners who wouldn't be able to hear anything if we couldn't get to the location.'

As the event grew even bigger in size, five different vehicles were being used, including a satellite uplink van, an extra mixing desk (as they had begun to include live performances by bands) and a large TV screen so that people at the back could see. 'It was a victim of its own success in a way,' says Beerling.

Along with the goodie mobile accompanying each show selling Radio 1 memorabilia, the DJs always made themselves available afterwards signing autographs – 'on anything to hand,' wrote Beerling, 'including on rare occasions the odd girl's breast!' At one Roadshow, a man became so incensed that he hadn't been able to get Noel Edmonds's autograph he jumped on the bonnet of his car in an attempt to stop the DJ driving away.

11

Radio 1 lost some key voices in 1976. Johnnie Walker had always found it a balancing act on his lunchtime show catering to mainstream tastes while at the same time giving expression to the more progressive types of music. He was constantly being told he ought to learn the art of compromise.

It all culminated with the Bay City Rollers and Johnnie's utter revulsion at having to play them. The previous year the Rollers had notched up six weeks on the chart with their song 'Bye Bye Baby'. As it was on the playlist, Johnnie was obliged to play it but he couldn't hide the sheer disgust in his voice and ten minutes later his producer walked in. 'The switchboard has been flooded with angry Bay City Rollers' fans. I think you'd better say something.'

Feeling in no mood to apologise, Johnnie opened his mic and said, 'Apparently a lot of Bay City Rollers' fans are complaining about the way I introduced "Bye Bye Baby". What do you want me to do? I played the record. You cannot force me to like it, because I don't like it. To be honest, I think they produce total musical garbage.'

This caused something of an outrage, and the next day it was widely reported by the press. Johnnie expected the nuclear button to be pushed but was modestly surprised when Derek Chinnery backed him publicly. 'We think he shouldn't have said it,' reporters were told. 'But he's entitled to his opinion.'

A year later, when it came time to renegotiate Johnnie's contract, Chinnery called him into his office. 'I want you to do another two years' lunchtime, but no more album tracks.'

'You want me to play more Bay City Rollers, don't you?' said Johnnie.

'If they're in the charts, yes.'

'I don't really want to do that, Derek. Why don't you give me a show at the weekend?'

Chinnery was rather taken aback by the suggestion. 'No DJ in their right mind would ask to come off a daily show and go to the weekend.'

'But that would give me the music freedom I would like.'

'Johnnie, you know what the trouble with you is? You're too into the music, man!' This was coming from the head of Radio 1 talking to a DJ on a music network. 'It's two years on the lunchtime show or nothing,' Chinnery said finally.

'Well, it better be nothing then.' And with that Johnnie left the office and Radio 1.

He never regretted the decision, only the burden walking out on a highly paid position placed on his wife and young family. He subsequently moved to California to continue his broadcasting career.

Despite all the difficulties, Johnnie loved his years at Radio 1. 'It was a great position to be in, to have a lunchtime show. People used to dash home from school to hear the chart rundown I did on a Tuesday. What was a new entry to the chart, and what was the new number one was a really important thing back then; it mattered.'

Replacing Johnnie at lunchtime was Paul Burnett, who wanted to put a different spin on the show, making it much more hit single orientated. As he says: 'Top 40 radio is where I've always felt most at home.' He also wanted to include some comedy. Growing up, Paul was a fan of *Hancock* and *The Phil Silvers Show*. In fact, he could recite entire routines from memory. Unlike other DJs who used quick bursts of comedy, or just a few lines, Paul's idea was to play sketches and routines in their entirety, and out of that, came 'Fun at One'. Lunchtime, he thought, was the perfect time for such a feature; with

130

people preparing or eating lunch or taking a break, they were that much more attentive.

Fun at One featured classic comedy routines from the likes of Bob Newhart, Jasper Carrot, Woody Allen and Ronnie Barker, and Paul discovered years later that many of the eighties generation of British comedians were avid listeners, with some hearing those routines for the very first time. So popular did it become that the BBC released two compilation albums. 'I even got a letter from the guy who fired the one o'clock gun at Edinburgh Castle every day. He said, "Do you think you could just knock it back thirty seconds." I had this image of this guy in his kilt firing the gun and then rushing back in, so I actually used to delay it for thirty seconds because that's all it took for him to get back from firing his gun.'

Other features included Is, Was, Should Have, where listeners were invited to name their current favourite hit, their all-time favourite track and a record that should have been a hit but wasn't, and Pub of the Day. Paul used to get a lot of mail from pubs, asking him to play a record for one of their regulars. 'One thing a new broadcaster has to look out for,' Paul stresses, 'is if somebody shoves a request in front of you – read it first.' One of the classics doing the rounds at the time was a request that read: 'Please play a record for all the gang at the Cock Inn, Tillet, Herts.' DJs certainly had to be careful not to read that one out on air.

Not long into his reign on lunchtime, Paul teamed up with Dave Lee Travis to release a pastiche version of C. W. McCall's hit 'Convoy', a paean to CB radio. They decided to go under the name of Laurie Lingo and the Dipsticks. It was Travis's idea to bring a bit of publicity to his friend, record producer Wayne Bickerton, who'd recently launched his own label, State Records. Paul liked the idea and wrote some lyrics. It was just a bit of a laugh but ended up selling like hot cakes and, when it reached the incredulous heights of number four on the singles chart, they were asked to perform on *Top of the Pops*.

Paul came up with the notion of using a split screen for their appearance, and dressing up as truckers with a light shining up on both

131

their faces as if from a dashboard. Travis wasn't having that; in the song his character was called 'Super Scouse' and Paul was 'Plastic Chicken', and that's who they were going to be on stage. 'I did point out that lorry drivers don't necessarily dress like their CB tags,' says Paul, 'but Dave didn't accept that. So, he got BBC costumes to sort out a Superman-type costume for himself and I had to dress up as a chicken. The only good thing about that was the dresser told me that Tony Hancock once wore the chicken costume in a sketch. "Oh nice," I said. "Bring it on." Anyway, we did it and I don't think we sold another copy.' The song did, however, reach number one on the Radio Luxembourg chart. 'Obviously, they hadn't seen *Top of the Pops*,' jokes Paul.

Along with the departure of Johnnie Walker, there was also to be no more Emperor Rosko. His principal reason for leaving had much to do with the fact that his father was in failing health in the United States and he wanted to be near him. He was also having battles with the tax authorities and, he says, 'being robbed left, right and centre by agents and management'. So overall it seemed like a good time to go. Looking back, though, Rosko calls his time on Radio 1 'the dream gig'. He explains: 'Back then you were the only pop radio station, so the fact that I might have five million people listening to me when I did my show was pretty heady stuff.'

Rosko was replaced on Saturday mornings by an eager new DJ who had made his name on Radio Luxembourg: David 'Kid' Jensen. Born in 1950 in British Columbia, Jensen grew up with a love of music and played trumpet in a youth orchestra. Realising early on he was never quite good enough to make a career as a professional musician, he switched to broadcasting, landing his first job at a local radio station near Vancouver. He joined Radio Luxembourg at the age of 18 in 1968 and within two years was presenting a popular midnight rock show. The youngest DJ at the station, it was Paul Burnett who affectionately coined the nickname 'Kid', which stuck for the rest of his career.

Jensen's popularity eventually reached the ears of Radio 1 and Doreen Davies travelled to the Grand Duchy to meet him. Doreen explained that first David needed the experience of living and broadcasting in the UK. This he did, moving to Radio Trent in Nottingham, where he stayed for a year before getting the call to replace Rosko. It was an invitation that he likened to being asked to join the Beatles. 'It was very exciting. I did a lap of honour round the streets of Nottingham.'

The Roadshow idea had done much to promote Radio 1 during the summer months; now it was intended to take that concept one stage further and bring the bulk of the daytime team out on the road for a whole week of activities. It sounded like a great piece of PR; in fact it was a totally cynical manoeuvre cooked up to nobble any new commercial radio station that was opening up. For example, if a new commercial radio station was about to start in Cardiff, Leeds, Birmingham or Glasgow, the plan was to flood that city with Radio 1. The first 'week out' took place in Manchester in February 1977 with Tony Blackburn, Dave Lee Travis and David Hamilton's shows staged in the shop window of W.H. Smith in the city's new Arndale Centre. This set the pattern for subsequent 'weeks out' where DJs would broadcast their shows from local factories or nightclubs, and money would be raised for charity.

Like the Roadshow, the DJs enjoyed the freedom of being taken out of their normal London routine, while the challenge of working together for the whole week created a great bond and sense of camaraderie. 'They were all like naughty school children away from home and no one would be first to bed,' reported Beerling. Often the senior producer would have to stand in the bar come 11 p.m. and order everyone upstairs.

There were a few drawbacks, notably having to wear specially made zip-up jackets with the Radio 1 logo and, for the DJs, their names embroidered on the back. Like a teacher on a school trip, Derek Chinnery would walk up and down the coach making sure that everyone was wearing them before they set off. If a DJ forgot to bring his then he'd be made to borrow one from a producer.

By far the most popular feature of any 'week out' was a charity football match organised between the DJs and usually a local BBC station. The Radio 1 football team had been running for a few years now and always drew an enormous crowd. 'We were pretty useless, really,' says Frank Partridge, a reporter on *Newsbeat* who was drafted into the team. 'But that wasn't the point. The DJs were so box office that we could fill stadiums just by turning up.' One match was held at Sunderland's Roker Park ground. 'Sunderland were then in the old second division,' recalls David Hamilton. 'We played against Radio Newcastle and the club had the biggest crowd they'd had all season.'

The team graced grounds like Carrow Road (Norwich City) and St Andrews (Birmingham City). 'I played at some great football grounds,' says Noel Edmonds. 'And scored some sensational goals, thanks to the relaxation of the offside rule because we were all so bloody unfit. After about twenty minutes we were all at walking pace.' Football nous or even skill was not a prerequisite to being picked to play for the team. Paul Burnett knew next to nothing about the game. 'My tactic when I was on the pitch was, whoever had the ball I ran at them. That meant that before half time it was all over, I was knackered.'

David Hamilton recalls one match at Old Trafford against a Manchester United ex-pros eleven featuring Bobby Charlton. The great man went to take a corner kick, an in-swinger that bent into the goal. 'Somebody on our team, foolishly, said, "Bit of a fluke there, Bobby." He said, "Oh, you think it's a fluke, do you?" And this guy said, "I bet you couldn't do it again." So, in the second half he took a corner with his left foot and did the same thing. And this time no one said it was a fluke.'

When the team played a charity match at Wembley, Paul Gambaccini became the first American to play on the hallowed turf. It was a momentous experience for others, too. When John Peel scored, he turned to Gambaccini and said, 'I could die today and be a happy man.' Paul played in midfield – 'I did the least damage there' – and his own most memorable goal occurred from a corner he took when the ball ricocheted into the net off Noel Edmonds' backside.

On another occasion, the Radio 1 team pitted their 'talent' against BBC Radio Scotland at Meadowbank Stadium in Edinburgh. 'I was born and bred within fifteen miles of the stadium,' recalls Frank Partridge, 'and I was keen to make my mark. After about fifteen minutes, a gap opened up and I managed to squeeze through it and open the scoring.'

The huge electronic scoreboard displayed it like this:

RADIO 1   1
SCOTLAND   0
PARTRIDGE (15)

Alas, even though many of Frank's family and friends were in the crowd, not one of them bothered to photograph the scoreboard for posterity. 'Shame! I'd love to have a photo of that!'

At half-time, a helicopter swooped into view, out of which emerged Noel Edmonds, in full football strip. 'I was captain by then, and told him where to stand,' says Frank. 'I don't remember what impact he made but that wasn't the point. The crowd loved the fact that he'd taken the trouble to turn up. He was stardust.'

The final score was 6–5 to Scotland!

One of the most interesting features of the Radio 1 football team was how the jocks themselves used it to measure each other's popularity with the public, especially by how voluminous the applause was as they came onto the pitch. After the matches, crowds always mingled outside the stadium and the DJs would come out of the dressing room and have to run to the coach. 'I remember Tony Blackburn used to stick his head out of the door to give enough time for everybody to recognise him, and then make this dash for the coach with everybody screaming,' recalls Johnnie Walker. 'It was like a competition: who could get the most screams?'

Paul Gambaccini was on the coach coming back from a match when he noticed that no one was sitting next to Noel Edmonds. 'And the reason,' he realised, 'was because it was the first time that Noel had got the biggest clap. It was the first time Noel got a bigger clap than Tony Blackburn.'

Radio 1 prided itself in highlighting the best in music, along with an earnest desire to try and spot new trends and the best up-and-coming bands. At the start of 1977, for example, musician Alexis Korner was given his own Sunday night show that was to turn on a whole new generation to R&B and blues.

The rise of punk rock, however, presented an almost unique set of problems and, by and large, the station chose to ignore it. 'I don't think families want to hear punk rock music on Radio 1 while they are having their breakfast,' Annie Nightingale recalled Doreen Davies announcing. Famously, the Sex Pistols single 'God Save the Queen' was banned from the airwaves. According to Chris Lycett, punk music was completely alien to those in charge. 'The management didn't have a clue about punk. It was like your father – "Get that bloody noise off."'

When Derek Chinnery read an article in the newspaper about punk fans with spiked hair and a habit of spitting everywhere, he called Peel's producer John Walters into his office to ask, 'We're not playing any of this punk rock, are we?' Peel was about the only one who was playing it. It's true to say that Chinnery never understood most of the music Peel played, nor the man himself. 'He disliked me intensely,' Peel later said, 'and took every opportunity to let me know that this was the case.' Chinnery reportedly described Peel's listeners as 'unemployed yobbos', yet at the same time he realised the DJ's cult value to the station.

It wasn't just punk that Radio 1 didn't appreciate. They missed the boat on reggae, too, when Chinnery declared, just as the craze for it started in the mid-seventies, that there wasn't much of a national demand for that kind of music. The rock'n'roll revival of the early to mid-seventies, represented by bands such as Showaddywaddy and films like *American Graffiti* and *That'll Be the Day*, both released in 1973, also caught the station napping. A musician/producer called Stuart Colman even organised a mass march on Broadcasting House in 1976 demanding the BBC play rock'n'roll during peak hours. The demonstration was such a success that Colman was asked to front his own weekly Saturday night rock'n'roll show that lasted until 1981.

While Peel was undoubtedly the true champion of punk on Radio 1, other DJs, such as Kid Jensen, and, joining the station in 1977, Peter Powell, were alive to what was happening, and later to the new wave scene. Born in Stourbridge, a market town in the west Midlands, Powell grew up with Radio Luxembourg; his father built him a small crystal set which he'd listen to under his pillow at night. Powell was just 16 when he tuned in to listen to Radio 1's very first breakfast show with Blackburn. 'I remember sitting there listening and saying, within about thirty minutes, "I'm going to be a DJ."'

Following school, Powell worked as a salesman but ran a mobile disco in the evenings and joined Radio Birmingham at the age of 19. His first taste of Radio 1 occurred in 1972 when he numbered amongst a batch of other young jocks given a trial run on the air, although he only lasted three months. Peter had much better fortune over at Radio Luxembourg where he stayed for five years. 'Then the call from Radio 1 – long expected, long hoped for, long prayed for – came,' he told the BBC. 'And that minute changed my life forever.' When the news came through that he'd been given his own weekend show, Powell jumped for joy, hitting his head on the low ceiling of his rented flat.

It was Doreen Davies who recognised Powell's potential in his energy and enthusiasm, even if initially Peter himself felt that he didn't have the music credibility to match it. For much of his time on the station there was a constant battle between being seen as purely a pop presenter and desperately trying to be credible. One night while listening to Peel, a song came on that Peter thought had to be the most exciting record he'd ever heard in his life. It was 'Teenage Kicks' by The Undertones. It wasn't on the radar of the BBC or being plugged by anyone at the record companies. The next morning Peter paid a visit to Peel's office and asked if he could borrow a copy to play on his weekend afternoon show. Peel sat heavily back in his chair and said,

'That's the first time anyone's ever asked me for a record from daytime in my life.' Peter made it his Record of the Week, and 'Teenage Kicks' went on to be a big hit.

Punk and new wave was hardly something one would associate with Simon Bates, who landed his big break towards the end of 1977, having arrived at the station a year earlier. A grammar school boy, Bates began his broadcasting career as a newsreader and presenter first on Radio 4 and then Radio 2. Making the transition over to Radio 1, he started out subbing for DJs on holiday. New presenters often sat in for their colleagues while they took a week or a fortnight's leave; it was one of the best ways to gain experience. The DJ filling in didn't have the pressure of maintaining the audience figures, so it was relatively easy and pressure-free to sit in and be good for a couple of weeks. It also got them heard by people of all demographics and at all times of day.

Bates, though, felt that his face just didn't fit. His colleagues were stars, many of them pin-ups on the walls of teenagers. He recalled taking a walk down Regent Street once with Noel Edmonds and being quite taken aback to see him mobbed by fans. But Johnny Beerling felt that there was something about Bates and gave him the mid-morning show where he was to reign uninterrupted until 1993, garnering at its peak an audience of 11 million.

Taking over from Tony Blackburn, Simon inherited some of the old features, notably The Golden Hour. This was an invention of Derek Chinnery that was an hour of records all of which charted in a specific year. Bates amended the format by turning it into a game, interspersing the records with news headlines as clues, so listeners could try and guess the year at home.

During his time, Simon was to interview some of the biggest stars in the business, from George Michael and Cher to David Bowie and Whitney Houston. One memorable encounter was at the home of Freddie Mercury. Sitting down with his tape recorder, Simon was offered some tea. It was soon obvious that the tea from Freddie's own personal pot was altogether different, a concoction of dubious liquids. During the interview, the star got quietly stoned.

By far the biggest hit with listeners was Our Tune. Devised by Ron Belchier, briefly Simon's producer when he first started on Radio 1, it began simply enough as a request for listeners to send their personal tales of love and loss and the record that gave sound to their pain. Expected to last just a couple of weeks, Simon was inundated with letters as the public embraced the segment and made it their own. People in offices and factories routinely stopped work in order to tune in and listen as Simon read out stories to the accompaniment of composer Nino Rota's haunting theme to Franco Zeffirelli's 1968 film *Romeo and Juliet*.

Our Tune covered a wide spectrum of issues, but it's best remembered for the more tragic stories, usually of a marriage or relationship ending, an illness or death. Russell Kyle of Glasgow's *Evening Times* spoke for many people in 1982 when he described Our Tune as 'dial-a-depression'.

The production team working on the show always took the greatest care, keenly aware that they were dealing with people's very personal memories and emotions. Indeed, Simon has revealed that on at least two occasions someone committed suicide following their story being aired. As a result, it was always a key priority to speak to the individual concerned to gauge their mental or emotional state before allowing their story to be told.

So successful did Our Tune become that any attempt to remove it from the airwaves was met with howls of protest from listeners. 'Half the country would stop work,' fellow DJ Adrian Juste said in a documentary about Radio 1 in 1997. 'You used to see lorries parked on the hard shoulder as soon as Our Tune came on.' The reason for its popularity was very clear to Simon: these were real stories from real people. He never tried to make them sound more exciting or more depressing than they were. And that was the secret.

With Bates taking over on mid-mornings, Blackburn, under something of a cloud, was moved to the afternoons. While still on mornings, Blackburn had suffered a kind of breakdown after his marriage to actress Tessa Wyatt had collapsed. For weeks, he made morose, meandering pleas on air, begging Tessa not to leave him. 'He was very down at that time,' recalls friend David Hamilton. It didn't help that Blackburn was on Valium. He'd play songs like Chicago's 'If You Leave Me Now' and 'Don't Throw It All Away' by Gary Benson, laying bare his private life in excruciating fashion. 'It was a little bit pathetic,' says David. 'And Derek Chinnery was not very happy.' At one point, Chinnery called in Blackburn's producer David Atkey to put a halt to the matter. 'I have no control over him,' said David. 'I can talk to him about it but the only way you can fix this is if the engineers put a time switch on the mic so he only gets five minutes to talk every hour.'

'You can't do that,' exclaimed Chinnery.

'Then you've got to give me the power to suspend him if he doesn't stop.'

'No, no, that's my job.'

'Well, there you go then,' said David. 'I can only talk to him and try and explain it to him but if he won't listen, and I don't think he will because of the state he's in, perhaps you should let him rest for three or four months to get over this and then bring him back.'

'Oh, no, he's too popular,' said Chinnery.

Despite these problems, David Atkey liked Blackburn and got on well with him. 'He's exactly the same guy off air as he is on the air. He still tells those silly jokes, but I always thought he was one of the best communicators that Radio 1 ever had. He might not be some people's cup of tea, but he was a great communicator.'

By the time Blackburn moved to the afternoons at the end of 1977 he'd managed to sort himself out over Tessa, with the help of friends like David Hamilton. 'I said to him, "Look, she's not the only woman in the world, there are other women out there. Let's go out and meet some and have a good time." So, I got him pissed most nights of the week. I like to think I helped him get through that bad time. And when he married again, I was his best man.'

★

As for Hamilton himself, he was about to get some bad news of his own. He was being taken off Radio 1 and moved to afternoons on Radio 2. He was devastated. 'I didn't want to leave. I wanted so much to be a Radio 1 DJ. I was doing *Top of the Pops*. I was doing all these gigs around the country. It was my life.' At the time, moving from Radio 1 to Radio 2 was seen as something of a demotion. 'Radio 2 was really quite old-fashioned,' says David. 'Radio 1 was THE station. It was the most exciting time of my life. It was a whirlwind and nothing can ever compare to it again.'

Fighting his corner, David wanted to know why he was being let go when his show was still attracting strong ratings. At first Derek Chinnery refused to answer, but when pressed by David he admitted: 'Basically, it's a matter of age.' David thought about that: he was 38, while Chinnery was well into his fifties. 'If I had been rude, I would have said, "Derek, if anybody's too old for the job, it's you. I think you're completely out of touch." But you didn't speak to bosses like that in those days, so I took it on the chin.'

On the day of David's final broadcast, Chinnery sat in the studio for the last fifteen minutes, something he'd never done before, presumably in case Hamilton decided to vent his spleen on air. The last song he played was Neil Sedaka's 'Our Last Song Together', which he thought was quite apt. 'And when the show was over, Chinnery carried my jingles out to my car. Bizarre.'

On his Radio 2 show, David continued to play much the same music as he'd done on Radio 1. One day his old producer came storming into the studio while he had an ABBA disc on the turntable. 'You're playing our music.'

David looked at him quizzically. 'I didn't know that you had ABBA under exclusive contract.'

The producer wasn't finished and went to see Chinnery, complaining, 'Hamilton is playing all our music.' In turn, Chinnery went to see his opposite number at Radio 2, Charles McLelland, demanding they back off playing all this pop music. 'Derek,' came the reply, 'you worry about your station, and I'll worry about mine.'

141

This was a period that saw a considerable overlap between Radios 1 and 2 musically and a competition for listeners. Andy Peebles was soon to start a Radio 1 afternoon show and remembers seeing a copy of David Hamilton's Radio 2 running order and discovering that half the records that were going to be played, he was playing as well. 'I remember saying to Derek Chinnery, "Surely this can't be right. Something's wrong."'

12

In the spring of 1978, Noel Edmonds voiced a desire to leave the coveted breakfast show. Over the last six years it had dominated his life and opened up many opportunities. If it wasn't for the breakfast show he would never have been offered *Multi-Coloured Swap Shop*, a huge hit with young audiences on Saturday morning television. Now there was nothing more to prove.

Derek Chinnery concluded that the perfect replacement for Noel on breakfast was Dave Lee Travis. With producer Dave Atkey moving across with Travis, one of the first things they did was a phone-in competition. It was all a bit antiquated; people were required to apply by letter, out of which a hundred were chosen and then informed through the post to stay by their phones in case Travis called them up. They used to get all sorts entering. One chap from Wimbledon told Travis on air that his parrot had plucked all its feathers out. Within days, listeners were sending in hand-knitted little jumpers for the bird to wear and Travis went down to Wimbledon to hand them over. 'Travis had a great connection with the public,' says Dave.

As for Noel, people were surprised when he requested a move back to weekends, specifically a Sunday slot that would allow him more musical freedom and creative expression to do what he wanted as a broadcaster. 'I think all of the successful broadcasters are only an extension of themselves. I frankly used to entertain myself and thankfully other people found it entertaining. If it didn't make me laugh, I wasn't going to do it.' A good example of this was the creation of the fictional Perkins Grange in the village of Dingley Dell. The story was that Brian Perkins had been left a stately home in a will and was so desperate for money, because the roof needed doing, that he tolerated Radio 1 broadcasting from there on Sunday mornings. 'Away we went with absolute nonsense and people loved it,' says Noel.

This approach went back to the time when a young Noel would be taken off into imaginative flight listening to *The Goon Show* or Kenneth Horne. 'It's about stimulating people's imagination,' he says, and it was something that carried over into his later television career, especially on *Noel's House Party*, which took place in another manor house in the equally fictional village of Crinkley Bottom. It worked. He says: 'People had their imaginations so stimulated that on *Noel's House Party* I had people asking me if that was really my house.'

There were also sketches and special guests like John Gielgud and Billy Connolly. 'It was a most unusual show. We even, on one occasion, in the next studio, organised a half-sized snooker table to be put in so I could play a game of snooker with Steve Davis while we were on the air.'

Noel's Sunday show became particularly well known for making chart hits out of obscure novelty records. 'Captain Beaky', a song performed by actor Keith Michell, based on a series of children's poems, was a prime example. Noel first heard Ed Stewart play it on Radio 2's *Family Favourites*, liked it and thought he could do something with it. After numerous plays, the song was in the Top 10 and people wanted to know whether Hissing Sid was innocent or not. Somebody even sprayed a bridge on the M1 with 'Hissing Sid Is Innocent OK.' Another success was Noel's repeated playing of 'Suicide Is Painless', the theme song from the film version of *M*A*S*H*, ten years after it first came out, turning it into an unlikely number one.

Making a welcome return from the breakfast show were the funny phone calls, which, if anything, grew more ridiculous. These prank calls were never pre-recorded, but carried out while the show was going out live. Noel would phone up the unsuspecting 'victim' while his producer took over the turntable. 'It could be quite challenging, doing it and then having to edit the piece to play later on in the show. Luckily most of them you didn't have to edit. They just rolled brilliantly.'

One great prank demonstrated the reach of Radio 1. A mother had set up her daughter, who was going in for a minor operation at the Bristol Royal Infirmary. She wasn't looking forward to the procedure and was expecting a call from the admissions person. Noel phoned up as Daphne, putting on his best matronly voice. 'Hello, we've got you down for seven o'clock in the morning,' he began, then proceeded to go through the details. 'Do you know what you're bringing?'

'Yes, just a nightdress and toiletries.'

'You might know we have some NHS cutbacks,' explained Daphne. 'Would you be able to bring some bedding?'

There was a slight pause on the line. 'What sort of thing?'

'A duvet and maybe a pillow.'

The woman started laughing, which set Noel off, too, but he kept going and when it got to the point when Daphne asked, 'Could you bring a bed?' both of them were in floods of tears. The next morning when the woman arrived at the hospital it was obvious that the staff there had heard the prank call because the nurses showed her into an empty room and said, 'We thought you were bringing your own bed.'

Another DJ who made a virtue out of using comedy on his show was Adrian Juste, who arrived at Radio 1 that spring of 1978 from BBC Radio Leicester. Growing up listening to Radio Luxembourg, it was really photographs he saw of the great American DJs like Wolfman Jack, surrounded by a plethora of hi-tech gear, that sowed the seed of his broadcasting career. Adrian was always more interested in the technology of the job and first bought two small tape recorders to begin mixing and doing voices. That eventually led to setting up his own home studio. It was basic at first, due to monetary constraints, but he kept improving it over time until it was the equal of any professional studio.

Too late to apply for the pirate ships, Adrian got his break with Leicester's local BBC station in 1969 and spent six years there as disc jockey and producer, interrupted by a two-year spell at the commercial BRMB station in Birmingham. All the time, he was sending out demos. When finally the call came, frustratingly for Adrian with just thirty seconds to go before a live link, it was Beverly Pond, Derrick Chinnery's secretary. 'Hello, Adrian, I've got Derek for you.'

'Hello, Adri....' The normally measured, slightly RAF tones got no further.

'Derek, I'm about to go on air, I'll call you back,' said Adrian and slammed the phone down. 'Rather like beating your boss at golf, it may NOT have proved a wise career move!'

Adrian, of course, duly called straight back, and thankfully, as an old radio man, Chinnery appreciated the situation and asked if he'd like to start on Radio 1 in four weeks' time as Kid Jensen's replacement on Saturday mornings.

Chinnery knew exactly the sort of show he wanted from Adrian. It was something he'd done before while at BRMB, dropping the odd comedy clip in amongst the music. 'Although I hadn't done a real structured music and comedy two hours before,' Adrian says, 'so he gave me Teddy Warwick, and a young, rather maverick producer called Dave Price, to put it together. We all hit it off immediately, and my initial six-week contract as Kid Jensen's replacement was extended right through the summer.'

Arriving from local radio, Adrian admits to being 'very starstruck', combined with a nervous fear of everyone taking one look at him and saying, "Who's this new competition?" 'But when they realised I spent four days putting a show together, they relaxed a bit because they thought, "Nobody else is going to do that." Once they found out I wasn't a threat to their opening supermarket capabilities, I was all right.'

While Adrian established himself on Saturdays, Kid Jensen graduated to his own daily drivetime show, or, as it was known then, the teatime slot. Given free rein to play pretty much what he wanted, it was Jensen's love for the energy and excitement of punk and new wave music that led to him championing the likes of The Police, Gary

Numan, The Stranglers and The Jam. David also took the helm of a revived *Roundtable*, the record review show that was dropped after the departure of Emperor Rosko. It was a show he loved doing. The format was simple yet effective. Artists always love talking about themselves and their music, but *Roundtable* gave them the opportunity to discuss other people's work and the show achieved such a high profile that artists often flew in from other countries to take part. Notably, one show had George Harrison and Michael Jackson, then in the UK promoting his *Off the Wall* album, and mystifyingly wearing a pith helmet throughout the recording. Stupidly, the BBC erased this historic encounter, but in 2019 word was put out on the collectors' circuit and someone came forward with a cassette recording of the entire broadcast as the two icons chat in a very rare informal style about life and their experiences in the music industry.

Shows like *Roundtable* were always popular with the listeners. *Star Special* tweaked the formula slightly by inviting a guest musician to come in and act as the DJ to introduce their favourite records. Broadcast on Sunday afternoons, *Star Special* lasted for just a few years but boasted an impressive array of guest DJs including David Bowie, ABBA, Joe Jackson, Frank Zappa and Bryan Ferry.

It was not unusual for pop stars to drop into the studio not just for an interview but to spin a few discs. Elton John memorably spun the platters in both 1975 and 1976 with his shows *EJ the DJ*. In 1992, Radio 1 invited Diana Ross to present her own show.

By the end of the summer of 1978, despite the popularity of Adrian Juste's show, a mini shake-up saw him removed from the schedules, leading to a vociferous and vocal group petitioning the BBC to reinstate him. 'When they write about you in the *Radio Times*, the Beeb know they've got problems,' says Adrian. Derek Chinnery had no alternative but to face the music and brought Adrian back, putting him on Saturday afternoon between 1 p.m. and 2 p.m. 'And despite a few short-lived moves to other slots, that's where I stayed for the next sixteen years.'

It was the ideal slot. People listened as they got ready to attend a local football match or go shopping, and Adrian's lively chat and popular mix of fast-cut comedy clips and music won a tremendous audience, as well as introducing a whole new generation to the likes of Tony Hancock and Kenneth Horne. Nor was it lost on Adrian that this was the old Jack Jackson slot. His producer often said, 'This is how Jack would do it,' leaving little ambiguity about what they wanted. 'Journos used to come up to me and say, "I bet you listened to Jack Jackson when you were young." I said, "Well, not a lot really." Had I known what I was going to do, I would have paid more attention.'

Having worked for a time in commercial radio and found it to be a hornet's nest of egos, Adrian instantly gravitated to the BBC way of doing things. Like a comfy pair of slippers, he always felt more at home at the Beeb. 'Probably because of my background. In the 1950s, I listened to the radio all the time, the Home Service, *Any Questions?*, *The Goon Show*, so I was more of a BBC man. It was like the RAF and I loved it. People like Derek Chinnery in his suede shoes: you sort of dreaded getting stuck in a lift with him, no conversation – but he knew his business.'

Egton House was, by this stage, a bit run down, 'but it had atmosphere,' says Adrian. As for Broadcasting House, that was special. 'You'd walk in and it was always a great buzz. There was so much history in the place and it automatically raised your game. Commercial radio could never compete with that.'

And there were his colleagues, whom he liked, although they didn't see all that much of each other. 'I suppose that's why we did get on – because we weren't living in each other's pockets all the time,' he says. The football matches did allow some of the DJs the chance to socialise together and Adrian was an active member of the team, even though he didn't know the offside rule and approached the whole thing as just a fun day out. 'But a lot of the teams we played against took it really seriously. We played at Carrow Road. "Oh, it's just a charity fundraiser, Adrian, a kickabout." They had four of the bloody Norwich first team in it, and those of us who could play got kicked to bits!' Some of the DJs did take things seriously, especially John Peel.

'We were doing an outside broadcast in Liverpool,' recalls Adrian, 'and they arranged a match at Anfield and Peel wouldn't play. He said, 'It's hallowed ground. I can't go on there.' I think we ended up playing at Tranmere Rovers' ground. We still got around 15,000 in there.'

Adrian was also the voice of the Roadshow – 'Today, live from Cleethorpes.' He did it for fifteen years, missing just one year when Tommy Vance took over. He also did a few Roadshows himself: 'I used to love doing them.' He did one with Janice Long at Haydock Park racecourse and was told by John Lennard, their Manchester-based producer, that they'd booked a knife-throwing act. 'I was put up against this board with all these blades flying at me. I thought, "I hope he wasn't out on the piss last night." They were quite close. I was sorrier for Janice because if one of those went through the jugular, she had to cover.' Years later, Adrian bumped into John Lennard and the producer admitted that he still had nightmares about the incident. 'It was bloody dangerous and I shouldn't have made you do it,' Lennard said to Adrian.

'Don't worry, John,' went Adrian. 'All those bloody knives coming at me – it proved invaluable experience for the BBC under John Birt!'

Andy Peebles joined the station at the close of 1978. Like many of his contemporaries, the radio was an integral part of growing up. Sunday lunchtime was especially important, consisting of almost religious devotion to the Light Programme, highlights like the *Billy Cotton Band Show*, *Hancock's Half Hour* and *Pick of the Pops* with David Jacobs. 'They were all incredibly important for me because it increased my fascination for what was coming out of the speaker.'

Having to come to terms with the early death of his father, Andy had won a scholarship to public school in Bishop's Stortford. He also began to tune into the pirates, especially Radio London, which led to a remarkable turn of events. One day a couple moved into the flat above his family's, and, over the next few months, Andy would see the man coming in and out. Eventually Andy introduced himself on the path one morning. As Andy remembers: 'The man said, "Yes, I know who you are and I feel very guilty that we haven't talked. But I'm only here one week out of three." I said, "Really, why is that?" And suddenly the penny dropped and I thought to myself, "My God, I know your voice."' The voice belonged to Paul Kaye, who had the distinction of being the first DJ heard on Radio London – and also the last when the station closed down.

Andy was to become very close with Kaye. During Kaye's shore leave, they spent a lot of time together and when he returned to the ship Andy would have his transistor tuned in to Big L listening to Kaye's show from nine till midnight. 'Sometimes he would say hello to me. It was a unique situation.'

Leaving school at the age of 18, Andy was taken on at a local hotel to run the bar. Kaye made a practice of coming in on his way back to the ship to order two or three bottles of Scotch – it wasn't difficult to reach the conclusion that the man had a drinking problem. Years later, when Andy was a DJ on Piccadilly Radio in Manchester, Kaye would do the occasional voiceover, but sometimes he was too drunk to work. 'I found this absolutely heartbreaking,' Andy says, 'because this had been a guy who, while he was never a substitute for my father, had great empathy and understanding, more than anyone else, about my simmering fascination with the world of broadcasting.' Kaye died in 1980 aged just 46.

Working as a club DJ, Andy got friendly with Emperor Rosko and was often invited up to Broadcasting House to sit in on his shows on a Saturday morning. Already a lover of soul music, Andy's visits to London were never complete without a rummage around the specialist record stores for the latest American soul imports. After a while, Rosko asked if he could buy a second set for him. Andy would arrive in the studio with a package of new singles under his arm whereupon Rosko, much to the annoyance of his producer, would rip up the carefully planned running order and play the new ones instead.

Andy's big breakthrough came in 1974 when the commercial station Piccadilly Radio opened in Manchester. He spent four happy years there with his *Soul Train* show, and it was the success of the show that drew him to the attention of Johnny Beerling, who asked him to join Radio 1. This was all done in a very cloak and dagger fashion, like tapping up a football player from an opposing team. Andy was advised not to tell anybody of the approach when he met Derek Chinnery for lunch in London. 'Derek was completely paranoid. When I said, "Let's get one taxi. I'll drop you back at Broadcasting House and then go on to Euston," because I had to return to do my evening show on Piccadilly, he said, "No, no, no. I can't have you coming anywhere near Broadcasting House, somebody might recognise you." I said, "Don't be ridiculous, nobody knows me outside Manchester." Anyway, he wouldn't have it and we got separate cabs.'

Tony Blackburn helped Andy settle in by inviting him to sit in the studio and watch him broadcast – an act of kindness Andy never forgot, and they became lifelong friends. 'Normally Tony hated people being in the studio,' Andy says. 'He didn't even like the engineers sitting through the glass. He was a really private person.'

Andy had been brought in to plug the two-and-a-half-hour gap that existed when Kid Jensen went off the air at 7.30 p.m. and the start of Peel at 10 o'clock, a gap previously filled by a Radio 2 programme. But it was an arrival curtailed by a strike from engineers who refused to work the extra hours on the new show. 'In the end, Derek Chinnery was so embarrassed and frustrated, because he was paying my fees and I wasn't doing any work, that he gave me a programme at teatime. Eventually my show got on the air and that's where it all started – thirteen of the happiest years of my life.'

Peel was amused by this new upstart coming down from Manchester radio and the pair enjoyed a mock adversarial relationship. 'We were always taking the piss out of each other,' says Andy. In fact, Andy was a huge admirer of Peel, going back to his *Perfume Garden* days on Radio London and was disappointed to discover that the broadcaster never enjoyed talking about the past. 'I remember getting close to a real argument with John when, out of sheer frustration, I said to him in the office one day, "God, Peel, why can't you face the fact that you're part of British broadcasting history and that the music you played on the pirate ships is very important?" But he wouldn't have it. All he wanted to talk about was today and tomorrow; yesterday didn't matter. I admire him for that, but he had sort of erased some tremendous history.'

Musically the two men were miles apart and their broadcasting style was vastly different, too. Andy, like many others, had been influenced by some of the great American DJs and saw value in the art of the voiceover, while Peel, being the great purist, believed you shouldn't talk over a single note in any record.

Something else bugged Andy, and that was Peel's 'man of the people' radio persona. 'I think it was an act. John Peel came from a very well-to-do family. John and his brother Alan were sent away to school at Shrewsbury, one of the top ten public schools in Britain. Alan, his brother, is incredibly well-spoken. I met him at a Radio 1 event and the introduction by John was in a stylised scouse accent, "You two will get on like a bloody house on fire. Public school boys united." This voice of John's was a complete fabrication. It was an image. I quite admired him for it, but I found it very amusing. He was certainly one of the great characters at Radio 1.'

David Symonds knew Peel when he was at Radio 1, sitting in with him on a few of his shows. Later in the seventies, David was promoting a couple of bands and once turned up at a club where Peel was the host. When David arrived, Peel was outside the venue, done up quite smartly, and polishing his Land Rover. 'Then an hour later when the gig started,' David remembers, 'John had gone into the dressing room and changed into the T-shirt with the built-in sweat stains, messed his hair up a bit, and put on his vegetarian loafers. John Peel was entirely self-created.'

It's clear that there was a constant battle between John Peel and John Ravenscroft, the name he was born with. For many of the people who knew him, the John Ravenscroft who was buried by this character called John Peel didn't really emerge on the radio until he started doing *Home Truths* on Radio 4 in the late nineties. 'And then you heard that character,' says producer Trevor Dann. 'That's the John I know sitting having a curry. John Peel was an invention of John Ravenscroft. They were not the same thing.'

★

Around the time that Andy Peebles arrived at Radio 1, the station also welcomed Mike Read. Unlike many of his contemporaries, Mike was never an avid radio listener; he was more interested in trying to make his way as a singer and a songwriter, with a passion for cricket and writing poetry. It was Neil ffrench-Blake, then starting Radio 210 in Reading, who wanted Mike on board. 'I assumed to play and sing,' says Read, 'but no... as a broadcaster... for three reasons, he said. One that I was very English, two that I was mildly eccentric and three that I was a good opening bowler and he was going to start a radio station cricket team.'

From Radio 210, Mike went to Radio Luxembourg where his easygoing style brought him to the attention of Doreen Davies, who always had excellent instinct when it came to judging and picking potential Radio 1 DJs. 'I was called over from Luxembourg to talk to Doreen and Derek Chinnery,' recalls Mike. 'I had a call later that day from my agent asking if I wanted the job. Was there any doubt? It seems that my laissez-faire attitude had led Derek to believe I was something of a dilettante and had a private income!'

On offer was just a single show on Saturday night, as opposed to the five shows a week he was doing on Luxembourg – and getting paid more than Radio 1 was prepared to give. Mike had a decision to make. As far as he saw it, this was like playing first team football for Crewe Alexander and then suddenly being told you're signing for Liverpool or Manchester United. You might not play every week or you might spend most of the season on the bench. It was up to Mike to decide whether or not he thought he was good enough to get into that first team, or stay where he was, pay the mortgage, be safe. Mike took the gamble.

When Mike arrived that November, Radio 1 was about to change its wavelength from 247 metres to 275 and 285 metres. While this didn't put an end to many people's demand for a permanent FM signal – only a select few shows went out with the benefit of stereo – at least the new frequencies gave the station better geographical coverage. Mike's first job at the station was to join with other Radio 1 DJs adding their voices to a song co-written by Peter Powell and the group

Showaddywaddy that was part of an awareness drive to alert the public to the frequency changes. As Mike recalled, the single was released 'to a wave of apathy'.

Very quickly, Mike started to host *Top of the Pops* and became a regular on Radio 1 'weeks out'. During an excursion to Plymouth, Peter Powell, who had a penchant for speedboats, took Mike and a few of the production team out for a spin round the coast. After half an hour, the boat began filling up with water and it became apparent that something was wrong. 'I couldn't swim, so I was given the lifebelt,' Mike recalls. 'The problem was we were half a mile out and the engine cut out. I went over the side with a rope round me and pulled the boat by paddling my legs. After a while, my feet started hitting the bottom which made it easier. Not easy... but easier. About an hour later, I made it to the beach, with quite a few rope burns, after dragging a boat with five people on board to the shore. My relief only lasted a few seconds before I received a serious smack around the back of the head from, it turned out, a handbag. The woman wielding it was stark naked.' Mike had inadvertently landed on a nudist beach. 'I was informed in no uncertain terms that 'You peeping Toms are always at it!' All was eventually explained. The nudists shared their sandwiches with me.'

That, however, wasn't the end of the episode, as Mike continues: 'Peter Powell and one of the nudists (a policeman apparently, although he wasn't in uniform) tried to limp the boat around to Looe Harbour, while our producer Paul Williams went for help. RNAF Culdrose was scrambled, as Paul had bafflingly told them, for some obscure reason best known to himself, that I had broken my leg! It was just as well they came, as the boat, now back out at sea with a fully clothed DJ and a naked police officer, burst into flames and they had to be winched off.' The following morning it was front page news in most of the tabloids. 'Derek Chinnery hauled Peter and me in to warn us against any more stupid pranks. He simply wouldn't believe that it was an accident and that we were nearly drowned.'

★

Before the end of the year a decision was made that Radios 1 and 2 should have their own separate controller. While Charles McLelland was asked to focus solely on Radio 2, the search began for the right candidate to run Radio 1. The talk around Egton House was that there were two candidates: Derek Chinnery and Teddy Warwick. The consensus amongst the so-called 'music-loving producers' was very much for Teddy. He was the music man and one of them. 'He was a very clear thinker,' says Tony Wilson. 'A very forward-looking modern guy who had little time for most of what the management of the station were up to. He was much more in our camp.'

The jocks loved him, too. Paul Gambaccini speaks for most when he says they all felt that Teddy had complete confidence and trust in them. 'I would walk up this little staircase from the third floor to the fourth floor and there was Teddy's office. Once I went up and said, "Do you think it's time for the Elton John story?" Because they'd had a Beatles story and a Rolling Stones story. He said yes, and he let me do it. That was it. Today, even if you get a commission, it takes about a year for the thing to be broadcast. I was 26 years old and just given a tape recorder. "Off you go, no budget, just do it." And that was Teddy.'

The attitude towards Chinnery was very different, with many holding the firm belief that his heart just wasn't in rock and pop music. David Hamilton recalls Chinnery holding a grand party for all the Radio 1 jocks at his house in Hampstead. During the evening, Teddy Warwick came up to David and said, 'Come over here and have a look at the old man's record collection.' They both flicked through it and there was the original soundtrack to *South Pacific*, *The Sound of Music*, that kind of stuff. 'He didn't listen to Peel because he couldn't understand what he was about at all.'

Amusingly, during an on-air debate about sexually transmitted diseases, Peel happily declared having once caught a venereal disease and that more should be done to educate teens about the risk of STDs. Chinnery went spare. 'I don't want to hear this type of comment,' he said at a meeting. 'If we go off in this direction, we'll be discussing homosexuality on air next!'

Tony Blackburn told a story about playing the Paul Anka song '(You're) Having My Baby' and Chinnery calling up on the studio phone. 'You can't play a song like that; it's about having a baby!'

'Well, people do have babies, Derek. And it's a lovely song.'

What Chinnery was, after all, was a BBC man, with his horn-rimmed spectacles and customary suit and tie. He was a safe pair of hands, having joined the BBC as a trainee aged 16 straight from school in 1941, and worked his way through the ranks. Almost inevitably, he got the job over Teddy Warwick. Many at Radio 1 were disappointed. 'He was the wrong man for the job,' says David Hamilton. 'Teddy was a man of the people. He should have been the controller.'

But to give him his due, Chinnery had played a significant part in the creation of the Top 40 chart as we know it today. In the early sixties, when he worked on the Light Programme, Chinnery diligently bought the four big music papers every Friday – the *New Musical Express*, *Melody Maker*, *Record Mirror* and *Disc*. Back in his office, he would study the chart pages and, in his bookish manner, copy out the numbers into an exercise book, awarding points, until he came up with a BBC Top 20. His system was completely unscientific and yet it became not only the foundation for the *Pick of the Pops* show presented by Alan Freeman, but also Britain's leading pop chart.

But for producers like Trevor Dann, Chinnery was 'very drab, a bank manager. He was not an unpleasant man. He once had to tell me off about something and he was almost apologetic about having to do it. He was just very cautious. Twenty years before he'd have been an air-raid warden.'

Johnny Beerling heard of the roundabout way Chinnery was offered the job as controller. Aubrey Singer, the managing director of BBC Radio, asked to see Chinnery and told him that after much thought they couldn't think of anyone else to give the job to. 'Derek wasn't sure whether to take that as a compliment or not.'

Chinnery's appointment can be seen as another round peg in a square hole. He did, however, make quite a good fist of running the station. Beerling, for one, quite liked him. 'He was very straight, Derek. During his management of Radio 1, Chinnery still used the term "gramophone records" in conversation. Not a man with a great sense of humour, but he loved radio. He was rather like a benign schoolmaster who regarded the DJs as unruly schoolboys that had to be kept in line.'

Taking over, Chinnery recognised that one of the common complaints about Radio 1 was its rather conservative nature and he did his best to rectify this. One decision taken was that no record should be played again within a four-hour time frame. He also relaxed the guidelines when it came to banning songs mentioning commercial products. In 1970, The Kinks had to replace the line 'Coca-Cola' to 'cherry cola' in order for their song 'Lola' to be allowed airtime on the BBC. Swearing, however, remained a big no-no. In 1982, Blancmange were forced to replace their lyric 'up the bloody tree' with 'up the cuckoo tree' in order for their debut hit 'Living on the Ceiling' to get played. This policy remained firmly in place for many years. In 1986, the George Michael single 'I Want Your Sex' was restricted to airtime post 9 p.m.

Chinnery had very clear ideas of the function of Radio 1, describing it as a 'personality station'. And he had a clear vision of exactly who their target audience was and broke it down into two specific groups. First group was the factory worker or labourer – a group of mechanics working in a small garage with Radio 1 playing in the background. Then there was the housewife, someone who perhaps a year or two before was a secretary working for a firm and is now married with a child. 'She wants music that will keep her happy and on the move,' stated Chinnery.

There was also a continued recognition of the importance of live music. The previous year, Radio 1 had launched *Sight and Sound in Concert*, an initiative to provide simultaneous pictures on BBC 2 along with stereo radio broadcasts. Long before the introduction of digital stereo and 5.1 Surround Sound, this series gave British television audiences an exciting glimpse of things to come and allowed rock enthusiasts to enjoy musical events with an improved sound quality.

In the lead-up to the series, the *Radio Times* handily suggested that 'for the best effect, viewers with stereo radio sound turn off the TV

157

sound and position their speakers on either side of the screen, but a few feet away'. Over the years bands that featured included Santana, Rory Gallagher, Jethro Tull, Thin Lizzy and Supertramp.

Many of the groups from those live sessions of the early seventies had gone on to achieve superstardom and were now too big to consider coming back to record in a BBC studio. And so, it came as something of a surprise to Jeff Griffin when he bumped into Roger Taylor and Brian May at a West End club one night and Taylor said: 'Do you reckon we could do a Peel session?'

Jeff almost spilt his drink. 'What! Are you sure?'

'Yes, John always used to say nice things about us.'

Jeff explained that he'd have to ask John Walters, Peel's producer. The following day, Jeff went to see Walters. 'I met a couple of the guys from Queen last night and they fancy doing a session for Peely.'

'What!'

'Do you reckon he'll have them?'

'Oh, I don't know,' said Walters in his laconic way. 'I'll ask.'

The answer was obviously yes and Walters asked Jeff to fix it up. 'I sorted out a date, booked the studio and they came in,' he remembers. 'It was fantastic – and it was the last in-house session they did for the BBC.'

This was October of 1977 and Jeff recalled that the band told him it was going to cost them more in petrol to drive their sports cars and equipment to the studios in Maida Vale than they were going to get in a fee.

In a bid to showcase up-and-coming new wave artists there was *Rock Goes to College*, which ran from 1978 to 1981. Presented by Pete Drummond, these gigs came from small venues such as universities, polytechnics or college halls holding a few thousand people. Again the fifty-minute live performance was broadcast simultaneously on television and Radio 1. The surviving footage captures bands such as The Police, The Specials, AC/DC, Siouxsie and the Banshees and U2 at their raw, early best.

The usual practice was for tickets to be given to the Students' Union to distribute for free. This led to an enormous ruckus on one infamous night in November 1978 when The Stranglers played the University of Surrey in Guildford. The band insisted that at least half of the tickets for the gig be made available to their local fans. Both the BBC and the university agreed to this request – then ignored it. When the band arrived at the venue, they learnt from fans outside that no tickets had been made available to non-students. Infuriated, the band thought about not playing at all, but instead went on stage in not the best of moods, thrashing through their songs in frantic style and deliberately antagonising the audience. After a few songs, some of the amplifiers were kicked over and lead singer Hugh Cornwell suggested that the audience 'fuck off'. With that, the band marched off stage and ignored requests from the BBC production team to return and finish the gig.

In the same month that The Stranglers were sticking two fingers up to Auntie Beeb, Radio 1 launched a new programme on Friday nights that was to run successfully for the next 15 years. It came about when Alan Freeman decided not only to leave the *Saturday Rock* show, but the BBC as well, feeling, as he put it, 'cocooned' within the organisation. After a break of about a year, Freeman popped up on Capital. After Freeman left *Saturday Rock*, his producer Tony Wilson took a couple of months off to decide what to do next. He wanted to put together a similar type of rock show but it had to be fronted by the right person. The name Tommy Vance sprang into his mind. Like Fluff, Vance had a punchy broadcasting style and an iconic voice, thanks to a mid-Atlantic accent acquired early on in his career when he worked on American radio in the mid-sixties.

Tommy Vance wasn't new to Radio 1, of course, having been one of those ex-pirate jocks first lured to the station. Heard in 1968 presenting *Top Gear* with John Peel, Tommy was soon let go and went to work in Europe before joining Capital in the early seventies, where he'd remained.

Wilson brought Tommy in and together a pilot show was put together. 'I took it to Chinnery,' Wilson remembers, 'who sort of rolled his eyes to the ceiling and said, "Well, if you must have these

159

old has-beens back, on your own head be it." And that's how *The Friday Rock Show* started.' The Friday 10 p.m. to midnight slot was taken from Peel, who now had to make do with just Monday through Thursday. 'I don't think he was entirely chuffed about it,' says Wilson.

For fans of hard-edged music, *The Friday Rock Show* became an institution. The new wave of British heavy metal of the early eighties would find its home under Vance and Tony Wilson's purview. All the major bands came in to record sessions – Iron Maiden, Def Leppard, Samson, Girlschool, Saxon, Tygers of Pan Tang and many more.

Tony enjoyed a good working relationship with Vance. 'He was a gentleman. We had a lot of fun.' The tradition in those early years was to meet up on the Friday at Broadcasting House, put the show together, head over to Tommy's flat in Maida Vale for dinner, and then return to the studio around 9 p.m. and get ready to go on air. 'After the show finished,' says Tony, 'we'd either go out to a bar or go back to Tommy's flat and stay up all night with friends having a good time. We were very pally. Great memories.'

13

Because the DJs on Radio 1 were always presented and promoted as a team, the public gained the impression that they were in each other's pockets and saw each other all the time. Far from it. 'I was quite a loner,' admits Noel Edmonds. 'I used to go in, do my show, and then go away again.' The DJs rarely socialised and, beyond things like 'weeks out', get-togethers were rare. 'We were all in at different times and tended to work with our own producers, so we rarely saw each other,' confirms Mike Read. 'There was no green room or place where people could hang out. Unless you had to record something or go to a meeting, there was no reason to hang around.'

One of the few instances when everyone met for a social occasion was the Christmas party, which began when the station first launched. The DJs all sat around a long boardroom table in the imposing, oak-panelled council chamber in Broadcasting House and were served a full festive dinner courtesy of the BBC canteen. 'They were all very amenable about doing these kinds of things,' recalls David Atkey, who produced many of the Christmas shows. 'Some of them weren't that keen to be there with other DJs they didn't particularly like, but they all did it.'

This event took place a couple of weeks prior to the festive season and was always recorded to go out usually on Christmas Day. Each year a different DJ was the host and went round the room chatting to his colleagues and asking for their favourite record of the year.

To make things a little more interesting, Atkey thought it would be nice to have a surprise guest. 'The first one was this waiter who came in and it was Andrew Sachs dressed up as Manuel from *Fawlty Towers*. None of them knew and they just fell about. Another guest we had was Paul Daniels and he came in all dressed as Father Christmas. He did a card trick with DLT on radio which actually worked brilliantly.'

The Christmas parties continued well into the eighties, and for many were seen as something more to be endured than enjoyed. 'It was a potpourri of egos,' says Noel Edmonds. John Peel referred to them as 'the most appalling event of the year', especially as part of the festivities meant being given a piece of paper with the lyrics to Christmas songs that they all had to sing.

Besides the potential for a massive clash of egos, there was a certain amount of paranoia about where each of them sat. Andy Peebles recalls that for quite a number of years Jimmy Savile was at the head of the table. 'In his own mind, he was in charge. He was the biggest star in the room. And he wanted to make sure that every one of us realised that.' He did this by also arriving later than everyone else. 'He didn't have an entourage,' says Adrian Juste, 'but everyone was supposed to bow and throw rose petals in front of him.'

By 1979, Jimmy Savile had been at Radio 1 for almost ten years and was a huge television star, fronting *Jim'll Fix It*, his own early evening children's show on Saturdays on BBC 1. Many of the old DJs had long ago made up their minds about Savile and the new intake were equally adept at arriving at similar conclusions. 'I learnt very early on that the only way to deal with Jimmy Savile was to play him, in cricketing terms, straight off the front foot and hit him back over his head over the boundary rope,' says Andy Peebles. 'And I consistently did that with him.'

Savile's work habits hadn't changed over those years. He continued to pop into Broadcasting House perhaps once a fortnight, keeping himself very much to himself. 'Savile separated himself from the rest of us,' says DJ Robbie Vincent. 'And for a very good reason, because amongst us might have been somebody who smelt something not quite right. He was such a devious pile of rubbish.' Once in the building,

Savile sat in a studio in front of a microphone doing the links for a couple of editions of his show, staying maybe half an hour, no more, and then he was out of the building again. 'It sickened me just how good he sounded on Radio 1,' says Andy Peebles, 'because technically he was a total, complete and utter incompetent. He knew that because the production team did such a brilliant job editing the things he did, he sounded like the consummate professional. He couldn't drive a desk to save his life.'

During the seventies, Ted Beston was Savile's producer for much of his time at Radio 1. His office was opposite Bernie Andrews' office and very occasionally Bernie would bump into Savile in the corridor and they'd have a little chat. On one occasion, Savile started talking to him about Broadmoor, boasting that he had the keys and could go there any time he wanted. 'Isn't that a bit weird?' asked Bernie.

'Then why don't you come with me next time I pay a visit,' offered Savile.

And that's what happened, Savile took Bernie in his Rolls-Royce down to Broadmoor. 'And it's quite true that he had the keys to get in,' says Jeff Griffin, who was told the story by Bernie. 'Savile didn't have to ask anybody else. He had keys to get in through the main gate, keys to get into the building itself, and he introduced Bernie to some of the patients.'

During the visit, a female patient came over to Bernie and pointed at a lanyard he was wearing round his neck. It was a present from the Beatles' record label Apple. Bernie was a sucker for free gifts that pluggers used to bring round to Radio 1. When Apple was launched, he'd been given a lanyard with an apple core on it. He often wore it because he loved it so much. The woman kept pointing at it and then started fondling it with her fingers. 'I like that,' she said. 'I like that very much.' Savile was watching all this and quietly spoke into Bernie's ear, 'I think maybe you should give her that.' Bernie didn't really want to part with it, but Savile insisted, 'I really think you should.' Bernie took it off and passed it over to the woman who went off holding it with a smile on her face.

When the visit was over, both men left the building and Savile locked the door behind them. 'Are those patients really as bad as people say they are?' asked Bernie. 'Well,' said Savile, 'that woman you just gave the apple core lanyard to. She strangled somebody with her bare hands.'

It wasn't long into Chinnery's reign as controller that he questioned Savile about rumours circulating at the BBC that he was sexually assaulting underage girls. Called into Chinnery's office, Savile was asked directly if these stories had any truth to them. The DJ told him that they were all invented nonsense and an occupational hazard for celebrities. Chinnery blankly accepted his word and didn't take the rumours any further. This in spite of the fact that in 1973 his predecessor Douglas Muggeridge had asked a Radio 1 press officer to check whether newspapers were planning to print a story about Savile having inappropriate liaisons with underage girls. These allegations revolved around his programme *Savile's Travels*. In the end, the story didn't run. Muggeridge was told that the papers were aware of such allegations but unwilling to print them 'whether they were true or not', because Savile did a lot for charity and was perceived as a popular personality. Whether Chinnery knew about this is unknown, but it's now clear that there were serious failings at the BBC when it came to investigating Savile's behaviour at the time.

Flash forward to 2009 when Savile was arrested after four women went to the police to claim that he had sexually assaulted them. Savile responded to these allegations in much the same way he did with Chinnery, by batting them away, coming up with the same excuses: the stories were invented and an occupational hazard for someone in his position. He said this in a police interview under caution. He also revealed that he had a policy for dealing with such complaints and that in the past he had sued five newspapers. A police log of the interview recorded Savile as saying: 'If this [these allegations] does not disappear then my policy will swing into action.'

The Crown Prosecution Service decided against taking any further action, for which they later publicly apologised, and a golden opportunity was missed to make Savile pay for his crimes when he was still alive. He died in 2011. A year later, after a television documentary made allegations that Savile had abused girls on BBC property, notably his dressing room on *Top of the Pops*, and other locations including various hospitals and his home in Leeds, the police launched a criminal investigation, Operation Yewtree. Bit by bit, the public learned of the horrifying scale of his crimes: covering a five-decade period, with the peak years being 1966 to 1976, he committed 214 alleged acts, some involving children as young as 8. Within the recorded crimes there were 126 indecent acts and thirty-four rape offences. Here was a man who used his fame and celebrity to hide in plain sight. Many of the women hadn't come forward at the time, citing the fact that they would never have been believed.

Many derided the fact that Operation Yewtree was set up years, indeed decades, too late, but it was seen as a watershed moment for child abuse investigations. While some commentors felt that it developed into a witch hunt with false accusations that ruined lives and reputations, it did subsequently deal with sexual assault cases committed by other celebrities such as Rolf Harris, Gary Glitter and Max Clifford.

After the Savile revelations, it was inevitable that Radio 1 would be placed under the spotlight and, in November 2012, Dave Lee Travis was arrested. When his case came to court in February 2014, he was cleared of twelve counts of indecent assault relating to incidents that allegedly took place between 1976 and 2008. However, in another trial later that year he was found guilty of an indecent assault dating back to 1995 and given a two-year suspended sentence. Travis always pleaded his innocence. He told the police after his arrest that groping behaviour was the 'norm' and described himself as a 'tactile' person, usually greeting both men and women with a kiss and a hug, but that he 'understood the line between being naturally huggy and making people feel uncomfortable'.

Travis and Savile weren't the only Radio 1 names associated with Operation Yewtree. Chris Denning, who numbered amongst the first recruits to the station back in 1967 and worked there for two years, had a long history of sexual offences going back to 1974 and had already served prison time in Britain when he was arrested in June 2013 as part of Operation Yewtree. Charged with forty-one sexual offences dating back to 1967, he pleaded guilty to twenty-nine charges of abuse against boys. Described by the judge as 'utterly depraved', Denning was sentenced to thirteen years in prison. Eyebrows were also retrospectively raised about John Peel's first marriage to Shirley Anne Milburn, when she was just 15 and he was 26. The marriage turned out to be doomed and an unhappy one that didn't last. Then Jane Nevin went public about an affair she had with Peel back in 1969 when she was 15 and he was 30. The relationship, which Jane insisted was consensual, lasted just a few months, during which time she became pregnant and had an abortion.

There was a weird kind of dichotomy going on at the BBC; it was innocent and outrageous all at the same time. 'On *Top of the Pops*, mothers used to do anything to sneak their daughters into the audience to stand next to Jimmy Savile,' says Johnnie Walker. 'And as we know now there was a very dark side to what was happening.' There was the case of Claire McAlpine, a 15-year-old dancer on *Top of the Pops*, who dreamt of a career on the stage. After she committed suicide in 1971, her diary revealed names of DJs and celebrities she had slept with and that she felt had exploited her. Although this information was reported after the coroner's inquest, neither the police nor the BBC took any action, which, given the climate at the time, comes as little surprise.

One of Radio 1's biggest icons was the next to fall, in February 2016. Tony Blackburn was asked to give evidence to an independent inquiry undertaken by Dame Janet Smith into the BBC's culture and practices during the years that Jimmy Savile worked there. However, he was viewed to have failed to fully co-operate and that his evidence, in the words of the BBC's director-general Lord Hall, 'fell short of the standards of evidence that such an inquiry demanded'. Blackburn was asked to leave the BBC. The veteran broadcaster, then presenting a Saturday show on Radio 2, was devastated and alleged that he was being made a 'scapegoat' and he would 'not allow them to destroy my reputation'. Eight months later he was reinstated, but the bitterness of his treatment remained.

Blackburn's case highlighted the problems inherent in judging an era when Britain was a very different place. Take for example the fact that Tony Blackburn had a 'kissing' slot on his breakfast show. The idea was that, on a designated signal, the listener was free to kiss absolutely anybody they liked. 'You might be at work at the moment,' Blackburn preached into the mic, 'and there might be that very attractive blonde there sitting over in the corner.' Permission was thus granted to go over and give her a kiss. 'She can't slap your face, so don't worry about that,' Blackburn continued. 'Or there might be a girl by the bus stop that you rather fancy, so you can just pull into the side there and give her a nice kiss. Are you ready? OK, stand by for it, off we go then, here it comes!' Even by the standards of the seventies, this feature raised the odd eyebrow. But Blackburn was of the opinion that it was just a bit of fun and his bosses obviously didn't see any harm in it either. And Alan Freeman once presented his show from a studio liberally decorated with bras. These had been sent in by female fans who had chosen to respond literally to the launch of a slot called 'Get it off your chest'. They were hanging everywhere. Political correctness was a long way off.

One of the BBC's policies at the time was to send some of its network radio producers around the country to check how things were going in the regions. One of these executives arrived unannounced one morning at Radio Nottingham and got chatting to producer Trevor Dann, who'd been with the station since 1974. They went out to the pub together where Dann confessed, 'I'd love to have your job, but they'd never look at a bloke like me.'

'No, you shouldn't think like that,' said the BBC man. 'You might be just what we want.' As it happened, there was a producer vacancy coming up and he urged Dann to apply. He did and got the job. 'I later found out I was the first new producer they'd had for five years.'

Trevor Dann was an only child and radio became his outlet on the world beyond his Nottingham council estate. The radio was always on at home, mainly music and comedy on the Light Programme. From the age of 10, he started listening to *Pick of the Pops*, writing down all the songs in the Top 20. As a present for passing the Eleven-plus, he asked for and was given a tape recorder which he used to record his favourite programmes. Out of that grew a determination to make broadcasting his career.

When Trevor first arrived at Egton House, he saw himself as something of a brash outsider. For one thing, most of the producers working at Radio 1 had been employed at the BBC in some other capacity. Trevor was one of the very few people to arrive from outside that rather closed world. 'That was a challenge for me,' he says. Added to that was his experience of local radio, where you did pretty much everything, from driving the radio car, commentating on football matches, making documentaries and recording bands. 'It was such a wide range of activities and that's great experience. So, I was pretty hands on when I arrived at Egton House to find a BBC where you couldn't even edit your own tape. You had to sit with an editor and say, "Mark it there and take that bit out." I was quite frustrated by the old heritage way of doing things.'

Worse than that, Trevor found Radio 1 a bit like a mixture of wartime Entertainments National Service Association (ENSA) and a Butlin's holiday camp. Except for Doreen Davies, all the producers were men, and comparatively well-educated. 'But they were working in the entertainment business, which was something they simultaneously wallowed in and despised. There was a very non-intellectual vibe at Egton House. Any attempt to try and argue that one particular artist or record was better than another was squashed. People like me who wanted to say "We should play Tom Petty because he's good and not play Shakin' Stevens because he isn't," well, that kind of debate was just brutally squashed because it was not considered our role. When I arrived, it was certainly a case of "This is how we do it and don't go rocking the boat, pal."'

A relationship that Trevor found fascinating was the one between producers and record pluggers. Although commercial radio had eaten into Radio 1's audience, it was still a national station and its ratings were large enough to make or break an artist. The record companies knew this, and so treated Radio 1's not terribly well-paid producers like gods. 'They ate at the finest restaurants,' says Trevor. 'They went travelling all round the world in business class. They had very nice hampers for Christmas. They were looked after. They were living in this fantastic bubble.' Like Tim Blackmore before him, Trevor never saw any kind of malpractice go on. 'I used to expect it. I used to think, "Somebody's going to come around and give me an envelope full of fivers or cocaine in a minute." But it never happened.'

However, there was a sort of grey area that existed which stretched the borders of legality somewhat. Trevor recalls a brief period when EMI Records was part of the Thorn Electrical group. 'EMI pluggers used to come around and make it clear that if we did happen to need a new fridge, that such a thing might not be impossible.'

Of course, there was no limit on the amount of records a DJ could receive. When Andy Peebles first arrived at Radio 1, he was being sent somewhere between 100 to 120 singles and sixty or seventy albums every week. 'If I kept all the vinyl and all the records that I was given in my thirteen years at the station, it would have filled Heathrow Terminal 5, from the ground to the ceiling. It was ludicrous.' Because the record companies were so desperate not to miss any opportunity to get a record played, there were perks galore. In all those years, Andy never paid for a concert ticket. 'In the end, Johnny Beerling, when he became controller, got very concerned about the amount of hospitality that was being offered, and indeed accepted, and we were told in no-nonsense fashion, "Be very careful what you accept."'

Andy had recently been moved from his evening show and replaced by Mike Read. 'That was fun,' says Mike. 'I would go and see bands and then recommend them to come to Maida Vale to do a live session. I really enjoyed that show, and of course John Peel followed me, so we were often recommending songs to each other.'

This was the post-punk era, just coming into the New Romantics, and what Mike played certainly reflected that. 'It was a great time because there was so much talent out there,' recalls Chris Lycett, who produced the show. 'And we were more or less left on our own.'

Chris was now a recognised producer in his own right. Moving from engineer to producer was sort of a natural progression at Radio 1.

Engineers, after all, worked with programme teams all the time, gaining knowledge of how the production side of the station operated and what made it tick. They still had to apply for the position, though, and go on attachment for several months to Radio 1 production where they trailed someone and cut their teeth, mostly in daytime. Chris went on to work with Peter Powell, Steve Wright and Noel Edmonds, and he launched Mike Smith on the breakfast show.

As a daytime producer, Chris was required to attend the playlist meetings, which he always thought were an effective way of managing and creating an overall sound for the station, while at the same time allowing the DJ and his producer some input to make their show different from those on either side of them. A few years later, when Chris moved into a more senior position, he broached the idea of revising the playlist meetings. He always thought it strange that the only producers attending them were from the daytime schedule. What they didn't benefit from was the knowledge and input of the more specialised producers. 'Clearly there were records suddenly popping up and floating round the charts which the night-time boys had been playing for weeks. So, I inaugurated the idea that at each playlist meeting we would have a visiting night-time producer with us and they would bring in a selection of records. It really worked and really changed it.'

Successful in his new slot, Mike Read joined the rota of DJs on the Roadshow. Always keen to bring something different and exciting to his shows, when he was in Porthcawl and found out that David Essex was the star guest, he racked his brains to come up with a stunt. Aware of the pop star's love of superbikes and racing, Mike called up Harley-Davidson and arranged for a bike to be delivered in the morning. Then he put a call through to the local coastguard to get some flares. He tied six of these massive flares on the back of the uninsured Harley, he and Essex hopped on and, from the back of the crowd, with a security guard forming a path through a throng of people, they raced to the front – no crash helmets, flares going off –

and shot up the hastily erected planks onto the stage. None of that would get signed off today.

Mike always loved doing the Roadshow. During a charity function at Buckingham Palace one year, Prince Philip came over to him and asked, 'Which stretch of the coast are you doing this year?'

For Peter Powell, the Roadshow encompassed everything Radio 1 stood for – all the energy, music and fun. It was one of the highlights of working at the station. 'I used to wait all year for it.' Powell was very much the Roadshow's action man. On one occasion, he abseiled down the Fiveways shopping centre in Birmingham. 'I'd do anything that was action or required a bit of danger,' he says, 'because I was so desperate to get my contract renewed at the end of every year.'

Dave Atkey, Peter's producer on the Roadshow, remembers the time Powell was air-sea rescued off a nearby building by a Sea King helicopter which generated so much downforce that Dave feared it was going to take the roof off the roadshow caravan. At Tenby, they met up with Royal Navy commandos who offered to set up a zip line at the top of the cliffs so that Peter could slide all the way down onto the stage. 'Yeah, I can do that,' said Powell eagerly. It was some entrance as Peter came hurtling down, only there was a rope across the bottom, used to stop people, but the commandos held it so taut that Peter flipped over and dislocated both his wrists. 'But he carried on and did the whole show and then we took him to hospital,' confirms Atkey. 'With the way health and safety is now, we couldn't have done a tenth of the stunts we pulled back then.'

In Plymouth for Navy Day, Dave and Peter bumped into some navy lads in the pub the night before the roadshow. Dave asked if it would be possible to go up in a helicopter with them and it was agreed they could do it in the morning before the show. Armed with a tape recorder, Dave, along with Peter, climbed into the craft and was slightly perturbed to see that each of the doors was stripped off. 'We go up vertically,' recalls David, 'and then the pilot just threw it over onto one side and I'm looking down and I've got the tape recorder and I thought, "I'm going to drop this." We did the whole thing and as we were coming down over a lake there was a big bang. After we landed,

171

I asked what that noise was and the pilot said, "Oh, we went a bit low there. The wheel went in the water."' Back in the hotel David played the tape. It was completely inaudible. Unperturbed, they got back in the same helicopter and did the commentary again, this time safely on the ground. With some added helicopter sound effects, the tape went out on air and no one was any the wiser.

Despite the huge popularity of the Roadshow, it had barely visited Scotland and Doreen decided it was about time that it did. Paul Burnett was chosen as the host, or as he puts it, 'I was used as the guinea pig to see how this thing would trial out. And they threw everything at it.' At the first stop the guest was Sarah Brightman, then enjoying fleeting pop fame with her hit single 'I Lost My Heart to a Starship Trooper'. 'We thought there was going to be a huge crowd,' recalls Paul, 'but we had about fifty people. Sarah came out with thigh-length silver boots on and did the whole performance, selling it big, to the mostly half-interested crowd. To add insult to injury, there were two dogs, doing what dogs do, at the side of the stage. And I swear they were doing it in time to the music.' Afterwards, Paul hoped to have a little chat with Sarah for the show but she'd already packed her bags and bolted.

Within his first year at Radio 1, Paul was put on the Roadshow, starting with a tour of north Wales. 'The weather was shit,' he remembers. 'For some reason they positioned the caravan so we were facing the sea, and we got all this salty spray in our faces. That was my first experience of the Roadshow.' He got to love it, though, especially when he was asked to do the West Country, since you always got the biggest crowds there. And it was there that Paul had a close encounter with a wasp, leading to one of the great Roadshow stories.

Before every gig, Paul would take a sip of beer, just to lubricate the vocal chords. He'd already done the warm-up and the crowd were reaching the peak of excitement as the clock counted down. 'I took another big sip out of this beer, with seconds to go, and I felt this lump going down my throat. I knew what had happened. It was a wasp. And it stung me halfway down the throat. I knew that wasn't good. I

172

collapsed on my knees, retching, trying to bring it up.' Paul explained to his producer Brian Patten what had happened and Patten immediately put out a call to see if there was a doctor in the crowd. There was and he bounded up onto the stage and advised Paul to eat as many ice lollies as he could.

In the meantime, the news had finished and they were on the air. 'I could still talk, and I announced to the crowd, "I'm sorry but I've just swallowed a wasp and it's stung me in the throat, but never mind. We're all having a great time, aren't we?" The whole place goes up. But after every link my voice was changing because my throat was swelling up. By the end, I sounded like Harold Wilson. But I made it through the show.'

It was all change for Tony Blackburn as he moved to Saturday morning, as well as taking over the chart show on Sunday. Ever since the start of Radio 1, the official singles chart had been presented on the station, starting with *Pick of the Pops* under Alan Freeman. In 1972, Tom Browne, a trained actor with a smooth, deep voice, took over from Fluff and the programme became essential listening for millions of people. Simon Bates took the reins in 1978 for just a year before the arrival of Blackburn. Despite its huge popularity, Blackburn didn't enjoy hosting the show all that much: it was too formulaic and proved a challenge to impose his personality into it. Besides, it was anti-climactic, since the week's chart was always revealed first on Tuesdays. But for many DJs, the chart show, along with the breakfast show, was the gig they wanted.

Andy Peebles found out just how nerve-racking an experience it could be when he took a call from Doreen Davies asking whether he would be happy to present the Top 40 while Blackburn went on holiday. At first Andy thought it was a wind-up. 'No, it's not,' said Doreen. 'We've had a meeting and decided we'd like to try you out.' These were the days when the final countdown of the Top 20 records went out simultaneously on Radios 1 and 2.

Bernie Andrews was the producer, and, as the time crept towards the point when Radio 2's audience was set to join, Andy saw him scribbling something on a notepad with a marker pen. Andy hit the pips dead on the nose, banged the jingle and went into announcing a new entry at number twenty. 'I closed the microphone, looked up and Bernie had written on this sheet of A4: "At this time last week, 22.75 million people were listening to this programme." At that stage probably my underpants should have needed changing, but they didn't and I got through it, and I did it the following week. They were quite clever the management team at Radio 1, because I think they did it deliberately, to test me out and give me a bit of confidence.'

Blackburn did the chart show for three years, coming off it in 1982 when Tommy Vance took over. Blackburn had no idea he was being replaced until he went into his producer's office and saw Vance's contract on the table. 'The only thing I was quite happy about was he wasn't being paid as much as I was,' he told fellow DJ Shaun Tilley.

One thing Radio 1 always prided itself in was its charity work, sometimes in association with the Variety Club of Great Britain to help disabled children or those in poverty. By 1978, the station had raised enough money to purchase ten Variety Club Sunshine coaches. There were often campaigns and appeals. During one summer Roadshow, listeners were urged to donate any bits of old vinyl. In all 150,000 records were collected and sold at a huge auction at Alexandra Palace.

It was always important to get the DJs to front these campaigns. In 1979, Simon Bates took part in a major charity event in aid of Oxfam and UNICEF, teaming up with a group of miners from Yorkshire who agreed to push him on a bed from one side of England to the other in a week. Bates even got to broadcast live from the bed and a total of £52,000 was raised. A few years later, Bates staged a charity bike ride from Manchester to Cardiff and was joined along the way by Madness, Kim Wilde and Chas & Dave, along with a large number of amateur and professional cyclists.

All of this fed nicely into the public service remit of the BBC, as did a raft of social action campaigns. These began in 1980 with *Action*

Special. Usually lasting a week, these looked at a particular issue and involved short bursts of information during programmes, mostly based on people's experiences, along with details about how to get more information. Campaigns that ran throughout the year ranged from advice about money, drugs, smoking, further education, safer sex and jobs. There were those within Radio 1 itself, like John Walters, who questioned the need for such action. He recalled: 'They'd say, "But we have to do Simon Bates saying, "Hey, kids, don't take drugs," because it's a public service." I mean, if Simon Bates said to me, 'Hey, don't take drugs,' well, give me the needle straight away.' What was that to do with us? It wasn't our damn business what kids did in their spare time. It was nothing to do with us at all, but they said, "We have to do it, it's public service."'

Repeatedly over the years, Radio 1 was criticised from various quarters – from MPs, from the press – for sounding too much like a commercial station. 'What's specific about Radio 1 as a public service station?' was the usual issue. That was one of the reasons for the creation of *Newsbeat*: no commercial music station would do fifteen minutes of news. It made Radio 1 distinctive. The same was true with the social action campaigns. Because Radio 1 had a mass audience, it could use that for messages, and these messages were packed into the mainstream of the station's output. The kids whom these campaigns were aimed at didn't watch the news and they didn't get this information from their parents or teachers. So where were they going to get it? How were they going to access it if not from a channel they trusted, that they felt was theirs because it played the music they liked, and then told them things they needed to know?

There was always a fine line to tread, of being a pop station and public service provider at the same time. The BBC is charged with being distinctive and doing things differently from the commercial stations, but, on the other hand, it also has to try and be popular to justify the licence fee. It wasn't always an easy balancing act.

14

At the start of the 1980s, Radio 1 looked healthy enough. It had managed to broaden the music base of the station and more than held its own against the commercial sector. But while Radio 1 was the dominant force around the country, it had lost the fight in London. 'Capital radio was absolutely massive in London,' says Andy Peebles. 'All I ever heard from my friends was, "I don't listen to the Radio 1 breakfast show, I listen to Chris Tarrant and Kara Noble." And I used to say to them, "Don't tell anybody, but so do I."'

The station was losing key staff to the commercial sector, too. Tim Blackmore left to join Capital as an executive producer. Despite being offered more money to stay at the BBC, his mind was made up. He felt that there was nothing left for him to do at the network and sought a new challenge. It was agreed he would work a three-month notice. The very next day Tim was producing a music session at the Maida Vale studio when the phone rang. It was Chinnery. 'I'm really sorry about this, Tim,' he said. 'And this is not me speaking, believe me, but I have to ask you to come back, clear your desk and leave the building.'

'What's this all about?' asked Tim.

'The hierarchy say that as you're joining the opposition, you can't be around because you might pick up information that would be useful to them. We'll pay you the three months' salary due.'

And that was it. Far from deflated, Tim rang Capital to say he could join them immediately, which he did. 'I had this fantastic period where I had two salaries for three months.'

He never regretted his decision to leave Radio 1 and looks back on his time there as phenomenally exciting and a huge privilege. 'It was the first time in my life that I began to understand what it was to have power and responsibility. To know that the decisions you make about what to expose to the public could influence what music they chose to buy.'

By 1980, the Radio 1 'weeks out' were still enormously popular and had raised more than £150,000 for the Variety Club. The events were also an opportunity for the DJs to let their hair down more and indulge in schoolboy pranks. Andy Peebles recalls one occasion in Bristol, where everybody on the team agreed they'd had enough of Mike Read, 'not in a nasty way, but we just decided that he needed teaching a lesson'. The plan was to booby trap his bedroom: lights were put of action, the legs of the bed were sawed and kippers were placed behind the radiator before it was turned on full. By the time Mike returned to his room, it smelled ghastly. 'I only had a few hours to sleep before the breakfast show,' Mike recalls. 'Got into bed… and the bed collapsed. I reached for the phone in the dark to call reception and the receiver was smeared with something that had clearly come from the rear end of an animal. I then heard noises in the bathroom and assumed the culprits were hiding in there to witness the result of their handiwork. I felt my way along the wall… quietly turned the handle and pushed really hard. The door had been taken off its hinges and I fell on top of it as a hell of a noise went up. I had no idea what was happening at the time but later discovered that the bath was full of chickens. I heard laughing outside the door and, without even thinking that I had no clothes on, found the handle and went into the corridor. Noel Edmonds and Simon Bates were killing themselves. I gave chase. Bates made it to his bedroom so I went after Noel. The corridor went round in a kind of circle, so when Noel passed my door with me close behind, he clicked it shut. I was now naked and stranded and had to go to reception in a mirrored lift and then find the night porter to explain the situation. I got very little sleep.'

But it was on the Roadshow where the art of the practical joke reached epic proportions. The main culprits were Noel, Mike Read and Tony Miles. One summer in particular saw a tit-for-tat war break out between Mike and Tony. It started in Barnstable when Mike went to get into his Mercedes sports car after breakfast only to find it on blocks with no wheels in the hotel car park. A few days later, two plain clothes CID officers arrested Tony, citing an irregularity in his car numberplates. He was handcuffed, put in the back of a squad car and told they were taking him to Cardiff nick. A few miles down the road, he was released and informed that Mike Read had put them up to it. Tony was not amused and began to plan his pièce de résistance. A capable musician, Mike liked to strum a tune on his guitar, whether people wanted him to or not. Tony went out and bought a guitar identical to Mike's and planted inside a small electronically triggered explosive charge, along with some red dye. He then orchestrated a 'break-in' of Mike's hotel room where, amongst the items to go 'missing', was his beloved guitar. That afternoon Mike had hoped to perform on stage with special guests Kid Creole and the Coconuts. But all was not lost. Tony made sure that at the appropriate moment Kid Creole handed over the 'doctored' guitar to a grateful Mike. A couple of strums into the song, Tony hit the detonator and bang – Mike was engulfed in smoke and dye – all live on air.

One of Mike's favourite pranks on Tony involved enlisting him into the army. 'He thought he was signing an autograph but the sheet under the carbon paper told a different story,' Mike says. 'We removed his clothes from the hotel so that he only had a scratchy uniform to wear all week and I enlisted a granite-faced sergeant-major and two squaddies to give him hell all week. I did let him take part in a military tattoo, but that was a tattoo on his bottom.'

Mike also presented Tony with the regiment's mascot, a small pig. At the end of the Margate Roadshow, everyone disappeared and there was Tony, left holding the pig. The next day at Eastbourne, Mike told the crowd that Tony had arrived at a local hotel with the pig and the manager shouted, 'You can't bring that in here!' To which the pig replied, 'Why not?' The true story was that Tony had left the pig en route to Eastbourne with an obliging farmer.

On one of the few instances when Tony and Mike teamed up to play a prank on someone else, the target was Simon Bates. This was when Mike was on the breakfast show and it was customary for Bates to phone in every morning to promote that afternoon's Roadshow. Tony and Mike managed to persuade a female member of staff in the hotel Bates was staying at to burst into his room scantily clad while he was on the phone. Unbeknown to Tony and Mike, Bates was prone to sleeping in the nude and when the girl walked in, she saw more than she bargained for. It's difficult to know who was the more shocked. Bates leapt into a wardrobe in a mad scramble to cover his embarrassment, still clutching the phone and carrying on with his conversation – 'Mike, please ask her to leave. I'm starkers.'

While still presenting the chart show on Sundays, Tony Blackburn was also asked to host *Junior Choice*, since Ed Stewart was moving across to Radio 2. Blackburn couldn't help but feel he was slowly being put out to pasture. No longer a weekday fixture on the station, he now suddenly found himself doing a kids' show and playing 'Puff the Magic Dragon' ad nauseum.

There was a definite sense of Radio 1 trying to shake things up a bit and bring in new blood. This was perfectly encapsulated by the arrival in 1980 of Steve Wright. London-born Steve started off in journalism in the seventies, working on various local papers. He then worked for the BBC in the record library, which consisted of two rooms: one was a room of filing cabinets that contained about a million index cards providing details of all the records the BBC held; the other room was full of stacked shelves of the records in question.

Steve then heard about Radio 210 opening up in Reading and decided to take a punt. 'I went along to see a man called Neil ffrench-Blake, who had an office in London, and he said, "I'll take a chance on you." I'd never done any radio before, apart from sending out tapes to odd stations here and there, and he hired me.' Neil ffrench-Blake was the first MD of Radio 210. An Etonian, Blake had also been responsible for giving Mike Read his first job on radio, and was always at pains to explain that he didn't employ disc jockeys at the station but broadcasters. 'I spent two or three years there,' says Steve, 'and learnt everything that I ever wanted to know about presenting radio programmes.'

Steve's work at Radio 210 led to him going to Radio Luxembourg and it was while he was on the air that a phone call came through to the studio from producer Stuart Grundy, asking if he'd ever thought about coming to Radio 1. Well, no, as it happened; Steve's intention was probably to work somewhere like Capital or one of the other big commercial stations. Grundy asked Steve to come and see him, and later offered Steve his own Saturday evening show. Having handed in his notice at Luxembourg, Steve arrived at Radio 1 with no real idea of what was required of him or how someone like him went about presenting a Radio 1 programme. 'I'd always listened to Radio 1 and loved it but never thought I'd actually work there. It was absolutely terrifying.'

Coming from commercial radio, with that economy of speech and banging out the records one after the other, Radio 1 was much more of a personality-led station. Every DJ was a star in his own right. 'I was this geeky guy,' admits Steve, 'and I thought, "Well, there must be enough room for geeky guys."' Steve already knew Mike Read from his days on Radio 210, but it was Tony Blackburn who perhaps made the biggest impression on him. 'He always made me laugh because he lived for the radio and still does. And he would actually wear a gold lamé suit in real life. He was a great character.'

Another big change in culture from commercial radio was the sheer scale of the Radio 1 operation. DJs weren't a one-man band but part of a larger team involved in putting a programme together. 'It was great,' says Steve, 'because having a producer and then having somebody the other side of the glass freed us up to be creative. The working environment was great. But bear in mind it's the BBC and it is a bureaucracy, so you can't just do anything you want. In local radio, I was able to answer the phones, go out and do a news story, make commercials, be the booker, and decide what I wanted to play. When you worked at a big station like Radio 1, you had to abide by the rules. I did find that a little bit of a struggle. I would frequently be in trouble for not sticking to the playlist, and "you can't say this and you can't say that". I took some of that on board and some I would ride against a little bit.'

Steve's Saturday show went well and he was offered other work on the station, too, such as an early Sunday morning show later that year and shifts sitting in for other DJs. All this time, he was learning how things worked at Radio 1. 'I still didn't know what I was doing, and I always thought that I was a phoney.' However, his big breakthrough was just around the corner.

To celebrate the release of *Double Fantasy*, John Lennon's first album in five years, Radio 1 had planned an ambitious five-part series on the ex-Beatle. But it was when his current record label Geffen got in touch saying that there was a chance of an interview that everyone sensed a major coup in the offing, given Lennon's retreat from public life.

An interview with David Bowie, then appearing in the stage play of *The Elephant Man* on Broadway, had already been secured, and a Radio 1 production team that included Doreen Davies, producer Paul Williams and Andy Peebles flew out to New York in the hope of also bagging Lennon. They arrived in New York on the evening of Thursday, 4 December 1980. The following afternoon a pre-arranged meeting took place with Yoko Ono at the palatial apartment she shared with Lennon in the Dakota building. It was made fairly obvious to everyone that any chance of an interview with Lennon rested purely on Yoko's say-so. It turned out to be a tense and tough negotiation, but after an hour she agreed to the interview going ahead the following day, Saturday 6 December, at 12 noon. The team celebrated that evening by going to see Bowie in *The Elephant Man*.

In the morning, news came though that Lennon and Yoko had been up all night recording and mixing, so the interview was pushed back to early evening. After doing a bit of Christmas shopping, the Radio 1 crew arrived on time at the Hit Factory studio in Manhattan and waited for the Lennons to appear. It was obvious to Andy, who'd grown up with the Beatles, why Lennon had chosen the BBC to talk to. At home in New York, the musician's radio was usually tuned into the BBC World Service, one of the few links to his homeland; when Liverpool got a mention, he often welled up and got emotional. Once they met, Andy was struck by the fact that the first person Lennon wanted to know about was Bernie Andrews, his old producer on the Beatles' live sessions in the days of the old Light Programme.

Yoko had stipulated that the interview should last no longer than an hour. In the end, Lennon talked for three and a half hours. Afterwards everyone – the Radio 1 team accompanied by John and Yoko – went out to eat. Realising what they'd captured on tape, a John Lennon who was just about as relaxed and candid as he'd ever been, Andy and the team carried out their interview with Bowie on Sunday, 7 December, and then made arrangements to fly back to London the following day.

The team were still up in the air when Mark Chapman fatally shot Lennon on the pavement outside his apartment block. Andy learned the devastating news when he landed at Heathrow and found himself in a media maelstrom. He was soon on his way to the sanctuary of Chinnery's office at Broadcasting House, feeling shattered and having hardly slept in the last twenty-four hours.

'You need to realise something,' said Chinnery, straightening himself up in his chair. 'You need to realise that because of what has happened, this is never, ever going to go away.'

Andy looked at Chinnery. 'Why are you saying that?'

'Because time will prove that it's true and that I am right.'

Andy's Lennon interview was subsequently broadcast, not just on Radio 1 but around the world. And Chinnery was right: as the last man to interview John Lennon, it never has gone away for Andy. 'There were times when I wished it would go away and then the other half of me would say, "Don't be ridiculous. What would other people have paid to have seven hours with John?" Now I feel incredibly proud and lucky to have been involved.'

15

The year 1981 kicked off with a major change to the schedule. Dave Lee Travis was moved from breakfast to make way for Mike Read. A few weeks earlier, Travis had come down with flu while on a 'week out' in Birmingham and Mike was asked to stand in for him. 'I left Broadcasting House after my evening show,' remembers Mike, 'drove away and straight into an unlit set of roadworks. I went back to Broadcasting House and started to see if there were any late-night trains, but Peely said, "If you can wait until midnight, I'll drive you up." And he did.'

Mike presented the rest of that week's shows in Birmingham and was then even more surprised to be offered the hot seat on breakfast. Happy on his evening show, doing sessions and discovering new bands, when the call came to do the breakfast show it wasn't really something he could turn down. There were mixed feelings, though, on his first day; excitement, to be sure, but also a nagging doubt whether or not he really deserved to be there. Talking to Chris Moyles for a documentary, Mike revealed that at the beginning he felt like a fraud. 'I thought, "This chair belongs to Tony Blackburn, Noel Edmonds, Dave Lee Travis. It's not really my chair."'

Things didn't get off to the best start when Mike decided to continue with the kind of music that he'd been showcasing on his evening show, including bands such as The Teardrop Explodes, OMD, Adam and the Ants and The Specials. Chinnery didn't like it at all. 'Why are you playing all this Teardrop Explodes stuff?' he'd complain. 'It's night-time music. It's not day-time music.'

'But it's just good music, Derek,' argued Mike.

It was a running battle that went on for about six months, during which time Mike thought he was going to get the chop at any moment. 'But I came through it and continued to play what I considered to be good music. I love music, whatever genre, as long as it's good.'

Mike also enjoyed a great deal of self-sufficiency. 'My producer tended to come in later, after the show, so I was basically on my own. There was no big team surrounding you during the show, like there is now at the BBC.' Saying that, Mike enjoyed getting out of the studio as often as he could, once broadcasting live from his own living room. On another occasion, he took on the role of a milkman delivering milk to Bristol Zoo. Walking past several of the cages, Mike heard this blood-curdling yell: "The gorilla's escaped. The gorilla's escaped." What to do, should he keep going or turn back? Then he heard this crashing through the bushes and froze as this giant gorilla rushed out. It turned out to be Noel Edmonds in a zip-up gorilla suit.

Mike also came up with the idea of a special week-long series of broadcasts following in the footsteps of Jerome K. Jerome's novel *Three Men in a Boat* which chronicled the journey on a narrowboat along the Thames from Hampton Court to Oxford. As he remembers: 'Doreen Davies's door was always open. She'd ask: "Any ideas?" I always had ideas. I suggested *Three Men in a Boat*, not thinking I'd be taken up on it.'

Mike immediately volunteered to be one of the three, but had no clear notion of who the other two should be. 'As it turned out it was Paul Gambaccini, who basically drove the boat, Noel Edmonds, who was in charge of the galley and did most of the cooking, and me as captain… doing… who knows what… being captain, I suppose. We had a lot of friendly rivalry with other boats, until we were told at one lock that we were to leave the river at the next lock as the authorities were severely displeased with our conduct. Oh, my goodness, we're for it now. But it turned out to be another Smiley Miley [Tony Miles] gag. I have no idea who suggested that we start in Hampton Court Maze. It took us most of the first day to find our way out.'

Naturally, as host of the breakfast show, Mike's public profile raised several notches. The fame game for Mike was a gradual process, from local radio where a few people would come up, chat and maybe ask for an autograph, to Radio Luxembourg where he really started to be more nationally known when he came over to the UK for gigs. 'Radio 1 was an extension of that, and the TV shows, *Pop Quiz*, *Top of the Pops* and *Saturday Superstore*, a further extension.'

Now one of the station's most recognised and high-profile DJs, Mike did become a target for the tabloids. Seemingly every time his car was clamped it was in the paper. Years after leaving Radio 1, Mike met a photographer from the *Daily Mail* who explained how he was told to spend many a night sitting in the woods outside his house to 'see who you came home with'.

According to Johnny Beerling's memoirs, there wasn't much love lost between Mike and Simon Bates, who followed him at 9 a.m. During the handover, there was usually a bit of verbal sparring going on. When it boiled over at one point, it was reported to Chinnery and a formal warning was delivered to the pair of them: 'This morning's effort was banal and embarrassing. Why two intelligent and supposedly inventive broadcasters on a national network should have to resort to unpleasant trivia I don't know.' The reprimand went further: 'If you cannot achieve a normal, civilised and occasionally humorous exchange then I will arrange matters so that you do not talk at all!' That put the matter to bed.

Taking over Mike Read's evening slot was *Newsbeat*'s Richard Skinner. During his seven-year tenure on the news show, Richard had never failed to send Doreen Davies an annual demo tape, hoping she might consider him as a music jock. Nothing happened until 1980 and one Friday night when he was sipping a pint in a pub near Broadcasting House. Suddenly Tony Wilson, producer of the *Friday Rock Show*, burst in and began scanning the room in a mild panic. Spotting Skinner he pushed his way over. 'Are you doing anything tonight?' Richard shook his head. 'Tommy Vance is stuck in

Gibraltar,' stated Tony. 'He went out to do a broadcast for the forces and the flights have been cancelled. He can't get back.' Richard looked at the clock on the wall. It was 8.30 p.m. 'You're doing the *Friday Rock Show*,' said Tony, grabbing Richard and marching him across to Broadcasting House.

The show went fine and Richard was asked to later deputise for Peter Powell. Now considered a safe pair of hands, Richard got the 8–10 p.m. slot, which, of course, meant doing the handover to John Peel. Respectful and enormously fond of Peel, Richard did sense a competitive edge with him as they battled over playing the latest bands. Peel was a sore loser which led to innumerable rows. He once threatened a band that if they did a session for Skinner, he would never play their record again.

Late 1981 into early 1982 saw a change in the way that the daytime shows were managed. After a lot of pressure, it was decided that the playlist would in effect be abolished and a new system take its place. The argument was that the playlist was making Radio 1 sound predictable and boring. At the time, there was a lot of pressure on the BBC from the Conservative government which had swept into power in 1979. From the earliest days of her premiership, Margaret Thatcher was a stern critic of the corporation. In May 1980 she had lunch at Broadcasting House with the main executives where she argued against the licence fee and suggested that Radio 1 should carry advertising. The network had to show it could do things commercial radio couldn't. It had to offer a quality alternative music service.

The playlist was replaced by something called the Grid which installed the most playable tracks, predominately chart hits, for instance Shakin' Stevens's 'Green Door', with the instruction that if a DJ wanted to play the record they had to do so in a particular half-hour slot, but if they didn't want to play it, they didn't have to.

This change coincided with Trevor Dann producing Dave Lee Travis's lunchtime show. Together Trevor and DLT began to play records that would not ordinarily get airtime on the afternoon schedule. For starters, they were the first to play Phil Collins' 'In the

186

Air Tonight'. It led to a stinging phone call from Doreen. 'Trevor, this is just exactly why I was worried about giving you a daytime show,' she said. 'What are you doing playing this progressive rock? And who is this guy?'

'He's the drummer in Genesis,' said Dann.

'The drummer in Genesis! Need I say more.'

Trevor received a reprimand for that. After it reached number two in the charts, Collins' first hit, Doreen bought Trevor a small present to say sorry.

Another example was 'Once in a Lifetime' by Talking Heads. 'I loved that whole album,' says Trevor. 'That particular song wasn't a single. I made Dave listen to it and said, "I think we should play this." Dave agreed and we played the arse off it. Warner Brothers came round and said, "Oh, shit, we'd better put it out then." So, they did and it became a big hit. And this happened with a load of other songs.'

This was a period of remarkable freedom (although the playlist did eventually return), but it did nothing to lift Trevor's current mood; playing this kind of music was one of the few distractions that kept him interested in what he saw as the stale environment of daytime scheduling. 'I was still living in Nottingham at the time on weekends and driving down to London. Every week I used to have to pack up my suitcase and walk down the stairs and get in the car. And I remember one day, just getting as far as the top of the landing, putting my case down and just going, "There's got to be more to life than this. This is just a horrible way to earn a living." I wasn't enjoying it. It didn't excite or challenge.'

Someone else who endeavoured to liven up the daytime schedule was Steve Wright, who, when he moved to weekday afternoons, was to revolutionise British radio by introducing the zoo format with its 'posse' of co-presenters, an approach that has been widely copied ever since. When he was first asked to take over on the afternoon, Steve realised what a huge opportunity it was, but had no clear idea of how to approach it. 'I really didn't know what I was going to do. I thought, "Well, I'll come up with a few characters." So, we came up with Mr Angry and Sid the Manager, and we did some sketch comedy and some true stories – anything if it was a light news day to fill it up. Then I'd heard about team radio from Australia and America so I thought, "We'll cast a few people." One would be a young person, another would be a woman, they'd be a slightly older person. We'd also use the engineers, and so the Afternoon Boys thing started. We combined all of that with the pop music of the day and some wacky jingles and made a show that I guess must have sounded a little bit different, interesting and unique.'

While both Kenny Everett and Noel Edmonds had used comedy characters to enhance their shows, the idea of a DJ helped out by a crew of people was something new on the station and came about largely due to Steve's belief that he still didn't quite belong at Radio 1. 'I thought, "If it's just me presenting a programme, I don't really have enough character or enough to make it work on my own. I need to interact with people to make it entertaining and they need to hopefully interact with me."' It worked brilliantly. 'We were able to talk about the news, movies and entertainment and gossip, but we were able to do that in a way that was conversational, that involved the audience and was sometimes funny and sometimes had a bit of attitude, and at the same time do a little bit of satire. That kind of programme stood out because there weren't many people doing that.'

Making way for Steve was Paul Burnett, who was devastated when he heard that he was being moved – after all, his listening figures were still good. 'But I know whose fault it was,' he says. 'It was mine. I took my eye off the ball and fell into an easy pattern of doing gigs, then doing the show, then doing gigs.' Paul's destination was Saturday morning, replacing the popular Peter Powell, and pitted against Kenny Everett, back at the BBC on Radio 2. Great, Paul thought. Actually, he more than held his own and when he happened to see some positive audience research about his show, he felt confident about his future. But no, Chinnery wielded the axe and Paul was gone from Radio 1. Meanwhile, though, he had been standing in occasionally for a few DJs on Radio 2 and had received such a good response that boss David Hatch was eager to bring him over full-time – that is, until Chinnery stole his fellow controller's thunder. 'When I left Radio 1, Chinnery organised a press release that said: "We wish Paul all the very best on Radio 2." Only he didn't check with Hatch whether it was all right to say that, and when he was told Hatch said, "Well, that's it, we can't touch him for a year." You talk about egos of DJs, actually it goes right up to the top.' Unwilling to wait a year, Paul worked for a couple of commercial stations before landing on Capital Gold where he enjoyed a ten-year stay.

Following Steve in the schedule at teatime was Peter Powell, promoted from weekend mornings. This was a period that Peter always looked back on as his favourite time working on the station as he managed to give the slot an identity of its own, helped by the new wave music scene and the New Romantic movement. As that metaphorical bridge between daytime and the nightshift, Peter could be more edgy in the new sounds that he played and, invariably, if a band sent in a good demo tape, he'd play it or invite them in to do a live session. Both Duran Duran and Spandau Ballet were encouraged by Peter and did live sessions for him prior to getting their breakthrough.

This was very much Peter's musical taste; he also helped bands like Adam and the Ants and Simple Minds. He was less enamoured of the dance scene and took it on trust when his producer Dave Atkey suggested that they hire a young, unknown DJ who had sent him an impressive audition tape. The idea was for him to do a fifteen-minute dance music feature every Thursday, informing listeners about the latest releases and news from the street. The man in question was 19-year-old Pete Tong. The segment proved a hit and was Tong's first break in the industry.

In the evening slot, Richard Skinner had given way to David 'Kid' Jensen, for whom much had happened over the last eighteen months. Approached by Ted Turner's cable channel TBS, David had moved to Atlanta, Georgia, to work as a news presenter. With an interest in current affairs, David felt it was an opportunity too good to dismiss. Although he enjoyed the work, after a little over a year it probably surprised David just how much he was missing the UK. A sympathetic Doreen Davies flew out to Atlanta to persuade him to return and he was welcomed back. 'I felt like I belonged, like going back to the family.'

For David, the BBC always represented something special, and Broadcasting House was a very evocative place to be. 'Everyone around the world knew the BBC and if you worked for the BBC then you had to be quite special,' he said. 'That entrance, which always reminded me of a big ship going down Portland Place, with the commissionaires in their uniforms and secret passages to here and there, I loved it. And I never went through those doors without thinking I was going to something special. It was an honour to be part of that.'

David's evening show highlighted a lot of indie music, along with championing new bands, often playing demo tapes that had been sent in. A case in point was an unknown band from Liverpool called Frankie Goes to Hollywood. Early sessions on John Peel's show led to the band being asked to record a session for Jensen, which would reach a far wider audience. The same thing happened when David heard Peel play a new band from Manchester called The Smiths. 'I thought they needed to be heard. They were so good, lyrically and musically very strong.'

David had a good relationship with Peel, who followed him at 10 p.m. Usually Peel would stroll into the studio for the last hour of David's show, often with a curry, and they'd happily chat in between the records. On one occasion, there was no sign of him as the clock edged towards ten o'clock. Worried, David popped out into the corridor to see Peel lying on the floor, crying with joy that his beloved Liverpool had won the European Cup. 'Kid,' he said, 'you're going to have to start the show. I can't go on.'

It can sometimes be a mystery why one DJ works and connects with an audience and another one doesn't. On other occasions, it's all too obvious. DJs have joined Radio 1 with high hopes only to quickly fall out of favour. In the case of Adrian Love, who came to Radio 1 from Capital in 1981, he brought with him his own demons. The son of the bandleader Geoff Love, Adrian made no secret of his alcohol addiction, something he occasionally shared with his listeners. But he was sacked from the station the following year for presenting his show drunk.

One interesting show Love presented was a news magazine on Sunday afternoons called *Studio B15*. This was a mix of items, including young contributors doing features or interviews, and covered the issues of the day. On one programme it daringly broadcast a complaint from a prisoner about conditions in his prison and the attitude of prison officers to the inmates.

Pat Sharp and Gary Davies were young, trendy DJs who both arrived at Radio 1 in 1982 with much expectation. Of the two of them, 20-year-old Pat Sharp was seen as the new, blue-eyed boy. 'He was the one everyone had high hopes for to be the next massive DJ on the station,' says Gary Davies. As it turned out, Sharp lasted just a year, moving on to Capital, while Gary stayed for more than a decade.

Gary was a massive fan of music growing up. His cousins owned the Twisted Wheel, one of the biggest live music venues in Manchester in the sixties and seventies. 'As a kid, where the rest of my family bought me boring presents like handkerchiefs, my cousins bought me the Top 10 singles. And when I was about 9 years old, they'd sneak me in backstage at the club and I'd see people like Wilson Pickett or Junior Walker and the All Stars. All the soul greats used to play there. It was mind-blowing.'

When Gary left school at 17, his cousins got him a job on the door. By that time, the Twisted Wheel was no more, having transformed into a huge nightclub, amongst the first in the country to have five different discotheques in one. During breaks, Gary used to stand in for the DJs. It was a great apprenticeship, especially how to deal with a live crowd. 'Working in a club and working on radio are two completely different things and different ways of communication,' he says. 'I just learnt how to read a crowd. During my time on Radio 1, I probably did more Roadshows than any of the other DJs, because I just had this great affinity for working with a live audience, which I really enjoyed.'

One night a DJ didn't show up and Gary was asked to take over for the evening. His deejaying career was up and running. He started to record demos and send tapes to radio stations around the country, including Radio 1, which, for Gary, was the ultimate dream. 'If you want to be a DJ that was, and probably still is, the station you want to work for,' he says. 'All my idols growing up worked there, from Kenny Everett to Emperor Rosko and Tony Blackburn.' All he got back, though, was a steady stream of rejection letters. This went on for two years and Gary's sense of frustration grew to the point where he decided to pack it in. But it was his father, who'd never been too keen on Gary being a DJ in the first place, who urged him to keep going. He made one more demo tape and sent it out, which led to an offer from Manchester Piccadilly Radio. 'So, thanks to my father's encouragement, the tape that I made actually ended up getting me the break.'

Gary worked at Piccadilly Radio for three years and, while he never had his own regular show, he was always covering for other DJs and appearing four or five times a week. One fateful afternoon he popped into a local clothes store and saw photographs of Radio 1 DJs plastered all over the walls, wearing trademark white jackets from the Roadshows. It turned out that the owner made them and Gary asked if he could do something similar for Piccadilly Radio. Out of this grew a friendship and, with his contacts at Radio 1, the owner was keen to try to help Gary's career. 'If you ever need a tape going over there,' he said to Gary one day, 'I know this guy Johnny Beerling and I'd be very happy to give it to him.' Gary put together an edit of one of his shows, Beerling liked it and asked him to come to London for a meeting. The result of that was the offer of a late Saturday night show on a three-month contract at £60 a week.

A celebrity in the Manchester area, Gary was unknown everywhere else and Beerling was taking a risk bringing him in. For Gary the gamble was even bigger. 'I had to leave Piccadilly Radio and give up everything in Manchester and move to London where it cost me a helluva lot more than £60 a week to live. But I just thought, "This is a once in a lifetime opportunity and you've got to take it."'

Not long after joining, Doreen Davies asked Gary if they could have a quick chat in her office. What she wanted to know from him was what Gary Davies was going to bring to the station: 'What's so special about you?' Listeners knew Mike Read because he always played his guitar in the morning. Steve Wright was crazy and wacky and had his crowd with him. 'So, who's Gary Davies?'

'I'm a youngish, single lad,' Gary began, 'who's just arrived in London from Manchester. I'm basically having to live in the spare cupboard in my sister's apartment and she treats me like shit.' Doreen told him to play on that and that's exactly what he did. Out of which came his catchphrase – 'Young, Free and Single'.

With his first few shows going well, Gary settled down into life at Radio 1. He had never really warmed to life at Piccadilly Radio, where there wasn't much of a friendly atmosphere. The jocks were very competitive, each with their own agenda, and there was a lot of internal politics going on. 'I just presumed going to Radio 1, which was massive, would be far worse – the egos and politics – but I found it completely the opposite. It was such a welcoming, friendly place. There was a real feeling of family there. And I think a lot of that came from Doreen.'

Doreen Davies was still very much the mother hen of Radio 1, looking after her boys. Gary remembers that whenever he did a *Top of the Pops* she'd always say, 'Wear something nice, dear.'

Doreen never lost her motherly instinct for her beloved DJs. 'Doreen was terrific,' says Andy Peebles. 'She had an innate ability to pour oil on troubled waters. She was brilliant with people, but she was also incredibly trusting.' Her husband was Derek Mills, then a senior executive at Radio 2, and between them they held some sway in radio terms.

Noel Edmonds especially loved and respected Doreen. In fact, when his first marriage was failing, he went to see Doreen and offered his resignation. 'I felt I'd let the side down because the story was about to appear in the newspapers.' There was nothing unpleasant going on: Noel and his wife had merely agreed to separate. Doreen saw it as such and told Noel she had no intention of accepting his resignation.

He recalls one cherished Doreen story. He had decided to create his own brand of perfume and give it to listeners as a competition prize. At the time, he had a Great Dane bitch and bought some anti-mate spray from the vet to use during the mating season. 'I went into Doreen and said, "Have a whiff of this." I'd covered the label of the bottle. "This is the essence I'm looking for." Doreen was a chain-smoker so I don't know how well she could smell. "For goodness sake," she said. "What's that?" I then pulled my hand away. "Oh, my God," she said. That didn't work out so we went down to Shepherd's Bush Market where she found a little vial of Indian perfume, and it was even worse than the dog spray. Anyway, we gave this out to people. We sent it as Essence de Noel.'

Doreen was also fiercely protective of the secretaries who worked at Egton House, instilling them with a confidence they needed. 'The last thing that most of my contemporaries would do is pick a fight with a Radio 1 secretary,' recalled Mike Smith. 'You would lose and they would not let you forget it.'

Mike was yet another new face about the place – well, newish. He'd first been brought in by Johnny Beerling to Radio 1 as a junior in 1975. The two men shared a passion for motor racing and Mike worked at Brands Hatch on the PR side. At Egton House, Mike made promotion trails, while during outside broadcasts he'd sit in the studio at Broadcasting House ready to play a record in case anything went wrong.

Having moved to Capital radio in 1978, in 1982 he returned to Radio 1 doing Saturday mornings, replacing the departing Paul Burnett, and also the pre-breakfast show during the week. The place, in his mind, hadn't changed all that much, especially how some of the DJs and other staff behaved. 'There were producers who would go out and get so drunk that they couldn't prepare their show – so the secretary would do it. Some of the male DJs were like schoolboys. Actually, my schoolmates were more mature than some of the idiots who got jobs as DJs. The secretaries were brilliant at putting DJs in their place.'

By the early eighties, *Newsbeat* had become a Radio 1 staple and a highly respected source of news gathering, with top journalists and presenters like Laurie Mayer and Frank Partridge. However, right from its origins, the programme had an uneasy relationship with the rest of the station. Those working on *Newsbeat* were well aware that the vast majority of listeners tuned in to hear music, and the intrusion of news and current affairs at regular intervals was a distraction at best. Every working day was always something of a challenge to make the bulletins sound as if they belonged alongside the normal output, which was a much harder job than putting out the news on a speech station like Radio 4 or LBC. And they had to make them sound as interesting as possible to a young audience, especially the fifteen-minute programmes, so that kids wouldn't switch off.

One of the ways *Newsbeat* tried to harmonise with the rest of the station's sound was to end each 'main' programme (12.30 and 5.30) with a pop interview – usually from an artist or band promoting their latest album or single – finishing off with thirty seconds or so of music that flowed as seamlessly as possible into the subsequent programme. As *Newsbeat*'s main presenter, Frank Partridge was delegated to do many of these interviews, either at Broadcasting House or elsewhere in London where the stars were staying or working. Over the years, Frank met just about every big name going, but was never to forget the occasion he was asked to interview Bob Marley and Genesis in the same week. Marley was staying in a very private hotel in the Marylebone area, and Frank turned up at 10 a.m. as arranged. 'I was shown up to his suite and while I was setting up, he casually rolled the most enormous joint I'd witnessed in my life,' remembers Frank. 'I pretended to ignore it, but after a few minutes, he offered it around – there were several "assistants" in his room – and then it came to me. It would have been churlish to refuse, but knowing that I was going to be on air within a couple of hours, I can't recall whether I inhaled or not. Unfortunately, the interview didn't go too well. The moment

I switched on the tape recorder, Bob lapsed into an unintelligible stream of Jamaican patois, which was completely unbroadcastable. I stopped the tape at one point and asked him to speak more slowly. Half an hour later I came away with something that made our "pop item" that lunchtime, but his opening outburst was saved for posterity – and appeared on various Christmas "funny" tapes for years afterwards! RIP Bob.'

Later that week, Genesis were in town. Phil Collins turned up at the studio with keyboard maestro Tony Banks in support, and the interview went well. 'But my abiding memory,' says Frank, 'is that Tony Banks arrived wearing a smart suit, with a copy of the *Financial Times* under his arm! While we were setting up and I was chatting to Phil, Tony was busily checking the performance of his investments! The contrast with what Bob Marley did during the set-up period couldn't have been greater.'

16

When a senior producer, Chris Lycett, moved from daytime and gravitated to the third floor, awaiting him there were several of the people he'd worked with before, like Jeff Griffin. Much of Chris's time was spent with John Peel and John Walters, and he appreciated what a great double act they were. 'Walters summed up their working relationship as: a man and his dog, each believing the other to be the dog,' says Chris. 'They were perfect together. They couldn't be better matched.' BBC management recognised this and while the usual practice was for producers to move to a different show and presenter after a year or two, just to keep things fresh, it was not even an option to split the two Johns up.

Chris always had a great deal of time for Peel. He recalls once being at an outside broadcast with him when two guys, probably in their twenties, walked over towards them. 'You are John Peel, aren't you?' one of them said. 'I just want to say thank you for making my life so much better.' Chris remembers what Walters used to say about Peel: 'We're all fucked if he ever grows up.' Probably the secret to Peel's success as a broadcaster was this insatiable appetite he had for the next thing. 'Not because he wanted to be proved to have found the next thing,' says Chris, 'but just out of sheer interest.'

Chris revelled in Walters' company, too, finding him a very funny man and an astute observer. 'He used to call himself the poor man's Peter Ustinov.' Together they drummed up the idea of doing a kind of arts programme. 'Walters had a fine arts degree and always had this big thing about Radio 1 not having to be just pop and pap, there could be a bit of culture, but it had to fit in with the format of the station.'

They came up with *Walters' Weekly*, a sort of layman's eye view of the arts, and even today Chris is amazed that they were allowed to get away with it. Each week Walters picked emerging artists to showcase or selected an off-beam subject. A perfect example occurred on the first show when a group of actors arrived at Walters' home to re-enact the film *Psycho*. 'It was a hoot,' recalls Chris.

Chris recalls another occasion he and Walters went to Bill Woodrow's London gallery to interview the artist. He was working on a piece, peeling metal strips off the outer case of a washing machine and turning them into a beaver. 'It was a comment on the environment,' says Chris, 'how the washing machine had destroyed the beaver but the beaver was getting its own back by eating the washing machine. I must say we had a ball doing that show.'

Walters' Weekly went out during Paul Gambaccini's month-long break from his American chart show on Saturdays, and incredibly it never lost any audience numbers. Cheered by its success, the arts programme was given a second series. However, towards the end of the second series, Walters was informed by management that they were being cancelled. This was a little awkward because a few days later he and Chris won a broadcasting press guild award for it. Walters bounced onto the stage to accept. 'I'm very honoured to be awarded this by our peers,' he said. 'And with supreme sense of timing the BBC has just axed us. Actually, to be fair not "axed"; they've told me they're "resting" it. "Resting" in the same context as a mother walking down the street with a little boy and they see a dead cat in the gutter, and the mother says to the boy, "Don't touch him, darling, he's just resting."' It brought the house down. *Walters' Weekly* did not return.

Meanwhile producer Trevor Dann had been poached by Noel Edmonds to work on his Sunday show. Trevor didn't like the idea of working on Sundays when Chinnery first raised it with him. 'But I was given the express understanding that if Noel wanted you, you did it,' he says. 'Noel was the main man. If he snapped his fingers, we all jumped.' Things began brightly enough. As Trevor was still living in Nottingham, Noel suggested he stay at a vacant property he owned in Notting Hill for some of the week. They could meet up on Friday and Saturday night for production meetings and then Trevor could leave after the show finished on Sunday to stay in Nottingham for a few days. Trevor agreed. 'And for three or four months it worked really well. But then Noel left his wife and came to live in the house permanently, which meant I was sharing it with him which was a whole different relationship.' With the press camped outside the door only adding to the strain Noel must have been under, Trevor noticed an understandable change in his colleague; Noel was moody and argumentative, and their relationship became more fractious for the rest of the short time they worked together.

Unwilling to produce Noel again, Trevor was being courted by television and announced his intention to leave the station. His final few months at Radio 1 saw him working with John Peel, a broadcaster he had always greatly admired. 'We had a really sparky relationship because I wanted him to play some old records as well. I had this argument with him, which was: "You're a great evangelist for new records, why don't you broaden that out and make it evangelism for 'new to me' records?" But he wouldn't do it.'

Trevor left Radio 1 to become producer of BBC's flagship live music programme *The Old Grey Whistle Test*. Almost ten years later he would return to the station in dramatic circumstances.

At the close of 1982, Radio 1 hired only its second ever female DJ, the first since Annie Nightingale. It had taken twelve years but better late than never. Before being approached by Radio 1, Janice Long had been working for Radio Merseyside, never used to listen to Radio 1 and had no real desire to move down to London. She loved what she was doing on her Sunday night show, helping to throw a spotlight on Liverpool's thriving underground music scene and featuring live sessions from the likes of Echo and the Bunnymen and Frankie Goes to Hollywood. When she interviewed Paul Gambaccini, the American jock went back to his bosses at Radio 1 telling them they ought to check her out. A small delegation went to Liverpool, met Janice, and a few days later her studio phone rang. It was Derek Chinnery. Janice thought that it was a gag and told him to get lost but Chinnery insisted that he really was the controller of Radio 1 and by the end of the next record wanted an answer, yes or no, did she want to join?

The BBC heralded the arrival of Janice with an introduction on *Top of the Pops* two days before her first Saturday evening show. But she felt she was under a great deal of pressure. She recalls bumping into Annie in the toilet early on and Annie saying, 'Thank God, another woman, and a fellow Aries.'

Walking into Egton House for the first time, wearing a black leather dress, high heels and fishnet tights, Janice expected an atmosphere that was cutting-edge and contemporary; instead what she experienced was something akin to an insurance office. Having been her own producer at Radio Merseyside, it was disheartening to see that women were not truly represented at Egton House, except in the typing pool. Yes, there was a female executive in Doreen Davies, but there wasn't a single female producer. When Janice asked why there were no women DJs broadcasting on weekdays, she received the reply, 'Because they're at home, doing the ironing.' Even her dress sense wasn't above scrutiny: she was repeatedly told it didn't befit her star status and that she was too working-class. It was once explained to her: 'There is a girl at Capital FM whom we really like, but she is fat, so you are lucky.'

Janice's producer was, like her, a new arrival at the station. Phil Ward-Large had been working at Radio Trent, Nottingham's independent local radio station, when he saw an advertisement for a position as a Radio 1 producer. He applied, had two interviews and got the job. Traditionally Radio 1 had drawn production talent internally but there was a feeling that the station could broaden its production base by bringing in producers from UK commercial radio, which by the early eighties had now been established for about ten years. Mark Radcliffe, who came from Manchester's Piccadilly Radio, and Phil Ward-Large were the first two producers to be employed under this initiative.

Besides the obvious excitement of joining Radio 1, Phil found it to be a hugely creative environment. 'Although I thought there might be some resistance to producers drawn from outside the BBC, that wasn't my experience at all,' he says. 'Everyone was very friendly and keen to make me feel welcome.' Apart from the famous DJs, Phil found himself in awe of established producers such as John Walters, Jeff Griffin and Bernie Andrews. 'These were names who had worked with musical giants including the Beatles, the Rolling Stones, Jimi Hendrix and David Bowie!' But, like Trevor Dann before him, Phil found the wider BBC experience somewhat different in that there remained a strong culture of demarcation where producers were not even allowed to edit tapes in the studio. That was a studio manager's job.

Phil quickly established a rapport with Janice Long and came to regard her as a consummate broadcaster, someone who was both knowledgeable and passionate about music. 'I can't believe there has ever been a DJ who attended more gigs than Janice. Every week she and I saw numerous new and emerging bands playing at London's clubs. Live music was an extremely important part of Janice's life at Radio 1.'

Meanwhile, Janice's trailblazing progenitor Annie Nightingale had become a television personality, after replacing Bob Harris as the main presenter of BBC 2's *The Old Grey Whistle Test*, opening up the show to punk and new wave. This was the kind of music Annie was passionate about and featured on her fondly remembered Sunday night request show on Radio 1. Originally broadcast on Sunday afternoons in the mid-seventies, the show moved to a slot after the UK Top 40 chart in 1982. Annie was always ambitious to work in the evenings, 'because that's when all the cool sounds were on,' she said in 2014. 'As a nighttime DJ, you aren't obliged to play the playlist. You don't have to be an entertainer. You have to really know your music, but you can also experiment.'

Initially the request show was commissioned to fill a three-month slot and ended up running until 1994. Annie's brief by executive Teddy Warwick was: 'If you play good music, people will ask for more good music.' And that's exactly what happened. The requests were notable for being on the quirky side since the show attracted a large student audience who listened as they finished their homework. When Annie wrote her memoirs in 1999, novelist and playwright Irvine Welsh asked if he could write the introduction since her request show had meant so much to him during his teenage years.

A lot of the requests were so off the wall that Annie regularly wondered, 'They're going to take this show off, it's too weird.' But it was the listeners' programme, as Annie always intended it to be. Equally strange were the lengths some fans went to in order to get their request noticed, such as sending it through the post on a brick; another did the same thing with a banana.

As for more standard requests, Annie's producer Bernie Andrews seemed to possess a sixth sense for spotting a phoney, especially if they were being asked to play a certain record too many times. He would sometimes track down the requestee and give them a good grilling over the phone to make sure they weren't a record company employee trying to get a free plug.

Annie and Bernie enjoyed a great relationship, even though many who knew Bernie and were close to him acknowledge that he wasn't always the easiest person to get on with, especially from the management point of view. 'He was very much his own man,' says Jeff Griffin. 'He was very uncompromising. He'd go to the wall on anything. Whenever he was doing a series of programmes and they were taken off, or something was changed, he would always take it as a personal insult. But he was a lovely guy and very funny.'

Bernie was always telling Jeff about his latest battle with management or argument with Derek Chinnery, which seemed to occur on quite a regular basis. One morning Bernie came into Jeff's office. 'I've just been in to see Derek,' he said.

'What happened?'

'We had another blazing row,' said Bernie.

'So then what happened?'

'Well, Derek said to me, "What would make you happy?" and I said to him, "If you left."'

'Christ,' went Jeff. 'What did Derek say?'

'He actually laughed because he was so surprised. And then he said, "I think it would be better if you left rather than me."'

Unfortunately, that's exactly what happened. The rebelliousness of Bernie's personality to the more corporate aspects of the BBC ultimately proved incompatible. He took early retirement in 1984; some reports suggest he was pushed out. 'It was a great pity because he still had a lot to offer,' says Jeff.

Pete Drummond couldn't believe the news when he first heard about it. 'When he said he was going to retire I said, "Bernie, for God's sake!" He was only 50 or something. He said, "I've got loads to do." I said, "Like what?" He said, "Chopping wood." I think he went to live out in the countryside somewhere. I never saw him again.'

In March 1983, Noel Edmonds announced that he was leaving Radio 1. 'I'd done it all. What more was there to prove? I'd done the breakfast show. I'd made a success of Sunday mornings. What else was there to do?' It was a decision very much influenced by his television profile which had taken off ever since the launch of *Swap Shop*. Jim Moir, a senior executive at BBC television, had said to him, 'You're on the radio, you're doing air shows for the factual department, motor shows for local TV. You're doing all this stuff, but what are you actually doing? Do you want to carry on doing that or would you like to come to my light entertainment department and I'll make you a star?' It was quite a compelling argument.

With Noel gone from the weekend schedule, Dave Lee Travis, one of the station's big hitters, was moved across and reigned there for the next ten years, building up a large and loyal fanbase. The Saturday morning show was known for its esoteric features, not least the snooker-based radio quiz *Give Us a Break*, complete with its 'quack quack oops' comedy sound effect when a contestant got a question wrong.

At its peak, Travis's show was pulling in a 15 million audience. A good example of just how far its reach extended occurred in 1990 when a request came through from a wife anxious to get in contact with her husband. The gentleman in question had been waiting for a kidney transplant for ten months. On this particular morning, he'd gone fishing when his wife received an urgent call at home from the hospital to say he was wanted for surgery. This was, of course, the days before mobile phones and she had no means of contacting him. She knew he took a radio with him because he always listened to DLT's show, so the hospital contacted the BBC and a call was put through to the studio. Wasting no time, Travis went on air with the information and the husband got in touch with the police and a helicopter was dispatched to bring him to the hospital.

Bolstering the weekend schedule was a new DJ. Robbie Vincent fronted a pioneering dance show on Sunday nights that featured soul, funk, jazz and fusion. One of the youngest Fleet Street journalists in the sixties, Robbie had covered the Kray twins' trial, but he'd always had an interest in radio and, leaving print behind, launched his broadcasting career as one of the pioneers at BBC Radio London in 1973. Bringing his journalistic expertise to the airwaves, he hosted one of the country's first phone-in shows which became an enormous success. A huge fan of black music, like the Philly sound and jazz-funk, which he thought was not being represented enough on UK radio, Robbie was given the opportunity to host his own soul show, which soon became essential listening to the capital's soul music fans.

It was Jonny Beerling's son, a fan of Robbie's Saturday show, who brought him to the attention of Radio 1 at a time when Beerling was pushing for a broader music spectrum on the station. 'Johnnie wanted me there to do what I'd done on Radio London,' says Robbie. 'I'll always be grateful to him for not interfering and letting me get on with it. There was no one at Radio 1 who understood what I was doing anyway.'

For Robbie, getting the Radio 1 gig was a big deal; the network was still enormously important, certainly in the way that it shaped the pop world. It meant that more people would be exposed to the kind of music he had such a passion for. 'Being a DJ is the same as being able to paint,' he says. 'When you paint and people look at it, they get all sorts of different feelings – pain, happiness, sadness, excitement. It's the same with a music show. When you pick that soulful voice telling a story about a broken romance, you know this is going to hit somebody emotionally.'

When Robbie arrived, he wanted as little to do with the showbiz element that surrounded the station as possible, particularly things like *Top of the Pops*, but especially the Roadshow. 'I would only have agreed to do that if I'd been dead and they had taken me there as an exhibit of misbehaviour, but not otherwise.' He felt much the same when it came to many of the daytime jocks, 'some of whom had no musical taste whatsoever and couldn't pick a hit if they tried. But that's what Radio 1 wanted. It wasn't the DJ's fault. You could open the doors of Radio 1 and be swept out by a tsunami of egos. I thought it was a load of bullshit. I hated it. To me they were a disgrace. But they were encouraged to behave egotistically.'

Robbie identified much more with the seriously minded music jocks. Someone like Peel, the deep music man, was much more to Robbie's taste, despite Robbie reaching the conclusion that a lot of what Peel played he didn't understand himself. 'He knew it was utter rubbish, and I think he enjoyed it. He enjoyed the fact that people out there would not understand it, either. But he had this way about him, which was the anti-egotist.'

Both men shared a love for highlighting music that existed on the fringes. While Robbie played plenty of mainstream material from the likes of Rick James, Brass Construction and Bobby Womack, he hunted out lesser known stuff that the clubs were playing. 'We used to call it funk missionary work.' Robbie always used to say that his show was an extension of the strength of the club scene. He also did a regular feature looking at the smaller independent labels and imports which required frequent visits to the various specialist shops dotted around London. 'I spent an absolute fortune and got no help with the cost at all. Probably a quarter of my weekly wage went on records.' He kept them in his home, stored in one of the rooms piled up to the ceiling.

Andy Peebles had every right to feel a little miffed that Radio 1 hadn't asked him to front a soul show, given that he was hired in the first place largely on the strength of his *Soul Train* show on Piccadilly Radio. Regardless of that, Andy had enjoyed numerous career highlights so far with Radio 1, not least flying to Russia to follow Elton John's ground-breaking 1979 tour. 'That was an incredible trip,' he says. 'This was just before the Moscow Olympics and Russian authorities were keen to show how open they were.' The final concert of the tour was held in Moscow and Andy introduced the broadcast live on Radio 1, marking the first stereo satellite link-up between the USSR and the West.

Andy later interviewed Elton for Radio 1 and was given a guided tour of his mansion. On a trip to the bathroom, Andy noticed a Rembrandt etching hanging on the wall. When asked if he was worried about intruders making off with his valuables, Elton joked: 'The constant Dorothy Squires records blasting out of the loudspeakers tend to drive people away.'

Andy was also proud that many of his records of the week ended up becoming hits, such as 'One Day I'll Fly Away' by Randy Crawford, 'Everybody's Got to Learn Sometime' by The Korgis and 'Just When I Needed You Most' by the American singer-songwriter Randy VanWarmer. Andy always insisted that if he was going to have a record of the week, it should be his choice rather than the producers. Even by the eighties, DJs still didn't enjoy musical freedom. 'That wasn't generally the way Radio 1 worked,' claims Andy. 'The responsibility of putting a show together still fell to the producer.'

In 1983, Andy was asked to host *My Top Ten*, a show which had been running since 1973. Derek Chinnery had come up with the idea of doing a hipper version of *Desert Island Discs* and asked Brian Matthew to present it. Going out on weekend afternoons under the original title *My Top Twelve*, Matthew could never forget the episode with Bill Haley. 'We were chatting about his whole life story,'

Matthew recalled. 'He admitted he'd had a serious drink problem, and that it had interfered with his work. Then suddenly he broke into tears in the interview, sobbing, because he'd made a mess of his life. We got it sorted out, that didn't go on air, but it was quite moving.'

My Top Twelve was later fronted by Bob Harris and Noel Edmonds, but Andy was to become its longest-serving host, putting in seven years and, he thinks, something like 300 episodes. He was also responsible for slightly changing the format, cutting it back to just ten records, thus allowing more chat with his guests. And what guests – Paul Simon, Debbie Harry, Cliff Richard, Morrissey, Phil Collins, Sting and Peter Gabriel. 'Even I go "wow" when I look at the people that I was lucky enough to talk to.' If he could pick his favourites, they'd be Keith Richards and Joni Mitchell. 'Those are the two most knowledgeable musicians it's ever been my honour to interview. Joni was extraordinary and Keith, likewise, he had an encyclopaedic knowledge of music and he had a passion for it.'

Nor was *My Top Ten* strictly the domain for musical artists. George Best did an edition. 'Fortunately, at that time he was off the juice and did a very good programme.' Best fitted in nicely with Andy's love of sport. Ever since joining Radio 1, he'd made it known that they ought to be covering more sport, and out of a conversation with Derek Chinnery emerged the chance to do his own Friday night sports programme, with the proviso that he attract big sporting names to appear. This he managed to do, bagging a trio of national English captains in Bill Beaumont, Kevin Keegan and Ian Botham – a particular favourite for the cricket-mad Andy. 'It was a lovely programme to do. The late Bill McLaren used to come and preview rugby for me. John Motson and Bob Wilson were also regular contributors. It became a bit of a club in a really nice way.' The show only lasted for around three years but managed to make a healthy impact as Andy discovered once when he met Princess Anne at an event and she confessed to being an avid listener.

17

The year 1984 began with one of the biggest controversies ever to hit Radio 1. Frankie Goes to Hollywood's debut single 'Relax' had been around a while, indeed the group had performed it on *Top of the Pops*. It was also being played happily on Radio 1. 'I'd been playing it for weeks,' says Gary Davies. 'I thought it was an amazing song. And I just knew it was going to be this big hit.'

Enter Mike Read, who refused to play it on his breakfast show. 'He actually did it off his own back,' says Gary. 'It wasn't that anyone had said to him, "You can't play this, we have to ban it." Mike decided to ban it himself. And that's the biggest mistake you can ever make. He's supposed to be there, with the kids, the guy playing all the cool new music. The last thing as a DJ you ever want to do is ban something.'

Mike has always insisted that his banning of the single was a myth and that what really happened was much less dramatic. He had a batch of records, including 'Relax', to play towards the end of the show, but with time running out one of them had to go and a look at the rather suggestive art on the sleeve made his mind up for him. Peter Powell's producer Dave Atkey had also taken against the song. After watching the video, he'd told Powell, 'I don't think we should play this on your show,' and Peter agreed. Despite protestations from pluggers about why it wasn't being played, Atkey stood by his decision.

In any case, a few days later, after the band came out publicly to confirm the sexually graphic nature of the lyrics, a memo went out from Chinnery's office to ban the song outright on Radio 1. Chinnery himself regarded the song as obscene, but did recognise later that the whole controversy just highlighted how out of touch the station was becoming. 'Perhaps we were a bit slow catching up with what was happening generally out there, but at the same time we were still trying to keep some sort of standard.'

Obviously, the attendant publicity was exploited to the full by the band's record company and the song became a number one hit. As for Mike, 'It became de rigueur at any dance, disco or party to play "Relax" as soon as I walked in.'

Like most 14-year-olds, Bruno Brookes listened to pop music and Radio 1. 'I remember vividly listening to Tony Blackburn when he used to do the breakfast show,' Bruno says, 'and he had this amazing, sunny, everything's happy disposition; there was something quite magnetic about that.' Inspired, he asked his dad for a twin turntable, but, Bruno explains, 'he didn't know what I was talking about, so I built one on my own and nearly electrocuted myself'. In the end Bruno's dad thought it wiser to give him £70 to buy a twin turntable that he'd seen advertised in the local paper. 'Friends used to come up to my bedroom, with bags of crisps and Coke, and I'd play them tunes.'

Bruno got to hear about an inter-school DJ competition in his hometown of Stoke. Although his own school didn't qualify for it, he managed to blag his way in. 'There was this enormous sound system on the stage – my dream. It was a multi-stack WEM system, with the most amazing kind of Rosko-looking deck. I went on last. And I won it. And that was the start of my journey.'

Leaving school, Bruno picked up money washing cars and deejaying at youth clubs and weddings. Then his dad came up with the idea of renting a local town hall. With a bit of clever marketing, Bruno's disco started to pack the place out every week with 1,500 kids. It became a thriving business. 'It enabled me to buy a phenomenal amount of equipment, a lot of it from a Genesis tour. And we had all of Mud's front-of-house PA. It really was everything I'd dreamed of.'

Word got around and Bruno was hired by BBC Radio Stoke. But his big break arrived when the host on the afternoon show called in sick and Bruno was asked to step in. That presenter never came back and Bruno hosted afternoons for the next three years. One day in the studio, the receptionist called through saying that Doreen Davies was on the phone. 'You're winding me up,' Bruno told her. 'Come on, I'm not having it,' he said and put the phone down. The receptionist rang again. 'Bruno, it's Doreen Davies, apparently she's from Radio 1.' Bruno knew exactly who Doreen Davies was and took the call, still believing it to be a wind-up, until he recognised the voice. Doreen was staying in a local hotel and had listened to his whole show. 'I want you to come and see us,' she told him. Is this for real? Bruno asked himself. He was only 24 but soon found himself going to London to cover for Steve Wright.

When Bruno first arrived at Egton House, he was told to see Johnny Beerling. Off he went down the corridor, passing a couple of staff and saying hello; no one knew who he was but rumours were circulating about this new DJ. 'I walked into Johnny's office. "Hi, I'm Bruno Brookes." He looked at me. "Oh, yeah. I heard you were coming in. Well, good luck. I personally wouldn't pay you in washers." I was absolutely stunned that he said that. It knocked my confidence hugely. I never forgot it. I think that was out of order.'

That confidence issue remained with Bruno even when he landed his own show, *Drivetime*, taking over from Peter Powell, which, says Bruno, 'I don't think he was very happy about.' Doreen pulled him into her office for a little bit of advice. 'Bruno, always do what you've always done, from the moment you were doing your discos. Just remember those kids coming back from school or from college, they want the pop stars, so I want you doing stuff around all the bands, your Duran Durans and Wham!' Bruno knew exactly what Doreen meant but it still took quite some time to really feel comfortable and to be able to be himself. 'I had two producers and one of them was trying to turn me into something I wasn't. I'm a great believer in that you can only be yourself. You cannot be manufactured in any way because if you restrain your natural personality, you're actually diluting your opportunity to be a brilliant communicator, whether you're a broadcaster or a CEO of a company.' It's especially important at a national station that has the capacity to reach every home in the country. 'They want to know that if you were to knock at the back door, you'd be exactly the same person as they're listening to on the radio.'

It took Bruno something like two years to relax into his natural self and really believe that the teatime show was made for him. He never saw himself as a muso-type presenter, although his greatest love is music and he did break a lot of artists. He never classed himself amongst the Peels and Gambaccinis of the station. 'They were so intensely detailed about what they played and why. That's fine but it wasn't naturally me. I just simply wanted to be the boy next door who likes a laugh, who is a bit cheeky with a little bit of unpredictability, someone who likes to party, but not too hard, and likes to wear nice clothes.' For Radio 1, always keen to promote a particular DJ's image, Bruno was a perfect fit for the time. And when the fame came along, Bruno worked hard not to allow it to go to his head. In a way he never really felt famous, which had a lot to do with how he'd been brought up and the kind of world he'd begun to move around in – the hanging out with pop stars malarkey. 'I remember one night I was invited to a private house in Mayfair and in the foyer were Rod Stewart and Elton John. I thought to myself: "I don't believe I'm standing here."'

While Bruno was trying hard to make an impression, young guns Gary Davies and Janice Long were racing ahead. After about eighteen months on the station, doing his Saturday night show, Gary Davies was given the coveted lunchtime slot. When he first joined Radio 1, Gary recalls Doreen asking him, 'What sort of DJ are you?' What she meant was, did he fit into the daytime guys, who were considered more just entertainment and fun, and not really that serious about the music they were playing, or was he a music specialist guy? 'I actually think I'd like to be both,' he replied.

'Well, it's very difficult to be both,' said Doreen.

'I don't think it is,' said Gary. 'I still think you can have fun, while taking the music that you play seriously.'

On his Saturday show, Gary had highlighted a lot of album tracks. Moving to lunchtime, where he had a much more mainstream audience, Gary was careful not to play anything totally unsuitable while at the same time pushing the boundaries. He always had a good relationship with his producers and could pretty much choose whatever he wanted to play. The producers were meeting the music pluggers every day, so a lot of times they were hearing more about new releases before any of the DJs would. Saying that, each DJ had their own pigeonhole where pluggers dropped the latest vinyl. 'I used to get into the office a couple of hours before the show every day, and most of that time was spent listening to new music,' says Gary. 'And it didn't matter how many records were there, I listened to everything, and if it grabbed my attention, I'd play it.' That was the real buzz of working at Radio 1, hearing a new band or a great new song and breaking it live on the air. 'I think I was the first person to play U2 on daytime radio.' When he played 'Creep', Gary was also the first person to play Radiohead on Radio 1. 'I had no idea who they were, what they did, where they came from. I just liked the song, so I played it.' He also did much to bring Tears for Fears to a bigger audience and championed Chris Rea. 'For me, it was all about the new music.'

In that respect, pluggers were still vital. 'There was a legendary plugger called Oliver Smallman,' recalls Gary. 'He'd think nothing of standing outside Egton House dressed up as a character related to a new song that he was plugging in the hope of getting your attention.' Gary only recalls being offered money to play a record once. 'That person was kicked out of Egton House and never came back.'

Gary's lunchtime show became famous for a host of features. There was the Day-To-Day Challenge, in which the same contestant went on air each weekday to answer quiz questions and try to upgrade their prize, and Willy on the Plonker, which required contestants to identify a hit song from a frenzied piano interpretation. This came about through the musical virtuosity of his producer Paul Williams. Outside the studio, there was a grand piano and Gary came up with the idea one day of getting Paul to play a few tunes on it as musical accompaniment to the weather forecast. This later expanded into a piano competition and became one of those novelty items that caught on with listeners.

The success of that lunchtime show propelled Gary to radio stardom and he was soon one of the most heavily promoted of Radio 1's DJs by what he called 'the Radio 1 machine'. Regular appearances on *Top of the Pops* merely added to his fame. 'If you were a Radio 1 DJ, you were pretty much as big as a lot of the artists that you were playing. Coming from Piccadilly Radio, where a few people knew me maybe in the nightclubs, but nobody else would know who I was or would care, all of a sudden, you're slap bang in the public eye. The newspapers are interested and you've got to be careful if you were out at night because of the paparazzi. You became a personality.'

During the eighties, Gary probably hosted *Top of the Pops* more than any other DJ. One lasting memory was the time Paul McCartney arrived to do his first *Top of the Pops* for years, in 1987. 'Usually the artists come in,' remembers Gary, 'they go to their dressing room, they stay in their dressing room, they go and do their rehearsal, then back to the dressing room, go and do the show and then go home. They don't mingle. Nobody really speaks to anybody. Yet Paul McCartney, the biggest of them all, came with Linda and spent the whole time just chatting to everybody. Just a nice guy.'

Gary's popularity led to a string of memorable opportunities such as being asked to host Wham!'s farewell concert and Michael Jackson's *Bad* concert, both at Wembley. 'That was surreal. The first night, Jackson had policewomen forming a corridor from his compound to the stage. On another night I think it was all nurses.'

And, of course, Gary did his fair share of Roadshows. Some DJs preferred to play their own records on the Roadshow, but most of them liked to be out front all the time. That was certainly the case with Gary, who got his producer or one of the engineers to run the desk while he mixed with the crowd, 'geeing them up and in-between the songs just having fun with them'. By the mid-eighties the Roadshow was even more of a mammoth operation. 'It was a bit

Hi-de-Hi! holiday camp, but it was phenomenal to be a part of it,' says Gary. 'There'd be five huge trucks in this convoy turning up somewhere and crowds of anything from five to 45,000 people.' One Roadshow in Birmingham's Bullring necessitated the whole place being closed down, with mounted police called in to control the crowds.

Janice Long had just become the first female DJ on Radio 1 to have her own daily show, which she presented Monday to Thursday at 7.30–10 p.m. It afforded her a greater opportunity to feature the kind of music that she was passionate about, such as Primal Scream, Lloyd Cole and the Commotions, The Alarm and James. She could go into her producer's office and say, 'I've heard this band and I think they're brilliant,' and he'd book them for a session. 'He'd just trust me,' she says.

As the show became more established, Janice carried out a survey to see exactly what her listeners were like, not just the kind of music that they wanted to hear, but what papers they read and how they voted. As a result, she was able to shape the kind of features she put on the show, from reports on current political issues such as the troubles in Nicaragua to covering party political conferences and on to social issues like racial harassment and homelessness.

One of the joys of doing the show for Janice was her nightly handover to John Peel. The pair struck up a playful friendship. She remembered him saying to her once, 'I'd get rid of everybody here at Radio 1 apart from you, of course. Bruno Brookes can go on reception, because I like him.' Their chemistry was transplanted over to *Top of the Pops*, where Janice was the first woman to present the show. It was during one of their appearances together that Peel uttered the immortal line, after Pete Wylie had finished a performance of his song 'Sinful': 'If that doesn't make number one, I'm going to come round and break wind in your kitchen.' No surprise to learn that the BBC received a number of complaints; the song peaked at number thirteen.

Janice had also moved into the area of documentary when she and her producer, Phil Ward-Large, approached Johnny Beerling with the idea for *Who's That Girl*, a six-part series where Janice interviewed and profiled some of the then most successful female musicians. The early eighties had seen an enormous number of women in the charts and it was time their achievements were celebrated. The six artists were Chrissie Hynde, Siouxsie Sioux, Alison Moyet, Alannah Currie, Joan Armatrading and Helen Terry.

Behind the scenes, things were changing at Radio 1. When Radio 1 and Radio 2 launched in 1967, each producer was asked which of the new networks they wanted to work for. By and large, the younger ones chose Radio 1 and the older ones went to Radio 2. That meant by the mid-eighties, those young producers working at Radio 1 had grown old along with the station. One of the senior producers, Teddy Warwick, had already retired, his position as Chinnery's chief assistant going to Johnny Beerling. Teddy's departure left a hole for many of the DJs who always saw him as one of the few management figures who was on their side.

Understandably, there was a drive for new blood, younger producers to come in and bring some fresh thinking. It was this policy that led Doreen Davies to find Martin Cox. Martin joined the BBC straight from university as a graduate trainee, doing time at Radio Oxford as a junior station assistant. Then he was whisked away to Radio 2, where he stayed for four years, before Doreen got in touch about coming over to Radio 1. 'It was amazing for me,' recalls Martin. 'It was paradise because I'd always been interested in music. For me as a young producer, I just had to stop myself and think, "Oh my God, I'm 24 years old, I am helping to run national Radio 1 and I've got Paul McCartney on the phone."'

The first show Martin was given was Bruno Brookes'. At the time, Bruno didn't get on with his producer and it was bringing him down. Martin came in, and he and Bruno just clicked. Here was a young producer prepared to take risks and drive the show, and they ended up doing some great radio together. 'In those days, it was wonderful because it really was up to the creative imagination of the producers

215

and the DJ to make it special,' says Martin. 'This is before we had playlist routines. You could choose all of your music, just so long as you used your intelligence to balance it between what's going to become a hit, what's brand new, what's not released yet and some classic oldies.'

That changed when the playlist returned and DJs and producers were more or less told what records to play. They still retained a modicum of freedom, but that was limited to a choice of just a few records per hour. Martin doesn't think the playlist necessarily damaged Radio 1, in fact it helped to give the station a more consistent sound. 'But I think it took away quite a lot of people's enthusiasm to get involved in the music. In those days we would get 140 new singles a week and we were only allowed to put ten of them on the playlist.' And that lasted for the whole week.

The playlist meetings hadn't really changed all that much. Each producer was obliged to go through all the new releases every week and pick their favourites. 'I did listen to every single record that came across my desk,' Martin confirms. There was always a temptation to pick out the big star artists and not pay too much attention to some of the others. In that way an indie band or a new band might be overlooked and the station miss out on a potential hit. The biggest example of this for Martin came in 1987 with Kylie Minogue's 'I Should Be So Lucky'. 'I took that record to the playlist meeting probably five or six times and people would say, "Who is this girl, Kylie Menogwee?" and "Oh, she's just some person from some Australian soap opera." I would bash the table and say, "No, this is going to be massive. This is such a commercial two and a half minutes, bright and familiar," which is always what Doreen used to say. It fitted the bill perfectly.' Martin did finally win the argument and, of course, it went on to launch Kylie's singing career.

Martin's main role as producer was to maintain and build the audience for the show. If ratings started to drop on a consistent basis, producers were moved off. Strangely, no producer at Egton House, save for John Walters with Peel, had their own regular office. Each office was for a designated show, and whichever producer was assigned to that show would go into that office. 'We never understood why they did that,' ponders Martin, 'because if we moved from, say, the Gary Davies show to Bruno's, you'd have to move one door along, and bring all your records and junk and everything else with you.'

Despite that inconvenience, Martin found that there was generally a very good atmosphere about the place. 'It was fun and exciting and everyone was doing great work. It was a play hard, work hard mentality,' he says. 'Yes, we would go out for an extended lunch with a plugger or an artist, or a reception for a new album release, and have a few glasses on the way. But when we got back, we made sure the programmes did not suffer in any way.'

There were the odd lapses, of course. DJs especially did have a habit of partying with musicians and industry people. Someone might catch their eye or the DJ himself would spot a musician with a new record out and say, "Why don't you drop by the studio tomorrow and we'll do a live interview?" Just such an encounter happened between Bruno Brookes and Pete Townshend. Martin was still producing Bruno's show and, as they were preparing to come off air at half past seven the following evening, and Bruno lined up his last record at 7.26, Martin took a phone call in the studio from the reception desk. 'I've got a Mr Pete Townshend for you.' This was news to Martin who hit the talkback button through to Bruno. 'We've got a problem. We've got Pete Townshend downstairs.'

'Oh, bugger,' said Bruno. 'Oh, shit. Get rid of him.' Bruno had forgotten all about it.

Martin went out through the heavy studio doors, along the corridor, into the lift and down into reception, which was empty apart from this rock legend. 'I'd always been a huge Who fan,' admits Martin. Townshend was sitting reading the *Evening Standard*. On seeing Martin, he stood up. 'Hello, I'm here for the interview.'

'Pete, I'm really sorry but...' Martin began, before explaining the situation. Townshend didn't take it well. 'He went apeshit,' says Martin, 'and left.'

About two years later, Martin was producing the breakfast show with Mike Smith and the same thing happened. 'We came off air at

9.30 and at 9.26, when Mike had just started the last record, the phone goes, "Hello, Martin, it's Reg on reception." Talkback to Mike: "Mike, were you out with Pete Townshend last night?" "Oh shit, I forgot to tell you. Can you tell him to go away?" Down the corridor, down in the lift, and there he is, sitting in reception, and he takes one look at me and says, "Not you again."'

The summer of 1984 saw the end of an era when Tony Blackburn was let go after seventeen years. It was a bitter divorce, with Blackburn feeling undervalued after everything he'd given. 'Tony held the opinion that the BBC owed him a job for life and he never wanted to go,' said Beerling. The first inkling that something was afoot came when Blackburn was in the reception hall of Broadcasting House one afternoon and the commissionaire just happened to mention, 'Oh, we will miss you around here, Tony.' Blackburn didn't know what he meant, but then his agent confirmed the news. 'I was very upset to leave, but I don't bear them any grudge at all,' he later admitted. Having turned 40, he did understand that Radio 1 was a young person's station, but it didn't make the departure any easier to swallow. As he wrapped up his last show, Blackburn put the final piece of vinyl onto the turntable, The Move's 'Flowers in the Rain', the first song he'd played when Radio 1 started all those years before.

Someone else leaving was Kid Jensen, who went across to Capital, looking for a new challenge. Kid was to look back fondly on his time at Radio 1, especially the moments he shared with Peel, although he never quite got to the bottom of why he was sometimes the target of practical jokes from his colleagues, memorably the occasion when Noel Edmonds set fire to the Top 40 script when Kid was doing the chart show live from Southampton University.

Things were to change even more significantly early in 1985 with the announcement of a new controller, as Derek Chinnery stepped down. The jury was to remain out regarding just how effective he'd been. 'I always found him to be a bit of a cold fish,' says producer Tony

218

Wilson. 'He did do some good things. He was a bit too much of a company man.'

To producer Dave Atkey, Chinnery always came across as 'very straight, not overly humorous'. His favourite Chinnery story took place during a 'week out' in Yorkshire, when Chinnery tagged along with Dave and Simon Bates. One of the highlights was meant to be a visit to York Minster, which had recently suffered a terrible fire and was at the time closed to the public. They'd received special permission to go inside and do a report. The radio car pulled up to the entrance and Bates and Dave got out, walked over to the huge doors only to find them locked. This was going out live on air. Back in the studio, the engineer put a record on – time enough for Bates to come up with a plan. 'I'll tell you what,' Bates said to the engineer down the line. 'Can you put some echo on my voice, and can you get a creaky door sound effect.' What the listener heard next was Bates knocking on the door and then, *errrrr*, followed by footsteps and an echoey effect as Bates described all this fire damage: 'Isn't it dreadful,' and so on.

'We come out,' recalls Dave, 'sound effect of a door slamming and the next record played. But Derek Chinnery went mental. "You're conning the public," he said. "You're not allowed to do that."'

When it was announced that Johnny Beerling was to be Derek's replacement, no one was surprised. 'He was a more communicative guy,' says Gary Davies. 'Derek was a bit stiff. And Johnny was really forward-thinking about where the station would be in the future. He was a great controller.'

By this point, Beerling had been with the BBC for almost three decades. In addition, for the past couple of years he had actively thought about the possibility of getting the controller's job and what he might do differently if put in charge. He knew things needed to change at Radio 1, facing, as it did, competition from expanding commercial radio and daytime television. He remained deeply disappointed about still being denied FM stereo and that the network wasn't a 24-hour service. He also felt that the DJs chattered far too much. 'While we expected our DJs to be a friend to the listeners, there was far too much inane egotistical chat and not enough about the music.' By this time, of course, needle-time wasn't anywhere near the problem it had once been.

When Beerling took charge as controller, market research calculated that Radio 1 reached 19 million people per week and was the most listened-to radio station in the country. And yet it was Beerling's belief that they had become stale and predictable. 'There was too much enthusiasm for the old nostalgia and not enough for the new.' Beerling had two options: to focus on attracting a much younger listenership or stay with the audience that the station had built up over the years. After much internal debate, the decision was reached to keep things the way they were, while at the same time broaden the range of music, news, entertainment and social action.

One of the first things Beerling did was bring in Ranking Miss P, who began her career on the pirate London station Dread Broadcasting Corporation and had recently made several guest appearances on Janice Long's show. Going out on Sunday nights, *Culture Rock* was Radio 1's first show dedicated to reggae and Ranking Miss P became only the station's second black presenter after New York-born Al Matthews, who in the late seventies had his own Saturday night disco show. Matthews was later to turn to acting, most famously playing the tough marine sergeant in *Aliens*. Ranking Miss P left in 1989, but the sound of reggae was carried on by former musician The Man Ezeke, who presented *The Sunshine Show* on weekday evenings from 1990.

There had always been a fine balance at Radio 1 between providing a public service and chasing ratings. As John Peel said, 'Don't give them what they want, give them something they didn't know they wanted.' Beerling felt that it was in the presentation of news that Radio 1 could really make a difference, acutely aware that for many younger listeners Radio 1 was their only source of news information. This is why he doubled the length of *Newsbeat* from fifteen to thirty minutes. 'Internal staff hated me for doing that but I thought it was the right thing to do,' he said. 'More people got their news from Radio 1 than they did from Radio 4, just by virtue of the size of the audience.'

The same went with current affairs and an increase in the network's social action programme, whether it was about youth unemployment or drugs. 'We were never dictatorial about, let's say, drugs,' relates Beerling, 'saying you must not do this or do that. It was saying, "Here are the consequences and here is where you can get help." One of the best things we did was set up free helplines, a common enough thing today, but in those days we had to get funding from various government sources and it would only be on for a week.' This scheme ran into trouble when the tabloid press complained that the station was not being censorious enough about the perils of drugtaking. There were similar problems later that year when the station launched an AIDS awareness campaign, promoting safe sex. The slogan 'Play It Safe' sparked fury from Roman Catholic bishops. 'The Catholic Church condemned me because I was advocating the use of condoms to stop the spread of AIDS,' says Beerling. 'We did all that pioneering stuff and nobody ever gave us any credit.'

Beerling's first major coup came that April when Radio 1 moved its entire operation over to Egton House. For Beerling, it was the culmination of many years of nagging and persuasion. People had complained that having the studios and the offices in different buildings gave the network little chance to cultivate its own identity. 'It should be run as a separate service,' Kenny Everett had argued. No one listened.

Others felt much the same, including Tim Blackmore. When Tim had made the move to Capital, he'd phoned Derek Chinnery to ask if he'd ever been to a commercial radio station and seen how it operated. He hadn't. 'Do you want to come over and take a look?' Tim suggested. Chinnery agreed and Tim gave him a guided tour. Tim wanted Chinnery to take particular notice of the difference in atmosphere in Capital's building compared with the atmosphere at Egton House. 'I've realised it's because the studios are there,' Tim told Chinnery. 'People walk in and out of the studio into where they work. I've never felt energy like there is here. We are all in this together. We are all working for the one thing.' The fact that at Egton the DJs all had to walk across the road to Broadcasting House to do their shows was an enormous handicap and the reason why Radio 1 never quite felt like an integrated entity, for many who worked there.

Chinnery never acted upon Tim's suggestion, so it was Beerling who finally organised the move. The entire second floor of Egton House was cleared to make way for the new suite of top-of-the-range studios. 'They were the best radio studios ever,' confirms Adrian Juste. 'They liaised with Steve Wright and me, probably the most technical ones, and got us in to help design it. They were absolutely brilliant. The station sounded better from the new studios. It gave us an autonomy and an independence, and we really flourished.' Having everything in the same building was a pivotal moment. 'It was the first time we felt like a proper radio station,' says Beerling.

One idea of Beerling's that didn't come to pass was to have a kind of viewing platform where members of the public could look in and see the DJs at work live on air. Due to the enormous popularity of the station, bosses didn't think such an idea was practical.

While the studios were all shiny and new, no one thought about sprucing up Egton House to match them. It remained, as it had always done, a bit of a dump. 'It was a very strange building which could have done with a spring clean when I arrived and probably could have done with about twenty spring cleans when I left,' says Andy Peebles. 'It was a very lived-in environment. But it had atmosphere.'

18

I In the spring of 1985, rumblings were spreading through the music industry of a major benefit concert going ahead at Wembley Stadium to raise money for famine relief in Ethiopia. Organised by Bob Geldof, it sprang from the Band Aid charity single 'Do They Know It's Christmas?' that had raised millions the previous Christmas.

Jeff Griffin had heard the rumours and spoke to Chris Lycett about them and at their next production meeting with Beerling raised the issue that if such a concert was taking place then Radio 1 needed to be at the heart of it. Things quickly snowballed after that and Geldof called a big meeting in London to prepare for the concert going ahead on 13 July. Chris and Jeff turned up representing Radio 1, but mostly it was TV people and the grey-suit brigade. 'It was all terribly "can't do",' recalls Chris. 'All of these grey men came up with stuff like, "Well, it's a very short timeframe." There was nobody saying, "It's a problem but we'll find a way of overcoming it." Geldof, who was clearly frustrated, slammed his fist on the table, "We're fucking doing this. I don't care what the fucking problems are. Pull your fucking fingers out!" These executives had never been spoken to like that.'

The technical issues on Live Aid were indeed immense. Yes, there were satellite facilities but nowhere as advanced as they are today. Up to the challenge, Jeff and Chris began putting together the nuts and bolts of what they needed in order to mix the concert properly and make it sound decent. Early on, there were intense grumbles from TV sound engineers who traditionally mixed their own sound for television broadcasts. In the end, it was agreed that Radio 1 would take sole charge of the audio feed that was to be heard around the world.

More than the technical issues, everyone had only been given six weeks' notice to get the thing planned and put on. 'Really,' says Jeff, 'this being the BBC, we would have wanted six months' planning for something like that, because it was such a massive undertaking. It wasn't a case of "It can't be done"; it was a question of working out how the hell we would do it.'

For Jeff in particular, the biggest technical issue arose from Geldof's vision for the concert to be like this global jukebox, with hardly any gaps in between the acts. 'It was a nightmare to work that out beforehand.' The plan was to have a circular stage divided into three sections: one section facing the audience with the band in performance, another section would be derigging the previous band, while the third section had been rigged, ready to come round with the next artist. The obvious solution was to have each of the three sections wired to individual sound mixing vans. 'Unfortunately,' says Jeff, 'because we only had six weeks' notice, it was lucky I could get two vans let alone three. We had one of our own London ones and the other one had to be brought down from Scotland.' In the end, the only way to work round the system was for Jeff's sound guys to keep plugging and unplugging the sound cables every time the stage rotated.

Jeff also planned to have a separate vehicle there in which to put the multitracks (separate audio tracks later used for mixing into a single audio track). Geldof had made it known that the bands and the managers did not want any multitracking done since this was just a one-off thing, it wasn't a commercial exercise, and no one was being paid. 'When that meeting ended, I went up to Bob and said, "I heard what you said then, but it would be criminal if we don't multitrack it. Unless you tell me, absolutely, categorically, that I'm not to do it, I am going to multitrack it. I can tell you that now."' And he said, "Do what you fucking like."' The fact that Jeff did multitrack the concert turned out to be an absolute godsend when the official DVD release of the concert was put together and released in 2004.

Leading up to the day of the concert, there were regular meetings at Wembley, attended, at times, by up to a hundred people, including representatives from American satellite companies, as all sorts of groups were involved putting in their halfpenny worth. At either the second or third meeting, music promoter Harvey Goldsmith announced a major coup. Mick Jagger and David Bowie were going to perform a live duet together, with Bowie performing at Wembley and Jagger at the American venue in Philadelphia. 'If anybody could have seen the look on my face,' recalls Jeff. 'I just sat there and waited till Harvey had finished and then said, "Harvey, I'm sorry to have to say this but you're going to have to tell them it can't be done, because they'd have to deal with a significant video delay." So that put the mockers on that straight away. Instead the two rock icons went into a studio and covered the classic Martha and the Vandellas' hit 'Dancing in the Street', along with an accompanying video. Later released as a charity single, it went to number one.

Due to all the logistics and availability of artists, there could only be one rehearsal, which took place the day before the concert, on the Friday. It did not go well. 'We tried running the first four bands,' says Jeff. 'That should have been no more than around one and a half hours, with a few gaps and links in between. In fact, it took nearly three hours. I pointed out that if this happened all through the concert, we'd still be on the air on Sunday morning.' The rotating system operating the revolving stage also broke down and had to be pushed by roadies. With an embargo that night for eight o'clock at the stadium, being an open-air venue and situated in a large residential area, rehearsals had to finish. But there was a lot of head scratching left to do and all the radio and television crews sat down for more than two hours afterwards trying to work things out, hoping to get it all functioning by the following day.

As for the Radio 1 DJs themselves, many of whom were to be presenters on the day, Paul Gambaccini recalls that they were only called in about it the week before. 'We had a planning meeting in the controller's office, and we were told, "This is going to happen, there can be no rehearsal, and this is what you're all going to do."'

The base of operation for the DJs was in the football commentary box, and of course it didn't occur to anybody that it would be like a sauna in summer. 'Everybody who went in there to do their links was just dripping like crazy,' remembers Paul. 'The temperature was approximately 100 degrees Fahrenheit.'

Other Radio 1 DJs involved in the event were Mike Smith, Janice Long and Richard Skinner. At the time, Noel Edmonds had a helicopter company based in Battersea and he shuttled many of the artists to the concert via London Transport's cricket ground, about 400 yards from Wembley Stadium. On the day itself, the climax of London Transport's cricket tournament was taking place and they refused to abandon it. In the end, the umpire, upon spotting the helicopter coming, would blow a whistle and clear the field for Noel to land.

For other DJs, it was a case of bitter disappointment not to be asked to participate. Gary Davies, for instance, was hosting a BBC corporate event that he couldn't extricate himself from. Missing Live Aid remains one of his biggest regrets. Bob Harris was no longer at the BBC but had a Saturday show on Norwich's Radio Broadland. Spinning the records, he thought to himself, 'I bet most people are watching or listening to Live Aid.' Going on air, Bob appealed for anybody who was listening to him rather than Live Aid to call into the station. Not one phone call came in.

Janice Long had been asked for by Bob Geldof and she was never to forget standing on the stage when the gates opened and the public flocked in. 'They were little dots in the distance,' she remembers, 'and they got bigger and bigger and you saw them with their hampers, bags full of pop, all trying to get to the front for this momentous occasion.' Before she knew it, the event was underway as Status Quo charged into their hit 'Rockin' all over the World'. Standing at the side of the stage, Janice felt a nudge: one of the television crew was telling her that if the pictures went down or if there was any kind of problem, she would have to go on. Janice thought to herself, 'I go on and do what? Tap dance, tell a joke, what do I do?' Luckily Quo's set passed off smoothly. 'Tony Hadley was standing beside me and we just looked at each other and burst into tears.'

Behind the scenes, Chris Lycett recalls there being a sense of calm rather than panic. 'In a funny kind of way, because it was put together so quickly, and we were all on this rollercoaster, I don't remember any of us being under any great pressure. In a sense, technically, so long as you've done everything you can to make sure it's right, it's in the lap of the gods.'

Amazingly, things did pass relatively smoothly, with only a few glitches. The first one, ironically enough, involved Bob Geldof himself, performing with his band The Boomtown Rats. 'We had six lead mics on the front of the stage,' confirms Jeff Griffin. And Bob got a bit too excited and accidentally pulled his out of the socket. The TV director in the control room shouted, "We've lost Bob's vocals." I looked over: "He's pulled his bloody mic out." That also meant that we'd lost that mic socket for the rest of the concert because he'd damaged the pins inside it.'

By far the biggest glitch occurred during the opening song of The Who's performance when the lights literally went out. Right from the start, Jeff had voiced concerns about the power supply at Wembley and whether it would be able to cope. He'd spoken to the stadium's engineering manager. 'We've got nine television vans, I've got two of my mixing vans, we've got a multitrack van. We're going to have about twelve or thirteen vans altogether.' This didn't seem to faze the manager at all. "Oh, don't worry about that," he said. "I work here all the time. It'll be OK." Of course, it wasn't: it blew the Wembley system. Luckily there was a stand-by generator that was put into action as quickly as possible so the majority of The Who's set was saved. Then just before the next act came on, which was Elton John, that packed up, too. Fortunately, the Wembley engineer had managed to work wonders and get the main power back, and just in time.

But the one gaffe everyone remembers is McCartney. The annoying thing is, it could so easily have been avoided. The set-up was fairly straightforward, with McCartney just at the piano and singing into a radio mic. Each radio mic had its own dedicated frequency, and for a good reason, as Jeff relates. 'Going back years when the BBC used to do things at Wembley, before they sussed all this out, some of the radio mics used to pick up the local taxi cab firm, so suddenly over the PA system you'd get, "Yes, control, I'm off to Hendon now."'

Jeff's team knew which radio mic McCartney was supposed to be using. Unfortunately, either his own roadie or one of the tech people had given him a different radio mic that they didn't know about. The result was, as McCartney launched into 'Let It Be', he was inaudible to everyone except the first few rows. 'What bloody mic is he using?' yelled Jeff. There was pandemonium. 'I had to get one of my guys to rush round and find out what radio frequency mic it was. Eventually we found it, but we lost, I think, the first one minute and twenty seconds. Obviously, I was really pissed off about that, but it was what it was and we carried on.'

On the Monday, after everything had settled down, Jeff spoke to a mutual friend who worked for McCartney. Jeff had no idea what was going to happen to the Live Aid material in the future, whether it would be repeated or be released on video. Either way, he thought it was a good idea if McCartney could revoice that missing minute and a half. By the end of the day, word came back that McCartney was happy to do it and by the Wednesday he was in a studio dubbing those missing vocals.

The repercussions carried on, though. A year after Live Aid, Chris Lycett was producing Simon Bates and they were going to interview Paul McCartney about his new album. 'We walked in and McCartney was there and Bates turned around and said, "This is my producer Chris Lycett. He's the guy who lost your voice at Live Aid."'

For Jeff and Chris, Live Aid was a career highlight, the product of amazing cooperation and teamwork. Backstage, everyone was working towards the one goal, and there were no clashing egos amongst the pop stars at all. Everyone got on and the atmosphere was electric. 'I would have to say, though,' adds Jeff. 'That it's just as well that Status Quo were on first because seeing the state of them an hour or so into the concert, there was no way they would have been able to do it.

But fair enough, they'd done a good job and got everything off to a great start.'

Dave Atkey, who was executive producer with Stuart Grundy, has his own special memory of that day. Dave was backstage most of the time, rushing to and fro setting up interviews with the artists performing. Then, after Bowie's set, that video came on of starving and dying kids, accompanied by the strains of 'Drive' by The Cars. 'We all stood there, including David Bowie, and we were all in tears. It was one of the most moving moments of the whole day.'

Put simply, no other broadcaster could have put Live Aid on. Today, it could be posted on YouTube, but in 1985 the only organisation from a broadcast perspective that had the resources to cover that kind of event was the BBC. Johnny Beerling was to call Live Aid 'probably the greatest showcase of popular music that there will ever be'.

One face amongst the throng of Radio 1 presenters at Live Aid was less recognisable than the others. It belonged to new boy Andy Kershaw, who arrived from *The Old Grey Whistle Test*. A young reporter from Rochdale, with experience in local radio and as tour manager for Billy Bragg, Andy was on the dole when *Whistle Test*'s producer Trevor Dann took a punt on him. In less than a year, Andy was on the radar of a few high-ups at Radio 1. Dann suggested the pair of them put together a demo. 'Get a box of your favourite records,' he told Andy, 'and we'll go into a studio and make a tape.'

After the demo was cut, Andy largely forgot about it until a fortnight later he walked into the *Whistle Test* office and Dann looked up from his desk. 'Congratulations, you're a Radio 1 DJ.'

It was obvious to people like Chris Lycett what the appeal of Andy was to BBC management, although it remained unsaid. 'They always considered him to be the heir to the Peel operation.' Peel himself later called Kershaw 'a kindred spirit' and 'almost the first person that I'd met at Radio 1 with a real interest in music'.

As a teenager, Andy listened religiously to Peel and so it was pretty overwhelming for him to arrive at Egton House and find himself shipped over to room 318, where John Walters and John Peel operated from. Andy was to describe his relationship with Peel as the two naughty schoolboys of Radio 1 at the back of the class. Andy loved hanging around the office, playing new records, booking artists for sessions and answering the mail, most of the time sitting on an upturned steel wastepaper basket because there wasn't space for a third chair. It did seem as if Andy, Peel and Walters were destined to work together. Walters described Kershaw's arrival within their inner sanctum as 'like an elderly couple nearing the twilight of their years who against all medical probability have a child'.

The office was cluttered with debris, piles of unopened mail sat on Walters' desk and the carpet was festooned with neglected demo tapes. Andy was there one morning when an officious BBC employer knocked on the door to hand over a piece of paper. It was a final notice from health and safety to the effect that room 318 constituted a fire hazard and endangered the entire building. Andy put the letter on Walters' desk, where it was probably never read and soon disappeared under layers of records and rubbish. The BBC health and safety man was never seen again.

The daytime jocks certainly knew to keep out of room 318. They weren't welcome save for a few 'chosen ones' like Janice Long and Kid Jensen, and musos like Annie Nightingale, Fluff and Gambo. 'The others knew their place and kept well away,' Andy wrote in his autobiography, 'possibly sharing Steve Wright's view that the occupants of 318 were "from another planet".'

Andy certainly saw his job at Radio 1 as a continuation of the Peel ethos. While their musical interests were not totally aligned, they certainly shared a distaste for what Andy labelled 'the smug rock mainstream consensus'. Soon after arriving, Andy made it plain that he had no intention of playing anything that the record companies sent him. He was always going to be looking to find those things that listeners wouldn't hear anywhere else. One of Andy's passions was for African music and there was an African record centre a short walk from Broadcasting House where he spent many hours looking for rarities to play. 'Very often, I'd go there and spend more in that shop in a week than I'd get paid for doing the programme,' he told *The Mouth Magazine* in 2018. Although Andy was brought in ostensibly to host a conventional rock show, within a year Radio 1 had on its hands, by default, a weekly 'world music' show. It turned out to be good timing, helped immeasurably by the 1986 release of Paul Simon's *Graceland* album, which highlighted the South African township sound of Ladysmith Black Mambazo, combined with the growing success of Peter Gabriel's world music festival Womad.

Trevor Dann had warned Andy that if he carried on with what he was playing he wouldn't last six months on the station, but at the 1987 Sony Radio Awards he won Best Specialist Music Programme and his future was assured. He remained on Radio 1 for fifteen years.

It wasn't just Peel who fascinated Andy, Walters did, too. He was capable of carrying on various conversations and yarn-spinning while fielding phone calls and dealing with pushy music pluggers and intrusive Radio 1 managers. Chris Lycett recalls one incident when Dave Price, chief assistant to Beerling, came in to complain about one of the stock rooms that over the years had become a dumping ground for old reel-to-reel tapes. 'We've got to do something about the archive cupboard,' demanded Price.

'Like what?' said Walters.

'We need more room.'

'Yeah.'

'Well, there's all of your session tapes in there,' said Price.

'Yeah,' repeated Walters.

'We need some shelf room.'

'How much?'

'I don't know,' said Price. 'Six feet.'

'OK,' went Walters. 'Will that be the six feet that goes from A to C, so we'll lose Bowie and Bolan, or from X to Z where we'll lose X-Ray Spex and XTC.'

This was just too much for Dave Price, who harrumphed and turned on his heel, muttering on his way out, 'Well, something's got to be done about it.'

★

Someone else keen to make an impression in Egton House was a young producer by the name of Jonathan Ruffle. He'd arrived by way of the World Service, where he'd been working as a studio manager, and, because of his interest in music, had been asked by the Mandarin service to write a monthly pop show that went out to millions of people in communist China – quite a thing to put on your CV when you're trying to move to Radio 1.

The BBC worked very much like the civil service in that staff could change departments for three months and try something else out, so Jonathan went over to Radio 1. 'I did stuff for every single show I could find, tried to make myself indispensable and when it came to "Are we going to get someone else in from another department or shall we keep this guy on?", they kept me on.'

Just a month into the job, Jonathan was asked to stand in for Simon Bates' producer while he took a two-week break. Suddenly, there he was choosing Our Tune and putting a running order together for one of the most popular shows on the station. 'You were blooded really, really quickly,' he remembers. 'And there was also an assumption that you actually knew what you were doing.'

Jonathan enjoyed working with Bates, as he did later with Steve Wright, because they'd both been journalists. Neither went into the studio without a whole sheath of things to say and do. They weren't going to start a show not knowing how it was all going to end because they still retained that journalistic discipline. 'These guys were lively-minded people and they worked really hard.' As far as Jonathan was concerned, there were three types of DJ working at Radio 1: first, those who had come up through being a DJ, who were technically brilliant, but a bit workaday. Then there was the group who had been on the pirate ships, such as Travis and Peel. 'Very occasionally you would see a gleam of the 20-year-old anarchic person who went and sat on a boat and played records when they were in their youth,' remembers Jonathan. 'They still had that pirate ship energy.' The final group, the ones Jonathan really liked, were the ex-journos. 'They really did the work. They understood it wasn't going to happen by magic.'

LEFT: Steve Wright, whose afternoon show became one of Radio 1's most popular, in 1980. *Keystone/Getty*

Peter Powell championed the new wave and New Romantic movements and, like many Radio 1 DJs before and after him, encouraged new music.

Denis Jones/ANL/Shutterstock

The annual Christmas party, captured here in 1980, was seen by many as something more to be endured than enjoyed. John Peel was to refer to them as 'The most appalling event of the year.' *PA Images/Alamy*

Andy Peebles, with Doreen Davies, interviews John Lennon and Yoko Ono, New York, 6 December 1980. Two days later Lennon was shot dead. *Mark and Colleen Hayward/Redferns*

LEFT: In 1982, Lenny Henry was invited to be a guest DJ, combining music with comedy. These shows proved so popular they ran for the next three years. *Chris Ridley/Radio Times/Getty*

Mike Read was one of the most high-profile Radio 1 DJs of the eighties and became infamous for refusing to play the Frankie Goes to Hollywood single 'Relax'. *United News/Popperfoto/Getty*

Radio 1 provided the audio feed for the Live Aid concert that was heard around the world. Janice Long joins Bob Geldof and assorted rock stars on the hallowed Wembley turf, 13 July 1985. *Landmark Media/Alamy*

In the 1980s Radio 1 promoted a series of social action programmes, be it on youth unemployment, safe sex or drugs, with free helplines, an innovation at the time. *PA Images/Alamy*

Ranking Miss P began her career on the pirate London station Dread Broadcasting Corporation before hosting Radio 1's first show dedicated to reggae, which started in March 1985. *Tim Roney/Radio Times/Getty*

Simon Mayo, just installed as the new breakfast show host, cycling to work in 1988 with his favourite teddy bear, as you do. *Steve Poole/ANL/Shutterstock*

Liz Kershaw, Bruno Brookes and Jackie Brambles were part of a new generation of DJs brought in to freshen up the schedules. *Shutterstock*

LEFT: Jason Donovan and Phillip Schofield have fun on the Radio 1 Roadshow, 10 August 1989. *Mirrorpix*

RIGHT: Simon Bates and producer Jonathan Ruffle return after their charity trip round the world, à la Phileas Fogg, where they broadcasted live from each far-flung location, 1989. *Bill Lovelace/ANL/Shutterstock*

ABOVE: Paul McCartney drops in on the Steve Wright show, 13 June 1990. *PA Images/Alamy*

'Young, free and single' Gary Davies, seen here with Kylie Minogue in 1992, had a great affinity for working with live audiences and probably did more Roadshows than anyone else. *Shutterstock*

The Radio 1 Roadshow started in 1973 and attracted tens of thousands of holidaymakers and fans every day of the summer. Shown here in 1995 with Simon Mayo, it ran until 1999. *Patrick Bishop/Alamy*

ABOVE: The man who changed Radio 1 forever. Matthew Bannister arrived as the new controller with the controversial task of booting out the old guard and making the station cooler and relevant for a younger audience. *Times Newspapers/Shutterstock*

LEFT: The big gamble. Chris Evans leaves his final rehearsal before first hosting the breakfast show in 1995, a desperate last throw of the dice to rescue the station's plummeting ratings. *Mirrorpix*

There was something about Egton House, too, that made it special, apart from the people who worked there. Jonathan puts it down to the fact that it was a separate building, that even though it was just across the street from Broadcasting House, they were worlds apart. 'That physical distancing from the BBC,' he says, 'imbued us with a sort of "We're the naughty schoolboys and girls across the road." We told ourselves we weren't allowed in the big boys' building.' It reminded him somewhat of a scene in the Beatles' film *Help!* when the Fab Four arrive at the terraced street where they all live next door to each other. 'The joke is that inside it's some massive psychedelic shag pad and I used to think that Radio 1 was a bit like that. It was a bit of a laugh to play pop records all day, that every morning the record delivery person brings several trillion records for you to listen to, and you can pick up a record and walk downstairs and play it on the wireless.'

Jonathan remembers working in his office late one morning, preparing for a weekend show and listening to all the records that had arrived in a big fat pile. 'I pick this record off the top. It wasn't one the pluggers had sent round, it was an amateur cover. I played it and thought, "That's really good." I went downstairs into Bates's studio. He's live on air, and I say, "You ought to play that, Simon. It's really good." And he played it. So, from the moment I put the needle on the record upstairs to it being played to his entire audience was only about ten or eleven minutes. Three weeks later, that record was number one.'

It would be nice to report that that record led to the discovery of a great band, or a solo artist of some import, but it was in fact a novelty record called 'Star Trekkin'' by a band called The Firm. 'Not, I suggest, a musical masterpiece,' reports Jonathan. But the story is indicative of what it was really like at Radio 1.

19

Sadly, 1986 saw the departure of the indomitable Doreen. Her post as head of Radio 1 was taken over by Roger Lewis, a young buck who had been the producer for Chris Tarrant's breakfast show on Capital before he was poached by Radio 1, where he rose through the ranks with alarming speed. At 32, he became Radio 1's youngest ever head.

Doreen retired at the same time her husband Derek Mills left his senior position at Radio 2, and her absence was mourned by many. 'She helped put Radio 1 on the map,' states Andy Peebles. 'She deserves massive credit.' What the DJs liked about her was her encouragement and truthfulness. Doreen always had her office door open: 'Come in and have a cup of tea,' she'd say. If a DJ happened to be a bit down, maybe a show hadn't gone well, she'd respond, 'Sounded fine to me this morning.' What she did was lift a DJ's spirits. Conversely, on another morning she might spot someone feeling a little bit too cocky. 'You look pretty pleased with yourself,' she'd say. 'Good programme this morning?'

'Yes, I feel great,' the DJ would answer.

'Sit down,' Doreen would suggest. 'Let me tell you how it could be better.'

Despite Doreen's departure, life still carried on at Egton House. The Top 40 got a revamp. Richard Skinner had been the voice of the show since 1984 and it had remained as popular as ever – and one of the toughest to produce. 'No radio programme calls for more discipline than a Top 40 chart show,' claims Phil Ward-Large, who deputised a few times for the regular producer. 'It obviously brings significant challenges and pressures. You've just two hours to fit in all the new entries, every record going up the chart, records holding their position and the countdown, as well as the DJ's introductions and back-announcements. Providing everything's correct, it's almost certainly the most satisfying show to produce.' When Bernie Andrews was producer, he always made sure that there were two copies in the studio of every record in the chart in order to avoid any mishaps.

Chart shows became something of a habit for Phil Ward-Large and he subsequently produced them for Kiss-FM and Xfm, as well as enjoying a long run on the Pepsi Network Chart with Neil Fox at a time when it attracted more listeners than the Radio 1 chart.

When Skinner was given his marching orders from the chart show, the obvious replacement was Bruno Brookes. Having grown up as a fan of the show, Bruno saw it as a huge honour and was only too aware of its legacy and continuing appeal. However, there were a couple of things of his own that he wanted to bring to bear upon the format. First, to inject more energy into the show, and that energy would build as the countdown neared its climax. And second, the issue of home taping. Everyone knew people at home recorded from the radio onto cassette tapes, despite campaigns by the record industry against it, fearing its adverse effect on sales. It was a rite of passage in the days before streaming. Some DJs even encouraged the practice. On her request show, Annie Nightingale often played 'Is That All There Is?' by new wave singer Cristina, and, because it was a particularly rare record to find, she'd always flag up the fact that she was putting it on in the next few minutes, 'so it gave people a chance to set up their tape recorders'. The difficulty for home tapers was the propensity for DJs, especially those who loved the sound of their own voice, to talk all over the intro and outro of songs. 'I remember saying to myself,' says Bruno, 'if I ever did the Top 40, I would never talk over the records, I'd just let people record it.'

Bruno hosted the Top 40 until 1990, and during his tenure audiences reached a whopping 15 million. He returned as host from 1992 through to 1995. Perhaps the incident he's most remembered for came in February 1993 when he accidentally played the full uncensored version of Rage Against The Machine's debut single 'Killing in the Name (Of)', which featured the F-word no less than sixteen times and culminated in a massive scream of 'motherfucker'. The mistake derived from the fact that Bruno always wrote his next link while the record was on, and with his headphones off was totally oblivious to the rain of obscenities pouring out of people's radios the length and breadth of the country.

The strange thing was, while the record caused great offence to many people listening, and the BBC was inundated by complaints, Bruno didn't get a single phone call into his studio, and after wrapping up the show with the number one hit of the week, still had no idea what had happened. 'It was only afterwards when I was walking through reception that one of the girls called after me, "Bruno, you realise we've been taking a lot of calls." I said, "Why? What's up?" And she said, "You played the sweary version of Rage Against The Machine." I said, "You're joking." I can't tell you how many people have patted me on the back for doing that.'

There was also a change on the breakfast show. Mike Read had been there for five years now and the general wisdom was that the show needed a freshen-up. Mike was moved over to Sunday mornings and also became host of *Roundtable*. The studio discussion programme reviewing the latest record releases still commanded its fair share of star guests, some better behaved than others. 'I remember the ratings going up when Pamela Anderson detrousered me under the table while I was broadcasting,' recalls Mike. Another favourite was with Elton John. 'He was full of innuendos and on top form.'

Whitesnake's David Coverdale, on the other hand, arrived at the studio demanding alcohol, only to be told that he could have a cup of tea. This did not go down well and he sat sulking at the back of the room, off mic and shouting his comments. After Coverdale had been asked repeatedly to sit at the table and join in properly, but had refused, the producer Phil Swern phoned security and, for the only time in his career, asked for one of his guests to be thrown out. Then there was Billy Idol. 'He was incapable of giving any sensible reviews,' Johnny Beerling recalled in his memoirs, 'because he was out of his head on something pretty toxic!'

Taking over from Read on breakfast was Mike Smith, who came in with a lot of ideas and quickly added 500,000 new listeners. *The Breakfast Show* now had a weekly reach of 18 million; Princess Diana was to declare that Mike was her favourite DJ.

One of Mike's producers was Martin Cox. 'Mike was a nice guy but he was not an easy man to work with. He was very committed and, as *The Breakfast Show* host, he was the most important person on air at that time. But we never became mates, as I did with Bruno and later Gary Davies. It felt like we were just doing a job and nothing more.' Mike was interested in the music but much more prone to playing golden oldies. 'He was quite critical of new releases,' says Martin. Smith was particularly averse to the factory sound of Stock, Aitken and Waterman. 'He definitely favoured, and he was probably right with this, bringing in classic old gold for the breakfast show.' Breakfast was probably the wrong time anyway to start experimenting. Listeners were waking up, having breakfast, getting ready and then driving to work. They didn't want to hear unfamiliar sounds; they wanted something safe and familiar.

One of the highlights of Mike's tenure on *The Breakfast Show* was a trip to Lapland with a group of schoolchildren, aged around 8 to 9 years old. It was a Christmas competition and the children were carefully selected, since they had to be young enough to still believe in Santa. None of their parents was allowed to come on the trip, so producer Chris Lycett brought along two female assistants.

The group flew to Helsinki and then caught another flight up to the Arctic Circle to Rovaniemi, the capital of Lapland, the 'official' hometown of Santa Claus. Collecting their bags, there was an announcement on the airport tannoy, 'Will the Radio 1 party please go to the information desk.' What greeted them was an ornate piece of wood with a message burnt into it from Santa himself: 'I'm sorry I can't be there to meet you, please go to my home. I'm rounding up the reindeer.' This was all being recorded and the kids were unable to contain their excitement. 'It's from Santa, it's from Santa,' they cried. For Chris, this epitomised the joy of radio. 'Somebody once said that the pictures are so much better on radio.'

Their accommodation was a log cabin set by a frozen lake and annexed to a hotel. Behind the cabin was a paddock, and on the gate hung another of the wooden boards with all the names of Santa's reindeers burnt into it. Cue more excitement. 'The following day we went to a reindeer farm,' recalls Chris. 'Don't talk about health and safety and all that malarkey. It was thick snow, it was 30 below, it was freezing. And there's a herd of reindeer and the kids' mindset is: "We'll help Santa with his reindeer." So they just flee from us, falling over in the snow, calling out all the names of the reindeer.'

The trip lasted three days, the last of which was broadcast live when the children finally met Santa Claus. Chris remembers it as an amazing experience for everyone, and not just the children. A year later, Chris received a letter from the mother of one of the kids, a young girl from Scotland who he remembered was quite reserved at first but after a day or so truly came out of herself. The letter read, 'I just want to say thank you because before she went Mary was quite shy and didn't play with other kids, and her ambition was to be a librarian. But after her visit with you she's come back and now she joins in, she's much more confident and not just that, she says she wants to be one of Pan's People!'

Beerling was a big fan of Mike Smith and admired his professionalism. Mike seemed to be able to do serious programmes along with the more light-hearted ones with the same deft touch. For Beerling, Mike epitomised the new breed of DJ that he was looking for, 'to bring a more intelligent approach' with less emphasis on the kind of showbiz personality Radio 1 was known for.

Someone else who fitted into that category was Simon Mayo, a young broadcaster learning his trade at Radio Nottingham. With a mother who'd worked as a studio manager for the BBC in the 1950s, Simon grew up around radio. He enjoyed listening to his mum's reminiscences and whenever the family drove through central London Simon always asked if they could make a detour to see Broadcasting House. As a child, he play-acted at being a DJ, with his sister supplying the jingles, and listened almost exclusively to Radio 1. 'I recorded shows like John Peel and the Top 40 onto a cassette,' he told *The Big Issue* in 2015. 'Then I would edit out the bits I didn't like with a razor blade and sticking tape.'

Starting out on hospital radio, Simon always aspired to work at Radio 1 and sent them endless demo tapes. Finally, one made its way to Johnny Beerling. As he listened to it on the Tube, Beerling noticed he'd missed his stop, a good indication of its quality. Simon was swiftly hired.

Walking into Egton House, Simon got the sense that Radio 1 was not quite the juggernaut that it had been back in the seventies. But it was still big enough that, as the new arrival, the newspapers were interested in him. The first thing Simon was asked to do was sub for Gary Davies on lunchtimes. 'This was a big deal because the Tuesday was famously when they unveiled the chart,' Simon says. 'As a kid, I would take my radio into school so that I could hear the Top 40. So to be actually announcing the Top 40 was head-spinning and genuinely terrifying.'

After that, Simon was given his own two-hour Saturday evening slot, going out before Dixie Peach, who presented a show called *Midnight Runner* which specialised in American style rock and funk. Dixie was relatively new to radio, having spent less than a year on the relaunched Radio Caroline prior to joining Radio 1. Previously a professional singer and musician, Dixie used his vocal talents and sang his introductions to a number of the songs in each show. He also liked to joke that he and Simon were the Crockett and Tubbs of Radio 1, a reference to the popular American cop series *Miami Vice*.

Helping Dixie find his bearings at Radio 1 was producer Phil Ward-Large, who over time had also worked with Paul Gambaccini, Kid Jensen and Gary Davies. Someone else he produced was Adrian

Juste, who Phil was especially impressed by. 'I don't think I've ever met a broadcaster who worked so hard and dedicated so much time to crafting their show as Adrian. He treated his programme as a full-time job, spending days in his home studio recording and editing classic comedy sketches.'

Later in 1986, Phil left the station, somewhat reluctantly since he would have been more than happy to remain there, but he'd accepted the position of programme controller at Radio Luxembourg. 'I'll be forever grateful to Johnny Beerling for giving me the opportunity to work at the "nation's favourite",' he says. 'My years at Radio 1 were without doubt the happiest times of my broadcasting career. It was an unbelievably creative environment and my office in Egton House became my second home. While I never had any interest in being a DJ, from an early age I always wanted to turn people on to the music I loved, to say, "Hey, you must hear this!" Being able to sit down with like-minded DJs and together build a musical plot, beginning with a blank piece of paper and crafting a two or three-hour show and then playing it to the nation was a dream come true.'

Over the years, *Steve Wright in the Afternoon* had become one of Radio 1's most popular shows. 'The idea always in my career is just to create a good mood,' he describes, 'and to be entertaining and try and be a little bit funny and try to keep people informed... I'm giving a performance, but it's a genuine performance.'

More than that, Steve had developed out of just playing records into basically presenting a lifestyle show. It's a bit of a cheesy word now – a satellite broadcaster might call itself Sky Lifestyle or something – but at the time it was a big innovation to start broadening out what you talked about and how you talked about it, from news and guests to showbiz gossip. This concept went even further under new producer Jonathan Ruffle.

Radio 1 had always been an idea-hungry environment, with people looking for input. And that was one of Steve's great strengths: he was completely egalitarian. 'He really did not care where any material came from,' says Jonathan Ruffle, 'as long as it was good and it was funny. It could be one of the technical operators or one of the sparks who can do the phone-in voice of Dave Double Decks, the send-up of a local radio DJ. Steve doesn't care. If he can do it, he's on the air and Steve helps them be funny.'

Things really started to change on the show after a young up-and-coming comic called Julian Clary came on. It went really well. Then Spike Milligan was a guest, 'because he's our hero,' says Jonathan. 'It was never intended for the show to feature star guests but public relations companies started to listen and began going: "I've got a comedian, I've got a TV star, I can put them on Steve Wright." This is what Steve did that was so new and different, not just having guests on to be interviewed but guests who got involved in whatever was going on in the programme. That included interacting with the production team, not the "afternoon boys" any more but the "posse".'

A good example of this occurred when The Monkees, who were in the UK on a reunion tour, appeared on the show. Rather than sitting down at eleven o'clock to do a boring twenty minute pre-recorded interview, they were in the studio surrounded by people who whooped and applauded every time they made a joke or did something. The recording was then edited into three-minute chunks, which Steve would play on air the same afternoon, split up by three or four records, other features or maybe the news. He would say something like 'The Monkees are coming back in about ten minutes, they're at the coffee machine,' or 'They're down in the record library looking to see if any of their records are there.' 'Steve created this impression that the guests not only came to the studio, but they came for the whole afternoon,' reveals Jonathan. 'Now, that sounds pathetic, but it was completely innovative at the time and a really brilliant idea. It suddenly made the content so fat; he didn't get one go at The Monkees, he got seven goes at The Monkees.'

Returning from a holiday in the States, Jonathan brought a bunch of comedy albums with him, including Robin Williams' *Live at The Met*.

Back at Egton House, he began editing what was roughly a sixty-minute album into two-minute chunks, resulting in thirty Robin Williams clips, enough for a month and a half broadcasting. 'Mel Smith and Griff Rhys Jones got wise to this,' says Jonathan, 'and they sent us the white label of their new album. So, before it was even released, we were putting out new Smith and Jones no one else had heard.'

There was one other vital component to all this, a man called Richard Easter, who had one of the most important jobs on BBC radio: he delivered the records. He was a postman, effectively. But he could also do a silly voice and Steve put him on the air. And, as it happened, he could write comedy sketches, too, such as a pastiche called 'At home with the Pet Shop Boys'. Ten of these were recorded, providing another two weeks' worth of broadcasting. Put that together with The Monkees interviews, followed by a comedy clip from Robin Williams and suddenly there was something on the radio that was very different. Added to all that was Steve chatting to the 'posse' with usually four topics of the day. Again, this was pre-recorded in order to make it sound good and editorially tight. 'And Steve's genius was to ringmaster that,' says Jonathan. And who were the posse? They included programme assistants, Jonathan Ruffle, the jingles producer, and Richard Easter, who later went on to write for Harry Hill.

The show was so popular that it achieved something quite staggering. The Radio 1 ratings always used to peak at around ten past eight in the morning, when most people were listening before going off to work or school, and would then tail off by lunchtime. When Steve came on in the afternoon, he actually made that peak go back up. Jonathan still meets people today who loved what they did. 'They tell you things like, "I was bored out of my mind. I was a rep driving around the M25 for a living, and every afternoon on came this show of people who seemed to be laughing and having a good time." And that's what we were doing, we were cheering people up. That was our sole aim.'

For Steve, however, the really impressive thing about Radio 1 was the Roadshow, the fact that it could go from town to town and pull in

242

25,000 people and it wouldn't necessarily matter who the host was. Steve had one character called Dr Fish Filleter, who was a source of much innuendo about fishy fingers. Jonathan recalls the time that he and Easter went up to Steve pleading, 'We simply cannot write any more Dr Fish Filleter, we just can't. It was a shit idea anyway and we've now been punting it for three months.' And Steve said, 'Love, it's going to be the most brilliant thing on the Roadshow. I've already got a bloke to deliver all this fish to the Roadshow in the morning, so you've got to run it for another month.' Steve knew how long it actually takes these things to penetrate the public's consciousness and Dr Fish Filleter became a highlight of his Roadshow appearances, throwing fish into the audience. Jonathan even remembers one person bringing a dead shark along to one of the Roadshows.

Steve always used to put on a show for the punters who had taken time out from their holidays to turn up or come down especially on a day trip. 'But I was always terrified when I heard those pips just before the announcement, "Today live from Bournemouth...". My hands would be shaking with nerves because you'd think, "OK, there's something like six million people listening and they're all waiting for you to come on." But in the end, you calm down and the people that came to the Roadshows were great. There was never any problems; it was always wonderful.'

Doing the Roadshow was a performance and in his early days at the station Steve learnt a lot from how some of his colleagues handled the live interaction with audiences, especially Tony Blackburn and Noel Edmonds. 'I just watched them and watched their stagecraft, their presence because I really didn't know how to do it. Gradually you start to learn it. I loved learning and I learnt a lot from the guys.'

One of the best things about doing a Roadshow was the sense of community amongst the production team, when everyone went back to the hotel and just chilled. 'One night,' says Steve, 'the Bee Gees flew in by helicopter the day before the Roadshow and stayed at the hotel with us. We were up until two in the morning with them. Maurice was at the piano, and we were all singing their hits. I will never forget that. It's a fantastic memory for me.'

The practical jokes remained an ever-present feature on a Roadshow outing and the main culprits hadn't changed either: Mike Read and Tony Miles. Producer Martin Cox did his fair share of Roadshows and never forgot one at Cannon Hill Park in Birmingham. 'Mike had got a bunch of local builders to put a breeze block wall around the goodie mobile, which was very funny and Smiley [Tony Miles] was furious. So, the following day, Smiley's revenge was to get Mike's pride and joy, his Triumph TR5, on the end of a crane and slowly lower it into the boating lake.'

One prank in Torquay led to producer Dave Atkey getting into hot water with his bosses. He and Peter Powell were staying in a hotel when Mike Read turned up. He just happened to be doing something in the town and asked if he could make an appearance on stage and plug the fact that he was hosting the Roadshow the following week. 'Only if you can think of something funny to do,' said Dave.

Tony Miles, of course, had an idea. 'Why can't we dress him up as a policeman?'

'Oh yes,' said Dave. 'You can come on and arrest the Roadshow for parking on a double yellow line.' Mike thought that was a great idea.

The next morning Dave and Tony headed into town early to find a policeman's outfit. They came across something that looked a bit like one in a joke shop where they were told by the man behind the counter, 'You're not allowed to impersonate a policeman. It's an arrestable offence.' A lightbulb went off in Tony's head. 'Really,' he said. The next stop was the local police station where the plot was hatched. Dave asked some of the officers if they could come on the Roadshow stage at a given signal to arrest Mike, live on air. It seemed like a laugh and they agreed.

The Roadshow went ahead and towards the end Mike came on in what was effectively a fancy-dress cop's uniform and started doing his bit. Suddenly there was a blast of a siren and a flashing blue light. A policewoman walked up onto the stage with another copper behind her. 'Are you Michael David Kenneth Read,' she asked. 'Yeah,' said Mike, tentatively, not sure what was happening. 'You're under arrest for impersonating a policeman.' Meanwhile Peter Powell is describing everything that's happening to the listening millions. 'So, Mike gets arrested,' says Dave, 'and is taken away. By this point the crowd is going mad. The police took him to the station, fingerprinted him, photographed him, and threw him in a cell, which was already occupied by someone else. And they left him in there for two hours.'

When the Roadshow finished, Dave tried to ring the BBC press officer to give him the chance to get hold of the story first but there was no answer, nor did anyone get back to him after he left a message. He then rang Johnny Beerling. Again no answer. Meanwhile word of what had happened reached the press so by the time Mike was released and Dave brought him back to the Roadshow site, a whole bunch of reporters was waiting. 'We got into every single [tabloid] newspaper in the country,' recalls Dave. 'I got the most severe bollocking of my life. Johnny was going mental. But we got fantastic coverage.'

These pranks and this kind of behaviour were by no means encouraged, but there was a school of thought about it helping to create a sense of comradeship amongst the team. Some producers did lay the law down – "There'll be no messing about on my watch" – but would be ignored. 'The temptation was always far too great,' says Martin Cox, 'because if someone started something it just kind of snowballed. It was "rugby club on tour stuff".'

Alongside the fun there was a lot of hard work, especially for the producer. The team would arrive at a town in the evening and everyone would have a meal together. But it was always the producer who had to be on site at six o'clock in the morning to put up all the fence barriers for the crowd control, then site the goody mobile, test the signal back to Broadcasting House, and generally make sure that everything was fine. Martin always found that, even this early in the day, fans would be waiting, hoping to get the best spots at the front.

Another role for the producer was as the warm-up act for the crowd. 'I remember one time in Brighton,' says Martin. 'We'd had a bit of a night of it at the hotel and I'd lost my voice. I still had to do the warm-up and went out there with "Good morning, Brighton" in this gravelly, barely audible voice. The studio manager, who was great fun but a real devil, kept my microphone level down so low that I had to croak even more for them to hear what I was saying. John Peel happened to be in the audience and found this so funny he wrote about it in his *Guardian* column.'

20

Robbie Vincent's soul show *The Sound of Sunday Night* had continued to be enormously popular, complete with his catchphrase 'If it moves, funk it', which came from one of his listeners. Weekends were always much quieter at Egton House and on a Sunday there'd be hardly anyone there at all. That suited Robbie fine, who never really socialised with the other DJs. He had his show, with its loyal audience, and that was it. He wouldn't compromise, even in the selection of music that he played. 'I could not, never have and never could play somebody else's choice.' Management knew also that Robbie was unwilling to move to other slots or do other programmes. 'I just couldn't face playing the pop stuff.' It was a principled stance that was to lead to his demise at the station towards the end of the summer of 1987.

Changes were afoot and Johnny Beerling had a tough call to make. One of his DJs had to go and he'd narrowed his choice down to two: Andy Peebles or Robbie Vincent. In the end, Robbie's contract was terminated. Beerling told Robbie it was because Peebles was the more flexible broadcaster. 'When Paul Gambaccini found out I was going he went in to see Beerling and said, "You must be mad. Why are you getting rid of our credibility?" I've never forgotten that.'

Robbie didn't want to leave and it was a bitter pill to have to take. Looking back, he admits that he was lucky to have had the opportunity to share with the nation the music he loves. He always enjoyed it when people got in touch to thank him for introducing them to a particular artist or song. 'It was a fantastic thrill to get all those letters and phone calls. That was my ego trip: that they'd liked something.'

Robbie numbers amongst a select few broadcasters who pioneered soul and funk music on mainstream radio. It was shows like Robbie's on Radio 1 that helped to create the climate for future stations such as Jazz FM, Choice and Kiss FM.

It was something of an irony that the man replacing Robbie on Sunday night was Andy Peebles. It had only taken nine years for Andy to finally do the *Soul Train* show that had proved so popular back in his Piccadilly Radio days. Like Robbie, Andy was a big soul fan. 'I absolutely adore it. It's my favourite form of music. It was something that John Lennon and I had in common and, over dinner that night after we'd done the interview, most of our conversation was just talking about soul singers that we loved.'

Soul Train was very much Andy's show, something he started back in the seventies and continued for forty years at various radio stations; it remains his proudest achievement. His listeners were loyal and Andy felt close to them. It fitted with his own approach to broadcasting, this belief that radio is one person talking to another person. When Andy did a morning show, to retain that feeling of intimacy, he used to close the blinds, shutting out the bright sunshine, and work in a semi-darkened studio.

For most DJs, the thing about radio, which is why many of them always preferred it to television, was the sense of speaking to one individual. Johnny Beerling always thought that the most successful DJs talked into the microphone as if it was a person. Communication is the secret, really. 'All a DJ has as a tool is their voice,' says Tony Brandon. 'They have to paint pictures in the listener's mind.'

For Johnnie Walker, it was trying to get a relationship going between himself and the listener. A trick taught to him by American DJs when he worked there was never to use plurals. 'DJs used to come on and start their shows, "Ladies and gentlemen, boys and girls," and they're all reminders that you're actually one of thousands, or maybe millions. These guys said to me, "Just come on and say, 'Hi, how are you?' Make the person think that you're only talking to them.'"

By this time, Johnnie had returned from the States and was working on a commercial radio station in Wiltshire. Out of the blue one day an idea popped into his head: go back to Radio 1. He picked up the phone and called Johnny Beerling, asking if they could have a chat. 'This is incredible,' said Beerling. 'We were having a meeting yesterday and your name came up. Can you see me on Thursday?'

After twenty years on the air, Radio 1 still went out in mono, except on Saturday when it 'borrowed' Radio 2's FM frequency, because they were mostly covering sport. Plans, however, were afoot for Radio 1 to finally get an FM signal and the idea was to do a Saturday afternoon programme that really highlighted the quality of stereo broadcasting. Producer Kevin Howlett wanted Walker to host it, but there was a lot of resistance to the idea of him coming back. Beerling thought that it was a great idea, having seen some recent market research that 70 per cent of listeners on Saturday were over 25: that made Johnnie an ideal candidate. Within 24 hours of that decision being made, Johnnie had that thought of ringing Beerling up. 'It was providence,' he says.

The Stereo Sequence was a huge undertaking. It all kicked off at 2 p.m. and finished at 7.30 p.m., including a documentary, the US chart show and a live concert. 'It was an amazing show to do,' says Johnnie. The American chart show element was by far the toughest to bring off since it required a live link-up with a DJ in Los Angeles. The problem was how to eradicate any time delay on the line. It was an American engineer who came up with a way of doing it but it was incredibly complicated. 'I used to do the main show from one studio,' explains Johnnie, 'and in the next-door studio was an engineer plugging up the connection with Los Angeles. And that was the studio I had to go into to do the chart show. It was so complex some studio engineers would feign illness so as not to have to do it.'

Having been away for almost a decade, Johnnie noticed a few changes around Egton House. 'I remember saying to Stuart Grundy, who produced my first ever daily show back in 1969, "What's the pub now then, Stu?" He looked at me a bit strange and said, "Well, there isn't one. We all tend to have sandwiches at our desks.'"

In Johnnie's early days, the main hang-out for the DJs was the BBC club at the Langham Hotel, just opposite Broadcasting House. It was the kind of place where you'd see Michael Parkinson or David Frost; everybody used to be in there. One senior producer liked to say that if the whole day went by and he didn't see one of his producers in the BBC club, then they were going to be in his office the next day and he would want to know the reason why. 'It's because he knew that's where all the good ideas came from,' says Johnnie. 'People are relaxed, they're having a chat, they bump into somebody, a subject comes up and the producer goes, "That's an interesting idea, we can do a programme about that." It was a very fertile place.'

It was the same with the Yorkshire Grey and the Green Man, the local pubs where the DJs and producers would meet up for drinks. Johnnie recalls having a ferocious argument with Teddy Warwick once about music policy. When it came to the end of the day, Teddy came knocking on the door as usual. 'Right, coming to the Green Man then?' Johnnie said, 'I didn't think you'd want to have a drink with me tonight, Teddy, after our row.' And he answered, 'That was business, this is personal.' So, they went off to the pub. 'That was just a way of having a disagreement about a policy but still retaining a friendship,' says Johnnie. 'And in the pub, who knows what ideas might have been born. I felt that was lost a bit when I came back to Radio 1 in 1987. It had gone a little bit corporate. That was kind of the yuppie influence of nobody goes to lunch any more, you've got to work and be at your desk. It's actually quite a good thing to step away from your workplace for a while.'

The Stereo Sequence paved the way for Radio 1 to finally begin its first regular broadcasts on the FM wave band starting that October. With the advent of the compact disc and clear digital sound quality, it was really only a matter of time before this happened. Indeed, on August bank holiday 1985, Bruno Brookes hosted the first compact disc show, where every song was played on CD and the whole thing went out in stereo. The reaction was extraordinary: Bruno was inundated with phone calls, not only from listeners but colleagues, producers and people he knew in the music industry, all of them saying how amazing it sounded. 'We got the stereo transmitters that day, because of that show,' Bruno recalls. 'I was privileged to be asked to do it. Everybody was just celebrating that the CD had arrived. Digital had arrived. There was such a dimensional difference in terms of the quality of the sound.'

Listeners still had to wait another two years for the national FM transmitter roll-out, first in London and then across the country, being broadly completed by the end of 1989. Radio 1 went out on the road broadcasting at various locations to publicise the shift to FM and garnered huge publicity when current teen idols Bros agreed to be involved. Boarding a helicopter, the band whizzed around the country to help switch on most of the new stereo transmitters in Glasgow, Manchester and Birmingham, finishing off at Egton House, where 3,000 fans were waiting for them. Such is the fickle nature of stardom that just a year later Bros appeared on the breakfast show and were taken up to the roof of Egton House for a few publicity shots. The number of fans outside this time barely reached half a dozen.

In the autumn of 1987, Beerling took on three new DJs, all of whom brought something different and vibrant to the station: Jeff Young, Mark Goodier and Liz Kershaw. By 1987 dance music was becoming a much bigger phenomenon in the clubs, with most of the music coming out of British independent labels rather than America. Robbie Vincent and Andy Peebles were doing their soul thing on Radio 1 and Gary Davies did his best to feature some of the big club records on his lunchtime show; he was amongst the first on the station to play acts like Black Box and Technotronic. As his producer, Martin Cox often had to hold him back on some of the music. 'There was a big issue at the time,' remembers Martin. 'Would Radio 1 play dance music? The answer was "no", and that came from above. So, if Gary wanted to play a record out of the clubs, it was very difficult to get that through the playlist.'

Jeff Young had different ideas. He'd been a club DJ heavily involved in the popular soul and jazz/funk scene and got his first break courtesy of Robbie Vincent at Radio London. After Robbie left to go to Radio 1, Jeff took over his slot and even filled in for him on Radio 1 when he took holidays. Jeff believed it had reached a stage where Radio 1 needed a dance programme. 'I wrote a three-page letter to Johnny Beerling, outlining how the dance scene had got to where it was and that particularly on a Friday and Saturday night there was a whole generation of kids in bedrooms and bathrooms getting ready to go out. And we could be doing a programme aimed at these people and it was something Radio 1 ought to be involved in.'

Jeff didn't hear anything for months and in the meantime had accepted a job offer at Capital; he'd even gone into the studios to carry out a bit of rehearsing. Then out of the blue Stuart Grundy called asking if he wanted to do an early evening dance show on Fridays. Jeff couldn't say no, which meant he had to resign from Capital before he'd even done his first show, which didn't go down very well.

Jeff's Radio 1 show was called *The Big Beat* and he had his own vibe about what he wanted to do with it. The problem, according to Jeff, was that his appointed producer, in this case Paul Williams, made the mistake of approaching the show like any other Radio 1 production. And Jeff, having just walked through the door, wasn't yet in a position to force through all of his ideas. As luck would have it, Williams soon departed to work on a big documentary with Paul McCartney, freeing Jeff up to develop the show the way he wanted it to be. 'I kind of turned Radio 1 almost into a pirate station for a few hours on a Friday night.'

This state of affairs went on for several months until Beerling asked Jeff how things were going with his producer. 'I haven't spoken with him for months,' the DJ answered. This came as something of a shock, so Beerling hurriedly brought in Mike Hawkes as a replacement. 'Now Hawkesie got it straight away,' says Jeff, 'because he'd produced specialist programmes like Ranking Miss P and he knew that you gave the presenter their head, particularly when it came to the music.'

Within its first year, *The Big Beat* carved out a large, loyal audience pioneering the new dance music by the likes of Mark Moore's S'Express and Bomb the Bass, pre-house and acid stuff, along with the early days of hip-hop with De La Soul, Ice-T and Public Enemy.

Given the notoriety of some of the tracks he was playing, Jeff experienced the occasional run-in with his station colleagues. During a drug awareness week, Jeff played 'I'm Your Pusher' by Ice-T. The verses carried very much an anti-drug message, but some of the chorus derived from an old Curtis Mayfield song called 'Pusherman', which dealt very directly with drug dealing. 'Bruno Brookes was driving around somewhere and got apoplectic about me playing this because he got the wrong end of the stick,' remembers Jeff. 'He ended up complaining because he had a younger brother who'd apparently written "ACID" all over one of his schoolbooks and got himself expelled, so Bruno said, "You shouldn't be playing this." Anyway, I had to go up to the powers that be with the bloody album with the lyrics on it. It took Bruno a long time to forgive me.'

These kinds of run-ins had much to do with the fact that Radio 1 was still viewed by many as a family-orientated station. And although some of the bands that he featured came stamped with controversy, Jeff didn't necessarily vet the kind of records he played. 'When you're listening to someone like Public Enemy, they're making a point. It's not necessarily racist or anti-white. Chuck D was very clever with how he went about things and so was Ice-T. It wasn't too gangsta then. It wasn't all about shooting, and stabbing, and bitches and hoes, thankfully.'

Born in Zimbabwe (when it was still Rhodesia), Mark Goodier moved with his family to the UK, settling in Edinburgh, and grew up listening to Radio 1 during its 1970s heyday. Having become, in his own words, 'infected' by radio at the age of 12, he often skipped school on a Tuesday lunchtime to rush home to hear Johnnie Walker run down the new Top 20 chart.

Running his own mobile disco, Mark began broadcasting on hospital radio before crossing over to local radio at the age of 18, spending five years at Radio Clyde in Glasgow. He thought he'd try his luck writing to Johnny Beerling to complain that Radio 1 had no DJs from Scotland, and included an audition tape. This oversight was rectified when Nicky Campbell, born and raised in Edinburgh, was hired, but Beerling still invited Mark to come and see him, offering him a thirteen-week contract, starting on Boxing Day. Mark was so nervous beforehand that he couldn't eat his Christmas dinner. It was the start of a fifteen-year spell with the station, beginning with a two-hour Saturday night show.

The third new DJ joining in autumn 1987 was Liz Kershaw, whose career began at Radio Leeds, where she managed to wangle a job after selling them a new switchboard on behalf of her employers British Telecom. When BT moved her to London, Liz compiled a demo tape and sent it in to Radio 1, keeping the fact that her brother Andy worked there a secret, not thinking for a moment they'd want two Kershaws on the same station. Her timing couldn't have been better: management were thinking young DJs were a bit thin on the ground, female presenters even less so, and on the strength of that tape she was hired to present a half-hour show on Sunday afternoons featuring interviews with artists in the chart that week. Called *Backchat*, it went on to win a Sony Award six months later.

Liz's casual and earthy style won over listeners as she grabbed interviews often on the hoof, with the likes of George Michael, Bon Jovi, Tina Turner and Run DMC. Her producer was Paul Williams. During one phone interview with Donna Summer in Los Angeles, Williams butted in asking Liz whether or not she thought Miss Summer was a lesbian. 'How about it, do you think she's a dyke?' It was calmly pointed out to him that not only could Liz hear what he was saying, but Donna Summer could, too.

Arriving at Radio 1, Liz was surprised by the comparative lack of management going on. 'Without any signs of supervision everybody just seemed to get on with it,' she wrote in her autobiography. 'The suits were hardly ever seen on the shop floor.' This seems to have been the method for much of the eighties. 'The BBC were interested in things like Radio 3 and the Proms,' says Adrian Juste. 'Because we were doing great business, they left us alone. We could do anything. Nobody during the eighties came up and said, "You can't do that." They just left you with a live microphone in front of 13 million listeners and you just did what you liked.'

Nor, according to Liz, was there much evidence of the more senior BBC types. This had been largely the state of play ever since the start of Radio 1 when the BBC as a whole tried to keep a discrete distance between itself and the noisy neighbours across the street from Broadcasting House. Occasionally some of the DJs were wheeled over to share a glass of wine in the governors' oak-panelled dining room. At such events, Liz was reminded of young Mr Grace from the BBC sitcom *Are You Being Served?* – 'Oh, you're getting 20 million listeners a week are you, jolly good. You're all doing very well. Carry on.'

In other more depressing areas, the mindset at Radio 1 appeared to be stuck in the 1970s. Incredulously, Jimmy Savile was still operating at the station, though it wasn't long after Liz arrived that Beerling finally made arrangements to get rid of him.

For Liz, walking into Egton House 'was like stepping into a rugby club locker room'. More than one executive was having an affair with a secretary. Liz recalls once opening a broom cupboard and interrupting one of her bosses in a compromising clinch. Too often, some of the secretaries had no choice but to put up with adolescent and lewd behaviour, along with unwarranted attention. Andy Peebles always thought that having the large open-plan area full of secretaries was asking for trouble, 'because DJs who think they can charm the birds out of the trees and the girls straight into bed, are going to go into operational mode'. It was the same at the Radio 1 'weeks out' when every morning at breakfast the rumours would start as to who might have been in whose bedroom the night before. 'But that's inevitable,' says Andy, 'in an enclosed society the like of which we were living in at Radio 1.' That was all well and good; there's nothing wrong with young, single people having fun. What went on was no different from any other institution or workplace, but there was a seedier side to it as well, as history was to show.

Secretaries working at Egton House were poorly treated in other ways, especially when it came to salary. When they decided to go on strike for better conditions the ringleader was called in by one of the executives, who laid out the secretary's career options. 'You're a pretty young girl. Why are you trying to be a man? Why don't you just wait and see who you meet? One day a nice pop star might walk in and ask you to marry him.' Liz Kershaw was so enraged when she heard about this that she joined the picket line.

Women, too, working in any capacity at Egton House, were still regularly disregarded when it came to promotion, especially climbing the ladder to being a producer. A female assistant whom Liz Kershaw worked with was repeatedly passed over. The last straw came when a younger man beat her to a producer's job despite the fact that he'd never worked in radio and she was the one being asked to train him up and lead him by the hand. The woman eventually had to leave to find more fulfilling work elsewhere in the industry. There was only one female producer at Radio 1 when Liz joined and now that Doreen Davies was gone, all the management were male.

The general attitude to women at Radio 1 perhaps explains the treatment of Janice Long. She had become pregnant and asked management for maternity leave. Beerling was concerned that after she came back Janice might be too busy looking after her new baby to carry on with her regular Monday–Thursday evening show. With this in mind, Beerling offered Janice a less demanding schedule of just the one show on Saturday instead. Not happy with the situation, Janice walked and went to the press. The headlines did not look good for Radio 1, essentially criticising the station for getting rid of a female presenter simply for being pregnant. Janice herself believed it was even worse than that, and that the reason was partly because she wasn't married to her partner. It smacked of discrimination and the Equal Opportunities Commission at the BBC contacted her with an offer to help. Unfortunately, due to Janice's contract, they were unable to do anything. Of course, today she would have had every right to pursue the matter through the courts.

★

In the spring of 1988, Beerling faced a major headache when Mike Smith announced his intention to leave the breakfast show after just two years in the job. Mike had been doing a lot of television and this was where he saw his future. Beerling made some discreet overtures to Chris Tarrant at Capital, but, when it seemed likely that the BBC would not be able to afford him, it was decided to promote Simon Mayo from weekday evenings. Simon was later to discover that the BBC's pursuit of Tarrant didn't stop until several weeks into his run as breakfast show host.

For Simon, the key to presenting the breakfast show was energy. If you happened to have a dead Tuesday, with nothing making the news, no guests coming on, no new releases, can you still make that Tuesday feel special for the listener? Much of that energy came from Simon adopting the zoo format to breakfast time, which hadn't been done before. There was another big difference, instigated by Simon himself and his producer Ric Blaxill. While other zoo formats were by and large noisy affairs and quite outrageous, a conscious decision was made to be a lot less in the listener's face. 'The tone of everything needed to be right,' says Ric. 'We were very aware that there would be a lot of people taking their kids to school, so we never wanted to be in a position where it would be an embarrassing moment for a parent because of something we said. We were always aware of the responsibility. That's why we decided never to do any crude humour, and we didn't take cheap shots at anyone. It was a different kind of zoo format. It was probably more measured, but that's what made it such a great listen.'

Simon brought in his own 'posse' that, over time, included Jackie Brambles, Caron Keating, Lynn Parsons and Philippa Forester. He always tried to make sure that the chats between everyone, the links, were really conversational, along with looking all the time for a way to make the audience a part of the show, which is a lot easier now with social media.

As a team, Simon and Ric stayed together for several years, all the time learning from each other. After every show, Ric would write down in a notebook everything they did in terms of content and then decide whether it had worked or not. A month later, he and Simon would go through all of it: 'Do you remember when we did that? Do you think we can possibly do that again at some point?' 'That was pretty forensic,' says Ric. 'But it seemed to be a good way of tracking what you were doing and what was working.'

Like Simon, Ric was new to the station, arriving from Capital where he was an assistant producer on the breakfast show with Chris Tarrant. Having applied to be a Radio 1 producer four years on the trot, without success, one morning in the Capital studio he noticed the *Guardian* open and that there was a job for a trainee producer at Radio 1. 'Chris had circled the ad and said, "You should go for that." I thought, "Well, if he thinks I'm good enough, maybe I should."'

Ric grew up a fan of Radio 1, so walking around Egton House it was very difficult not to be starstruck. 'These voices had been the soundtrack to my life and now suddenly there they are, they're your colleagues. A month in, I thought, "Come on, I've got to get a grip."' It was always great fun walking into that building every morning. The energy was always incredible. 'That was right from Clare being on reception all the way up. It was a team. Even though there was competition between shows and presenters, which is healthy, there was a real team spirit without a doubt.'

Like most new producers, Ric was seconded to several shows, just to get a feel of the place. He worked with Gary Davies, Mark Goodier, Adrian John and, fleetingly, on DLT's Saturday morning show. 'That was very surreal,' admits Ric. 'Just being in the studio when he was doing *Give Us a Break*, and all those "quack quack oops". I'd been listening to that show for years. It was mind-blowing.'

Just 25, Ric was under no illusion that that was partly the reason for his employment. Like any organisation or company that targets a younger audience, and that was its remit, there needed to be a steady flow of new blood coming in to freshen the place up a little bit. 'But there were still things that were very traditional, part of Radio 1's history and heritage,' says Ric. 'It was a brilliant hybrid at that point because you did have people like Simon Bates and DLT, and then there was Simon coming through, Nicky Campbell and Mark

Goodier, all quality broadcasters. They were obviously looking to reposition the station because we were all pretty young and all came in at roughly the same time.'

Another fresh face was Phillip Schofield. Already a familiar face on television, as host of the BBC's popular Saturday morning children's show *Going Live*, Phillip was on Radio 1 on Sunday afternoons. Schofield quickly became one of the most used Roadshow presenters, something he loved doing, remembering how as a kid in Newquay in Cornwall, he'd always be the first on the beach when the Roadshow arrived, sitting there fascinated as he watched them set up.

Phillip made the headlines in 1990 at a Roadshow when star guests Bros were pelted with eggs. When one of the eggs missed its target and hit a woman in a wheelchair in the front row, Schofield lost his temper and charged onto the stage, grabbing a microphone and yelling, 'I don't normally use language like this, but you're a bunch of wankers!' Afterwards Schofield remained unrepentant and refused to apologise. The BBC backed him up in a press statement: 'Phillip doesn't regret using the word. In the heat of the moment it was entirely justified.' The incident actually did him some good, denting his squeaky-clean image.

Jackie Brambles was just 21 when she joined Radio 1 in summer 1988. Growing up with a love and passion for music, Jackie never entertained the thought of being a DJ, largely because there were so few female voices on the radio. As it was, she fell into broadcasting by accident. Looking for a job – any job – she wrote to her local radio station in Ayrshire, Scotland, and was taken on as a general dogsbody. Then, at night, she'd practise on the desks when no one was about.

One evening when Jackie was on her own at the station, a DJ failed to show up and she was hurriedly put on the air. It was some introduction and led to her own show. Word of Jackie quickly reached the ears of Richard Park, who ran a station in Glasgow. When Park was asked to take over as programme controller at Capital, he brought Jackie to London with him. Within a year of being on Capital, she was poached by Radio 1, thanks to producer Ric Blaxill, who remembered Jackie from his time at the station and who had, during a random conversation with Johnny Beerling about them looking for younger female presenters, suggested they check her out.

Jackie was under no illusion that politically the BBC was under pressure to put some more female voices on air, and she benefited from that affirmative action. But her rise was certainly meteoric: within two years of standing in for a missing DJ, she was on the biggest music station in the country. 'Who gives a 21-year-old, a clueless 21-year-old, a microphone to the nation and says, "Go, do what you like." It was amazing.'

Jackie started on the early morning show and was also part of Simon Mayo's breakfast posse. Her exuberant personality led to a job as presenter on *Top of the Pops* and several Roadshows. Doing the Roadshow for Jackie was the closest thing she ever came to feeling like a rock star, especially being escorted through the crowds to the stage by burly security guards. She enjoyed the whole thing, from the audiences that showed up even when it was bucketing down with rain to hanging out with the crew. 'It really was like going on Cliff Richard's *Summer Holiday*,' she said. 'It was a road trip with your buddies in these massive trucks, this convoy of people. It was brilliant fun to be a part of that.' Jackie was to carve out a brilliant career at the station, becoming in many ways a role model to the new generation of female DJ stars to come, such as Zoe Ball, Jo Whiley and Sara Cox.

As new faces arrived, inevitably old faces faded away. Peter Powell left, after a long stint on the weekend breakfast show, and Beerling was facing the loss of Johnnie Walker. *The Stereo Sequence* had proved a big hit and one of the station's flagship shows, but just doing that one show per week rather than more regular work was placing a huge strain on Walker's finances. 'My wife and I divorced and I was trying to fund her house and the children and also a flat in London on a very small weekly programme fee. Then I got offered a lot of money to go to Richard Branson's Radio Radio satellite project, which offered overnight service to the whole Independent Local Radio network. I remember going to Johnny Beerling and him saying, "I know what you're going to tell me, you're going to join Radio Radio. Very sad

Johnnie, I don't want you to go. But I understand. I just hope you get paid." Which was a very perceptive comment actually, because mostly I didn't.'

Looking for someone to take over *The Stereo Sequence*, Beerling heard on the industry grapevine that Roger Scott, a fixture on Capital since it started, was becoming disillusioned with the station's music policy. By that time, Capital was a very focused, Top 40 contemporary hit radio station and for Scott it just wasn't exciting any more playing what was on a computer printout that an anonymous executive, or a piece of market research, had determined were the safest records to play. 'Not records that will make people listen,' argued Scott, 'but records that will prevent people turning off. So, you don't play anything dangerous, you just play things that won't chase listeners away so they will be there and they'll hear the ads.' Scott firmly believed that BBC radio was 'the last refuge of the free spirit'. Yes, they had playlists and, yes, there were restrictions, but for him it wasn't anywhere near the rigid controls exercised on broadcasters in the commercial sector. In this regard, Scott was proven right when Beerling gave him almost total freedom about what music he played and the artists he wanted to interview.

Three months after taking over *The Stereo Sequence*, Roger was rewarded with another show – *Scott on Sunday*. And it was around this time that Roger came up with the concept of doing a series on classic albums. It was a simple yet effective idea: Roger would interview an artist or band about their career-defining work, complemented by selected tracks. Some of the albums that featured included *Synchronicity* by The Police, *Rumours* by Fleetwood Mac, *The Joshua Tree* by U2 and *Dark Side of the Moon* by Pink Floyd. The first series made its debut in May 1989, but the second series went out posthumously after Roger tragically succumbed to cancer. He had been bravely fighting the disease for a long time and continued to broadcast way past the point most people would have given up. When he couldn't come to the studio any more, the mic went to him and he recorded the links to his show at home until the time came when even that was too much for him. Roger died in October 1989. He was 46.

Johnnie Walker was not alone in describing Roger Scott as 'the DJs' DJ'. He was immensely respected amongst his peers. Johnnie met Roger's wife Lesley years after his passing and she told him that Roger used to come home after doing *The Stereo Sequence* and say, 'I cannot understand why Johnnie Walker gave that up. It's the best radio programme I've ever done. It's absolute broadcast heaven.'

Roger's natural successor on *The Stereo Sequence* was Bob Harris, returning to the station after fourteen years. At the time, Bob was on British Forces Broadcasting Service, and had actually sent a tape to his old colleague Jeff Griffin to see if there was any chance of him finding a route back to Radio 1. 'I'm really sorry, Bob,' said Griffin, 'but the reaction was, "Oh what, Bob Harris is going to come in and say, 'Wow, man, listen to The Colours.'"' Bob then gave up on Radio 1, but Johnny Beerling happened to catch one of his shows on the Forces network, loved what he heard and brought him in as Scott's replacement. 'Coming back was an incredible feeling,' Harris wrote in his memoirs. It got even better when a few months later Bob was offered the late show, 12 till closedown at 2 a.m., Monday to Thursday. He was in his element, playing folk and blues, country and rock, along with live sessions, and very quickly he built up a strong relationship with his audience. 'It was like an intimate, exclusive club, with a membership of approximately one and a half million.'

21

Bruno Brookes had been breaking bands and records since he first started on the station, beginning in 1985 when promotions man Gary Farrow came into his office urging him to listen to a single by an unknown duo called the Pet Shop Boys. 'Never heard of them,' said Bruno. As soon as the propulsive bassline of 'West End Girls' began, Bruno knew that the song worked. 'And a couple of hours later it was on air,' says Bruno. 'None of this "We'll plan it for next week's show."' 'West End Girls' went on to top the UK chart and launched the band to international fame.

In the mid-eighties it was not unusual for Radio 1 to receive almost 200 singles a week. Bruno's producer at the time was Malcolm Brown, whom he liked enormously, but he kept a messy office with vinyl offerings strewn across the floor like dirty washing in a teenager's bedroom. Killing time one morning, Bruno noticed a particular acetate that read: 'Swing out Sister "Breakout".' 'I liked the name so much I put it on and within twenty seconds I knew it was a hit. I took it down to the studio and played it.'

But it was in late 1988 that Bruno pulled off his biggest coup when he championed 'Stakker Humanoid' by electronic group Humanoid, a single later described by the *Guardian* as 'the first truly credible UK acid house record to break into the mainstream'. When it came into Bruno's hands, the record was the only copy in the country. 'When I heard it,' he says, 'I thought, "Jesus, that's different. That is amazing."'

The following day, he played it twice on his show – still a rare thing for a DJ to do – confident that there would be a response, and there was. 'Everybody started talking about it. My phone was going mad. Sony called me up at one stage asking, "What's that track you're playing?" I got the feeling they were sending people around town trying to find this artist to sign them up. It wasn't even supposed to be released. It was a white label. The next minute it's in the charts and it did start a musical revolution in this kind of sound.'

Bruno was then on the *Drivetime* show and was followed by Liz Kershaw. It wasn't unusual for there to be a lot of banter and fun during the handovers. Looking back, he says: 'Probably somebody upstairs was thinking, "That's the best part of Bruno's show. This could really work." So, Liz and I were offered a weekend breakfast show.'

Double acts are rare in radio, maybe because two egos in the same studio aren't worth the hassle, but more likely because it's so difficult to get the chemistry right. When they do work, such as with Dave Cash and Kenny Everett on the pirates, the public warm to it. Such was the case with Liz Kershaw and Bruno Brookes. 'We approached that show not as DJs but as two people just having a bacon sarnie and a cup of coffee in a café,' says Bruno. 'The idea was: "We'll sit here, play some records and take the piss out of everything; mainly I'll take the piss out of Liz and Liz takes the piss out of me." The fact that nothing was really planned was what made it funny. We smashed Capital's numbers. At the time Capital was big in London, it was a beast, and we smashed them at the weekends.'

This playful 'love-hate' relationship won them plenty of PR in the tabloids, including a story of when Liz took umbrage over Bruno playing the latest Wet Wet Wet, grabbed the heaviest object that she could find and smashed the 7-inch live on air, along with the turntable. Hauled in to see Beerling, Liz's wages were docked every week until the damage was paid for.

The pair even went on Roadshows together. When Tom Jones turned up as a guest, Liz, recalling how much of an idol the singer was for her mum, made her way into the crowd and took up position in the front row. During the performance, Liz playfully grabbed at the star's tight trousers and wouldn't let go, leaving Tom to shake his leg as if he was trying to rid himself of a rutting dog. 'Get security, get her off,' he said off-mic through gritted teeth.

'What?' said Bruno. 'She's our presenter!'

In 1989, Beerling decided to considerably up the station's comedy output, which certainly helped people like Adrian Juste. His *Saturday Show* had evolved beyond its early stages of Tony Hancock clips to become much more topical and satirical. With a budget increase, he'd been able to build up a superb team, including two writers from the ITV comedy sketch show *Spitting Image*, and Steve Wright's former producer Malcolm Brown. Adrian was also moonlighting on the Steve Wright show as 'the pub singer', an idea that came out of his dissolute youth in Leicester. 'Every working men's club on a Saturday night, there he'd be,' remembers Adrian. 'A couple of beers and, bingo, he was Tom Jones! I was doing him one day in the corridor and Steve said "I think we could use that."'

In recent years, Adrian had also begun to highlight a lot of American stand-up comics such as Emo Philips, Jim Carrey and Steven Wright, often exposing them to a British audience for the very first time. It was his routine after the show to visit the big record stores in the West End and hunt out the best import stuff. 'They'd fly all the planes back from America to Heathrow and use records as ballast, piles of them, and Tower Records used to flog it all and I got some lovely American stuff and it went down really well.' He dug out some up-and-coming British talent, too. When Victoria Wood recorded a live album at the Edinburgh Festival, she sent Adrian a note asking if he would consider playing some of it on the show. With another comedian, Adrian remembers: 'I saw a video of a soft-spoken Liverpudlian chap and asked him if I could use some of it. It was Lily Savage. He said, "You really want to play it?" I said, "Yeah."'

Radio 1 had always had a reputation for bringing comedy onto the airwaves. In 1971, when John Peel left for his summer break, John Walters brought in Vivian Stanshall from the The Bonzo Dog Doo-Dah Band as replacement. Cue two hours of music mixed with

Stanshall madness, including spoof advertisements, bizarre characters and sketches, along with a lampoon of Dick Barton-esque radio serials that presented Stanshall as the upper-crust Colonel Knut, with his trusty sidekick Lemmy, played by Keith Moon.

It was to Moon that Walters was to return in the summer of 1973 when Peel was away again. The result, *Touch of the Moon*, basically consisted of Moon playing records and linking them with surreal whimsy and skits, all pre-recorded in the mornings when the drummer was most likely not to be incapacitated.

In the same year, Walters presented Monty Python's Eric Idle with the chance to do his own show, prophetically called Radio 5. It was produced by Dave Atkey. 'Eric did it with John Walters and they'd come in each week, read me the script and have me in stitches – every time,' remembers Dave. 'What was good was that by the time I'd heard it in the office, then we'd gone to the studio and recorded it maybe a couple of times and edited it – and I still found it very funny.' The show was such a success that Idle returned in 1974.

Then, in 1982, Lenny Henry was asked if he fancied doing a series of shows as a guest DJ, combining music with stand-up and sketches. These proved so popular they ran over the course of three years. Again, Dave Atkey came in as producer. 'That was a privilege to work with him,' Dave says. 'Lenny was a great guy.' Oddly, Lenny wasn't happy sitting behind the desk in a studio, with the engineer playing in all the records. He didn't want any of that. 'I'd like to do it as if it's a Roadshow,' he told the producer, who saw how to make it work. 'I got on to the outside broadcast guys,' Dave says. 'They weren't doing the Roadshow at the time so the whole deck was in storage and we set it up in a room at the Langham Hotel. Lenny used to do the show in there and play all the records in himself.'

This time, Beerling wanted the emphasis to be much more on contemporary or 'alternative' comedy, with its specific appeal for younger listeners. That included personalities like Victor Lewis-Smith, a noted journalist and TV/radio producer. 'He was outrageous,' says Beerling. 'Some of the edits I had to make on his show and the rows we used to have. He did one sketch where he phoned up some big hotel in New York and pretended, in a terribly camp voice, to be the aide-de-camp to the Queen Mother telling them he required a cucumber and a large pot of yoghurt in her fridge. I said, "Victor, you can't get away with that!"'

There was also The Mary Whitehouse Experience, which started that spring and launched the careers of David Baddiel, Rob Newman, Hugh Dennis and Steve Punt. The show later transferred to television and achieved even greater success.

On the day of its launch, Beerling was away on a weekend management seminar, which also happened to coincide with his birthday. During dinner, he was told that there was an urgent phone call for him: it was Mary Whitehouse. Calmly picking up the receiver, Beerling got the full force of the venerable lady's wrath. He tried to calm her down, explaining that he'd cleared the use of her name with the BBC's lawyers. She wasn't having any of it: 'I have instructed my lawyers to issue an injunction to stop the programme,' she wailed. 'It will be with you before the show goes out at nine tonight.'

'That's your prerogative,' replied Beerling. The line went dead. Processing what had just occurred, Beerling put a call through to the studio and spoke to the show's producer about recording an alternative opening, just in case. He then quietly returned to his table and carried on with his meal.

Suddenly, at 8.30 p.m., a motorcycle dispatch rider in black leathers and helmet burst into the room. 'By this time, I'm shitting myself,' recalls Beerling, thinking it was the injunction. 'I opened the envelope – it was a birthday card from the whole team. The whole thing had been a practical joke and they totally fooled me.'

Even more bravely, and as it turned out foolhardily, Beerling asked rising satirist Chris Morris, later of Brass Eye and The Day Today fame, to do a Christmas show in 1990 mixing comedy and music. Morris recalled saying to Beerling, 'You're putting me on at three on Christmas afternoon. I'm going to say things that you're not going to like.' Beerling casually laughed off the warning. 'Oh, I think you rather underestimate us.' Or maybe, as Morris was to confess, 'I just didn't recognise the sound of someone handing me a great big lump of rope.' Morris told the festive listening millions that the Pet Shop Boys, who were making a habit of performing with older divas like Dusty Springfield and Liza Minnelli, were about to record the song 'Little Children' with Moors Murderer Myra Hindley. Beerling did not invite him back.

Morris did return to Radio 1 in 1994, when Beerling was no longer controller, and managed to cause an even greater stir, most notably when he falsely announced that Conservative minister Michael Heseltine had died. The BBC suspended him for two weeks, after which Morris was allowed back on, pre-recorded and pre-checked rather than live. He struck again on his final Radio 1 broadcast on Boxing Day reporting that Jimmy Savile had dropped dead at Stoke Mandeville Hospital. Listening at home, Savile sued the BBC, claiming that the false report had ruined his Christmas.

Undoubtedly the event of 1989 was the fall of the Berlin Wall and Beerling was eager for Radio 1 to make its presence felt in amongst all the celebrations. Simon Bates was duly dispatched for a special show broadcast from the Brandenburg Gate. It almost didn't happen when the driver of the radio truck ended up parking on the wrong side of the wall! Luckily it was sorted out and the show went ahead. More hysteria followed when Bates realised that somebody was shooting at him from the crowd. 'Get off the stage,' he yelled and dived for cover. It turned out that a member of the audience was shooting pellets from an air rifle and he was quickly apprehended. Later that night, Steve Wright called Beerling up. 'I understand Bates was shot at today. I don't want to speak to him but to the man what done it and complain bitterly because he missed!'

Steve and Bates had something of a playful and mischievous relationship. Bates once hid some Arbroath Smokies in Steve Wright's console before going off on a trip and they were only found once the all-pervasive smell of fish filled the studio. Other DJs were less predisposed towards Bates. 'He was a good guy but a lot of people didn't like him,' says producer Dave Atkey. 'He had a great voice, was great at self-editing, technically really good, but he couldn't stand anybody who was inferior to him. Once he had a real slanging match with me and I thought we were never going to speak again. I got on with him for the most part, but a lot of the other DJs didn't like him particularly.'

At one Christmas lunch, which took place during the miners' strike, Andy Kershaw took umbrage over Bates' political position on the dispute and they got into a raging argument. After one remark too far, as Kershaw recalled in his autobiography, he snapped and lunged across the table, 'intending to seize him by his ample self-satisfied chops'. Andy was restrained by Peel and Walters, and then Chris Lycett frogmarched him out of the room and across the street back to Egton House.

It also got physical once between Bates and Tony Blackburn, as David Hamilton remembers: 'We did a twenty-fifth anniversary *Top of the Pops* and there was a spat between Bates and Tony before we went on. I almost had to pull them apart. The next minute when the cameras rolled it was: "Hi and welcome to this special edition of…"'

John Peel's animosity for Bates equalled that of his wrath for Blackburn, with both epitomising everything he hated about the cheery end-of-the-pier jollity of Radio 1's daytime output. When Bates appeared as the villain in a pantomime in High Wycombe, Peel booked out the entire front row with family and friends to boo him. 'It was a pathological hatred,' reveals Robbie Vincent. 'I never understood how somebody like Peel could dislike somebody so much. He disliked this guy so much that he planned to beat him up in the car park at Broadcasting House. I thought, "John Peel couldn't beat up a kipper." But he disliked this guy so much.' Another time Peel was so angry with Bates that he went into the car park and broke the windscreen wipers off his car – on a day when it was pouring with rain.

Despite the feelings that Bates could incite in his colleagues, and the pranks that he'd pull, there was little doubting his ability as a broadcaster. Dave Atkey recalls being on an outside broadcast with him and receiving a traffic bulletin. Bates didn't have time to look at it. 'Just read it to me,' he told Atkey, so Atkey read it to him down the talkback. 'He was saying it verbatim on the air two seconds after me – unbelievable,' says Dave. 'I've never seen anybody do that.'

Bates never fell into the muso category. His shows had always been a mix of news, gossip and music, with Bates more interested in the news and gossip than the music he was playing. 'After a record he would never say, "Oh, that's nice,"' says one of his producers, Martin Cox. 'Only occasionally would he say, "Have we got the new one from…?" He was always keener to give the latest news scandal. It was more of a *Daily Mirror* approach to radio than a *Sunday Telegraph* approach to radio. But he was a great communicator.'

Bates wasn't a particularly social animal, either, when it came to his colleagues. The show would end and he'd get in his car and go home. 'Nor did he come up to the office and sit around and joke with people,' says Martin. 'He would keep himself to himself.'

Saying that, Bates was always up for his fair share of challenges. A prime example was the year Radio 1 paid tribute to the fiftieth anniversary of the Battle of Britain. One bright spark thought that it would be a grand idea for Bates to fly in an old Lancaster bomber and then to be a passenger in a modern Tornado jet. The Lancaster was fine, but the Tornado took off, it seemed to Bates, almost vertically. He was soon 35,000 ft in the air, 'at which point,' he recalled, 'I threw up over millions of pounds' worth of equipment.'

By far the biggest and most rewarding challenge was hatched by Bates and his producer Jonathan Ruffle over a few pints in the pub. The idea was for Bates to travel round the world, à la Phileas Fogg, by foot and by ship, no plane journeys, and to broadcast live from each far-flung location. Some cynically believed the real inspiration for doing it was partly to avoid that summer's Roadshows, which Bates never really enjoyed because he felt he never mastered it. Back at Broadcasting House, enquiries were made with the Outside Broadcast people who said that the whole thing was impractical and couldn't be done. Undeterred, Bates did a bit of digging and came across Inmarsat, a satellite telecommunications company that would make it possible to transmit the show pretty much from anywhere on the planet. The only problem was that Bates and Ruffle had to lug around with them two suitcases of equipment that weighed 40 kilograms each.

The plan was to go around the world in record time, the target being sixty-seven days. Every Monday to Friday, Simon and Jonathan had to erect the equipment, including a dish aimed at a satellite orbiting 22,000 miles in space, in order to broadcast live to the UK at 10.30 in the morning. 'My key memory of that trip is just being terrified the whole time,' admits Jonathan Ruffle. The potential for failure was literally on a global scale, not just the technical issues but how were they going to fill airtime when, for example, they'd been on the same ship for five days! 'That was the fear,' says Jonathan. 'How are we going to fill that bloody half hour a day. This is a complete nightmare. We looked forward to the weekends on that trip like you wouldn't believe because that was two days where we didn't have to be getting the thing out and broadcast.'

With the potential for technical glitches and things going wrong, the crew did have a 'We can't get hold of Simon and Jonathan' card up their sleeve, but there's only so many times you can pull that one out. There was also another Radio 1 DJ ready to fly out at a moment's notice if Bates fell ill. Fortunately, that wasn't required. Besides being an interesting travelling companion, Bates, with his journalistic background, was perfect for this kind of programme. Whenever Jonathan was struggling with the technology, Bates was the one with the cool head, advising, 'I've got a short-term, mid-term and long-term plan, so you concentrate on what you're doing. Don't worry, I know exactly what to do if you can't make it work.' In the tightest spots, it was incredibly reassuring.

In spite of the ulcer-inducing logistical problems, and the danger of passing through countries like Nicaragua, hoping not to bump into the Sandinistas, there were some inspiring highlights. In Bangalore in India, Simon and Jonathan visited a blind school for children run by Oxfam. Here the children could sort silkworms by touch, they could plough a paddy field with water buffalo, recognising which buffalo was theirs by feeling the animal's face, and they could climb trees and knock down coconuts. Simon and Jonathan also watched them playing a game of blind cricket, with a bell in the ball. 'I've been to plenty of refugee camps in all sorts of places in the world,' says Jonathan, 'but that was one of the most humbling things that ever happened to me. It was an incredible experience. That was "round the world" for me.'

Equally inspiring was approaching the southern Indian city of Chennai (then called Madras) at dawn by commercial ship, with India this smudgy line on the horizon. Situated down in the bowels of the ship, well away from the engines, it was utterly silent. 'I don't think we said this to each other,' recalls Jonathan. 'We just intuitively knew that this experience was utterly extraordinary. We'd been gifted it, and we would never experience that again. That was a transcendental moment.'

In the end, they didn't break the record, managing to navigate the globe in seventy-eight days. This was hardly a surprise as at some points progress was inevitably slowed down by unforeseen circumstances, such as having to wait several days in Singapore for transport out. Far from being meticulously thought out, nothing was booked in advance. All they had was a representative from Cunard, lining up ships as they went along and advising things like, 'If you arrive in Kuala Lumpur on this day, we should be able to get you out on a ship to Tokyo. However, if you arrive at Kuala Lumpur on that date, well, you might have to wait a day or so.'

'It got to the point where you're thinking, "This thing is going to go wrong,"' says Jonathan. '"The days are going to expire and we're going to be in Malaysia making up shit programmes because we literally can't get out of this country on a ship."'

Still, it was an impressive feat, covering 25,000 miles through twenty-seven countries and raising £300,000 for Oxfam. When the pair arrived back in London, 'Welcome Home' banners were erected outside Broadcasting House and a large group of fans was there to greet them. Beerling was to call the endeavour 'one of the outstanding events staged during my time at Radio 1'. The satellite equipment they had used was later displayed at the Science Museum in London.

22

R adio 1 faced the 1990s in a buoyant, bullish mood with Johnny Beerling determined to make sure that it continued to be the most listened-to radio network across the country. As always, that meant promoting new talent and in 1990 Beerling brought Jonathan Ross over from television to host his own Friday night show live from Ronnie Scott's jazz club in Soho. Mixing music with comedy and audience participation, it enjoyed a thirteen-week run and Beerling was sorry that Ross couldn't be persuaded to do a second series.

There was also a determination to continue Radio 1's legacy of carrying the best live music, both in-house sessions and concerts. The station had a bumper year in 1990 with live concerts that included Eric Clapton, Phil Collins, David Bowie, Fleetwood Mac, Tina Turner and, most infamously, Madonna. As part of her Blond Ambition world tour, Madonna performed three shows at Wembley Stadium. The second night was broadcast live on Radio 1. Jeff Griffin was producing and warned his bosses that it was probably not the wisest thing to do. 'I'd been to see her in Italy and she'd been swearing in English and Italian,' he says. 'I told Johnny Beerling and the head of Radio 1, Roger Lewis, that we should pre-record it, but Roger in particular said, "No, no, it'll be great to have her live." I said, "There's nothing we can do if she starts swearing."'

Madonna was warned beforehand not to use any obscene or inappropriate language and had agreed. The result was predictable, of course, as Madonna used no fewer than twenty-one obscenities in less than three minutes, including variations of 'Fuck' nineteen times. This was an all-time record, although Beerling can't recall there being many complaints. The BBC still had to issue an apology and Madonna was banned from performing live on the station again. This ban was eventually lifted.

One definite highlight of 1990 was the Nelson Mandela: An International Tribute for a Free South Africa concert. There had been a previous Mandela concert, held in June 1988 at Wembley and broadcast live on Radio 1, that celebrated Mandela's seventieth birthday. It was a concert seen by both the African National Congress (ANC) and the anti-apartheid movement as having placed increased global pressure upon the South African regime to release Mandela from incarceration. Less than two years later, in February 1990, Mandela was released from prison. Two months later he was at Wembley in person to watch the festivities surrounding the new concert held in his name.

Behind the scenes, producer Ric Blaxill recalls a hectic schedule getting everything organised. Since Live Aid, these 'event' concerts, while not the norm, had enabled people to gain more experience and the technical infrastructure was a lot stronger. 'I remember the energy and adrenaline that day was absolutely incredible,' says Ric. He has never forgotten being in a room for a security briefing when Nelson Mandela walked in and gave a small speech. 'It was very emotional listening to this incredible man. And his generosity of spirit. I can remember thinking, "How can this guy be so kind and compassionate after what he's been through?" It was a pretty amazing and very special day.'

One of the most memorable live concerts Radio 1 ever broadcast took place under their own roof, at the BBC radio theatre. It was September 1993. Simon Bates' producer Fergus Dudley took a call from the management of Prince, saying he wanted to come in and do a short live set in front of a small invited audience. A suitable day was arranged and it was agreed that Prince and his band would arrive at nine in the morning. Fantastic, brilliant. It was only after the call ended that Fergus realised he'd forgotten to ask for a contract or some form of written commitment that Prince would in fact show up. In spite of that, preparations went ahead, even though Bates' office never received another phone call from Prince's people. The day arrived and Bates and Fergus sat on the fourth floor of Broadcasting House looking out of the window, down Regent Street. 'If he doesn't bother to get out of bed this morning, we're stuffed,' said Fergus. Just then, two huge articulated trucks came into view and the two men breathed a gigantic sigh of relief. In front of a largely invited audience, Prince and the New Power Generation raced through a blistering six-song setlist that included '1999' and 'Peach'.

Radio 1 was also to begin its long association with Glastonbury. Previously the station had sent a van down to record a few bits and pieces that were sometimes broadcast months later. The festival's organiser Michael Eavis thought it was all well and good for Radio 1 to put out the odd highlight after the event, but what he really needed was pre-publicity and exposure. Glastonbury didn't necessarily sell out in those days, certainly not quickly. To this end, Eavis spoke with Martin Elbourne, a manager and agent who booked some of the acts for the festival, to see if he knew anyone at the BBC. Elbourne did, he knew Jeff Griffin, and got in touch to see if Radio 1 wanted to become involved in a greater capacity.

Keen on the idea, Jeff met Eavis over a few pints at his local pub. First, Jeff required a few certainties. 'If we're going to do it, I've got to know that we're going to get the rights to record the bands. If the bands are going to say no, we don't want it going out on Radio 1. There's no point in us coming down.' Eavis said this shouldn't be a problem. He was less enamoured by the idea of the Radio 1 publicity department insisting that all manner of Radio 1 banners be placed near the stage and around the festival site. Anyway, a deal was sorted.

Jeff let BBC Television know what he was going to be doing, in case they wanted to get involved themselves, but they weren't interested. 'Instead Channel 4 came to me and asked, if they brought their van down, could they do a deal and buy the sound off us. We did this a few times, supplying the sound to Channel 4. But then a more enlightened person was suddenly in charge of BBC 2 and said, "What the hell! Why is this going to Channel 4 when BBC Radio's down there?" So, they then came on board and it's been on BBC Television ever since. And it just got bigger and bigger every year.'

In 1989, Radio 1 staged a week highlighting green and environmental issues, and in the nineties, continuing to support a programme of social-action broadcasting was as important as ever to the station. A recent action special for jobs had taken more than 10,000 calls in a week, demonstrating to Beerling the need for a permanent, free Radio 1 telephone helpline. Prior to 1990, each campaign was run with the help of various agencies for a specified amount of time. After a lot of hard work and lobbying, the BBC found the funds to set up a permanent service that allowed listeners to find information and support for issues covered in any recent programmes. As time went on, this service was extended beyond Radio 1 to the whole of the BBC and became known as BBC Action Line. In 2019, it supported more than a million people.

And finally, one of Beerling's biggest bugbears remained unresolved: that despite its national prominence, Radio 1 wasn't providing a 24-hour service. The station was still shutting down at 2 a.m. after the Bob Harris show. Bizarrely, it was the advent of the first Gulf War in 1990 that won the argument for Beerling.

In August 1990, Bob Harris was about to go on air at midnight when a newsflash came through that hostilities had begun. Within minutes, Beerling arrived in the studio and took the decision to keep the network on air through the night to inform listeners of the latest developments. 'The long-term impact of this programme was immense,' Bob wrote in his memoirs. 'The circumstance of our all-night broadcast was the lever Johnny had been looking for to force through his desire to make Radio 1 a 24-hour station at last.'

The year 1990 also saw a new head of daytime in Paul Robinson. Paul had started his career in hospital radio, before becoming a presenter on Radio Tees and Mercia Sound and later switching over to management as programme director at Chiltern Radio, an independent radio station operating from Luton and Dunstable. It was his success at Chiltern, turning an underperforming station round in three years, that brought him to the attention of Radio 1 and Beerling decided to approach him. 'We met in a pub on the Isle of Dogs,' Paul recalls. 'That was my Radio 1 interview.'

Coming from local radio, it was a huge leap for Paul to go to a national station, but after ten years in the business, three in management, he was confident that he had enough ability and experience to do the job. 'Johnny saw something in me and gave me that chance. I will always be grateful to him for that,' he says. Still, it was a bit of a culture shock. This was the station of the stars – Simon Bates, Steve Wright, Dave Lee Travis. 'Suddenly,' Paul says, 'I was their boss. It was extraordinary.' In his thirties, Paul was also dealing with producers, some of whom were in their fifties and had been there for twenty years. 'I remember one of them saying to me, "You were in short trousers when I was doing this job." And I was his boss.'

As head of daytime, Paul was chairman of the weekly playlist meeting. These had previously taken place in Doreen's office, but now that she'd left, they were held in a conference room in Broadcasting House where the producers and DJs sat for the bulk of the morning. The aim was always to reach a consensus on what records were chosen. 'If we couldn't get a consensus then I made the final decision,' says Paul. 'It was an amazingly powerful position.' After the meeting, Paul's assistant would type up the new playlist and take it down to the lobby of Egton House where about forty pluggers waited with their mobile phones ready to call the office to report whether their record was on the list or not. 'Then in the afternoon I knew I would get the phone call from the managing directors of the record labels saying, "Why is my record not on the playlist?"'

The responsibility was very much to give breaks to new artists, particularly British talent, and to have a diversity of music. Also important was to make sure the playlist wasn't dominated by the big record companies, since hospitality and other incentives remained an issue. 'There was something called the "Tuesday club",' reveals Paul.

'On Tuesday afternoons, there was no producer in the building because they were all out having lunch with record executives, normally a very liquid lunch.' Paul started to visit the record companies, too, with the intention of making sure that no producer was captured by a particular label and that they were pitching records because they believed in them, not because they'd been told to. 'I always wanted to say that every record on the playlist was decided purely on editorial merit.'

However, the playlist records appeared at the discretion of the producers, with the result that there was sometimes no continuity between one show and the next. The problem was perfectly illustrated one afternoon during the handover between Gary Davies and Steve Wright. 'Gary and Steve didn't particularly get on,' says Paul, 'and as they didn't listen to each other, Gary played a record at the end of his show and then Steve played the identical record at the start of his show. That convinced me that this was not working terribly well and I made sure the playlist records were properly rotated and spread around the day.'

Paul had been appointed because Beerling wanted to bring someone in with commercial radio experience and introduce some of that practice and nous into Radio 1. One innovation Paul came up with was around travel news, especially during the breakfast show. At Chiltern, the travel news was much more localised, and what had always annoyed people about Radio 1 was how the travel seemed to be so London-centric, that listeners in, say, Newcastle heard constantly about the M25 and Tube delays. Paul decided to split the travel bulletin, with one for the London region and then another for the rest of the country, both going out at the same time. This required Simon Mayo to record one of the bulletins while he was on air during the preceding record, and then do the second one live, careful to match the timing of both to the absolute second. And he had to do this twice an hour. 'But it sounded great,' says Paul, 'because it meant, in London, Radio 1 sounded more London, which helped us compete with Capital, and outside London, suddenly that negative had been taken away.'

★

Simon Mayo was now firmly established on the breakfast show. As far as music policy was concerned, it was a completely straight bat because one had to appeal to so many people. 'But when the moment was right,' recalls producer Ric Blaxill, 'we did try something left-field.' Just like Noel Edmonds seemed to have an uncanny knack for turning novelty songs into major hits, Simon, too, had a run of popularising quirky songs. 'These were songs we just went for and thought, "Let's see what happens with this,"' says Ric. 'They just gave a bit of personality to the show through the music.'

'Kinky Boots' for example was originally recorded in 1964 by Patrick Macnee and Honor Blackman, stars of the television series *The Avengers*. When Simon began to feature it on his show, the Deram label reissued the song and it was a Top 5 hit. The same pattern was followed with Scottish comedian Andy Stewart's 1960 comedy song 'Donald Where's Your Troosers?'. Simon played it and was inundated by requests to play it again. When the song was reissued in time for Christmas, he continued to give it airplay and the song reached number four in the UK Singles Chart, much to the surprise of Andy Stewart himself.

Most notably, though, Simon was responsible for resurrecting the Monty Python song 'Always Look on the Bright Side of Life', taken from their comedy classic film *Life of Brian*, released in 1979. Featuring numerous times on the breakfast show, Virgin took the decision to reissue the track as a single in September 1991, it became a Top Ten hit and has stayed part of the British zeitgeist ever since.

Then there was the time Simon made 'Bring Your Daughter... to the Slaughter' by Iron Maiden his record of the week. 'It was just brilliant because it was such a polarising song,' says Ric. 'Clearly not what people expected from the breakfast show. So, every now and again, we dropped something in like that.'

Simon's breakfast show also included the Confessions series, one of radio's most enduring and popular features. It started innocently enough, when Simon ran a record amnesty on the show, inviting listeners to apologise for records they'd borrowed from friends over the years and had never returned. From that, Simon asked people to come on and apologise for other misdeeds, too – something bad that they'd done and wanted to get off their chests. The whole thing just took off. It wasn't unusual for the office to receive a sack full of mail every week.

Nobody bothered to check these 'confessions' for authenticity; Simon just picked the best and read them out. Typical examples included the man on a train with no working toilet who out of desperation pissed out of a window just as they were passing a station and sprayed those waiting on the platform. Or the man who found negatives of his brother's wife naked and sent them in to the 'Readers' Wives' section of an adult magazine.

Of course, Simon was careful not to read out any of his listeners' 'sins' that related to crime or anything serious, although many did cause a stir, especially those tales relating to animals. The more notorious included a goat that ended up at the bottom of a well and a sister's hamster that was borrowed from its cage, placed in the cockpit of a remote-controlled aircraft and flown around before disappearing to its doom behind some trees. These would certainly not be allowed on air today.

The Confessions feature continued for several years and proved so popular that there was a tie-in book and even a television series. Simon was to relaunch the series in 2010 on his Radio 2 show.

Meanwhile, rising star Mark Goodier had moved from weekends to the prestigious early evening slot, Monday to Thursday. It was here that Mark was to come into his own as a Radio 1 DJ, although at the beginning he had no clear idea what to do. His brief was to create an evening magazine programme for young people. Instead, along with his producer Jeff Smith, Mark devised a show that focused on new talent. Yes, they would still play mainstream music, such as the latest Madonna record, but the emphasis was more towards material that they thought was groundbreaking or might prove popular if it got airplay. Out of that ethos emerged the *Evening Session*. Evenings had always been an important time in the schedule, when listeners felt that they could rely on DJs who were passionate and connected to the music and open to playing more alternative sounds. The *Evening Session* was built on that tradition and ran between 1990 and 1993, until it was revamped and presented by Steve Lamacq and Jo Whiley. It was Mark Goodier, however, who first built the show into a safe haven for the emerging indie and grunge scene of the early nineties. Goodier championed the likes of Radiohead, Blur and Teenage Fanclub, and was the first DJ to play Happy Mondays on the radio. A lot of bands came in to play live for Mark at the Maida Vale Studios, most notably Nirvana. Their 1992 odds-and-sods release *Incesticide* featured several songs recorded for Goodier's *Evening Session*.

Mark also took over from Bruno Brookes to present the Top 40 on Sunday. Like Bruno, Mark had grown up listening to the show and was initially terrified at the prospect of hosting something that was now a broadcasting institution. He hosted it for two years, then returned in 1995 through to 2002, becoming the longest-reigning presenter of the official chart show.

There were arrivals and departures in 1991, too. Johnnie Walker was back, yet again, on weekends, while Mike Read had decided to leave. 'I was offered the breakfast show on Capital,' he says, 'as it was thought that they would get the first national commercial licence.' As it turned out, that never happened and Mike was sort of stuck there. He was later heard on Capital Gold and Classic FM. He looks back on his time at Radio 1 fondly, and with a sense of justified pride. 'I remember being told that you weren't only a DJ, but an ambassador for the BBC, and it's something I've always remembered.'

Jeff Young was also leaving. He had recently moved to a senior position at A&M Records but was finding it increasingly difficult to handle both jobs, to the point where it was affecting him physically. 'I was just trying to do too much,' he says. 'I was basically losing it.' Jeff decided to continue only with the A&M job and resigned from Radio 1. Beerling took it well, even asking if Jeff could name someone who might be a good replacement. 'Just go and get Pete Tong,' said Jeff. Tong was currently hosting a dance show on Capital. Beerling brought

Tong over to Radio 1 on Friday nights where he created *The Essential Selection*, broadcasting to the nation's club-going youth.

A new arrival was a young DJ then at Capital radio called Paul McKenna. Paul began his broadcasting career DJing on Saturdays in the Oxford Street branch of Topshop. There also an early connection with Radio 1 when his dad managed to get him the chance to sit in on Tommy Vance's show. 'Tommy was a lovely guy,' remembers Paul. 'At the time I was at college doing art and I said to Tommy, "I've made a T-shirt for you with the *Friday Rock Show* on it." He wore it and people started asking where he got it, so he came back to ask if I could make some more.'

Vance was one of numerous DJs, including Adrian Love and Kenny Everett, whom Paul managed to contact, who shared their expertise and offered encouragement. 'By basically being this anorak fan,' he says, 'I got to watch all these really great DJs broadcast.' But it was Vance's producer Tony Wilson who suggested that if Paul made a demo tape, he'd make sure Radio 1's then controller Derek Chinnery heard it. 'I got this phone call,' recalls Paul, 'saying Derek would like you to come up and see him, which was exciting but also a bit daunting. Derek was a headmaster figure, but very nice to meet. He said that my tape was very promising but I was a bit younger than he'd expected. "I hope you didn't think I had a contract waiting for you to sign," he said. "No, no, no," I said, but secretly, "Yes, yes, yes." He said, "What you need to do is go off and get some experience."'

That's exactly what Paul did, including a stint at the recently relaunched Radio Caroline, broadcasting from a new ship that was a former Icelandic factory fishing trawler. Then, still just 20, Paul got an offer to join Chiltern Radio (before his future boss Paul Robinson joined). His first job there was to cover for the breakfast jock who was away on holiday. 'I really enjoyed that because it's the most important show on a radio station,' says Paul. 'Also, when you play that record at eight o'clock in the morning, that's the best it's going to sound all day. By the time the listener has heard it for the eighth time in the afternoon, it's not quite the same.' There was something else, too.

Traditionally the breakfast jock is a personality DJ, who can do jokes, competitions and a host of other things rather than just play music. 'And even though I liked music,' says Paul, 'I saw myself as a personality DJ.'

By this time, a second career path had begun to open up for Paul thanks to his growing interest in hypnotism. It began innocently enough, hypnotising friends for fun at parties or trying to help them quit smoking or lose weight, and soon led to putting on his own shows above a London pub. Digging deeper into the craft, Paul followed the same pattern he'd done with DJs: seek out the best in the field, watch them, talk to them and learn from them.

Now at Capital, given the old Saturday afternoon slot that Kenny Everett used to do – 'so no pressure' – Paul was thinking of striking out big and hiring a London theatre for one of his hypnotism shows. He went to see Capital's boss Richard Park to ask if he had any objection to his using the station to promote his show, if he paid for the airtime. Park sat back in his chair, mulling the proposition over. Finally, he said: 'I'll back you.' For Paul it was a destiny moment. 'I believe a lot of success in life comes down to people backing you.'

Paul took a huge gamble and borrowed a hefty sum of money to rent the Duke of York's Theatre on St Martin's Lane on Sunday nights. The first run of shows barely broke even, but audiences began to pick up until it was selling out. Things were starting to move fast. Paul Smith, a television producer, was keen for Paul to front his own hypnotism show on prime-time TV, while his agent had been approached with an offer to join Radio 1. He'd finally made it, almost ten years after that first meeting with Derek Chinnery.

Working on the early shift at weekends, Paul quickly observed how things ran at Radio 1 and the BBC, and just how different it was from Capital. At Capital, particularly under the stewardship of Richard Park, the format was the star, while Radio 1 was a station of stars: the DJs and the music were just as important as each other and people tuned in sometimes just to listen to their favourite DJ. Coming in, Paul was still very much in Capital autopilot, doing rather tight links in-between all the records because that's what he was used to. One day a producer took him to one side. 'It's all very well,' he said, 'but could you speak a bit more, Paul. We want a bit more of *you*.'

Unlike the very narrow Top 40 format that Capital was doing, Radio 1 had a very wide music policy, particularly when it came to new music. While Paul had a lot of free rein in what he played, there was an obligation to give new bands a try. He even complained, 'Do I have to play this? Can't we just stick with the big hits?' His producer replied, 'No, you've got to play some of this stuff. It's the way the culture works here.' A lot of things one did in the commercial world that seemed like common sense just didn't apply at the BBC because of its public service remit, and there were a lot of boxes that needed to be ticked. For Paul it was something of a culture shock, and, as others had observed, a bit like being in the civil service. For example, every studio had a control room and the engineer would set things up on his side and the DJ would self-op in his studio. One day Paul went round to alter something on the engineer's desk. 'Oi,' said the engineer. 'That's your side of the glass and this is mine.' Paul apologised. 'Just remember that, OK,' finished the engineer. 'That was the culture,' says Paul. 'We all had our particular roles and had to stick to it. It didn't work like that at Capital. We just got on and did it. But that was the protocol at the BBC.'

There's another incident that symbolises the BBC for Paul. He hadn't been at the station for long when it was announced that Radio 1 was to be renamed 1FM in readiness for the loss of the medium wave signal in 1993. Paul Robinson asked Paul to come up with some promotional trails. As he worked on them, Paul wanted a particular sound clip. Robinson told him it was probably held in the archive and the chap who ran it would know where it was.

I went round a maze of corridors and into this guy's office. It was like the TV show *Hoarders* where people have got about 12 square inches in their house to sit down and nothing else because the entire room is filled with stuff. There were boxes of tape and cartridges from the floor to the ceiling, even the guy's desk had no more room left on it. 'I'm looking for this,' I said. He went, 'Mmm,' thought about it for a few minutes, then off he went and started rummaging around and pulled one of the tapes out. 'That's what you're looking for.' It was almost surreal.

At the same time that Paul was doing his 4 a.m. to 7 a.m. slot on Saturday and Sunday, as well as occasionally standing in for Gary Davies and Steve Wright, he was still doing the hypnotism shows. One night the venue might be in Hull or in Brighton or perhaps London's West End. It was gruelling, and he was finding that he was suffering physically with bouts of tiredness and sickness. 'I was beginning to feel conflicted,' he says. 'I wasn't giving 100 per cent to either job. I needed to make a choice. But it was really difficult because I'd wanted to be a DJ since I was a teenager and there I was at the biggest radio station you could possibly be on.'

Elsewhere, Paul's decision was almost being made for him when Paul Smith came back into his life. He'd managed to get ITV to back a pilot show and, when that went down well, executives began talking about the possibility of a series. In his heart, Paul knew that this was the path he wanted to follow. 'I was getting more excited about doing my hypnotism shows than I was about playing the new song from Talking Heads. That's when I knew it had to change.'

It was a gamble because by then Paul was making good progress at Radio 1. Each DJ was given the ratings for his show, but there was also something called the Audience Appreciation Index, which was a score out of a hundred and was used as an indicator of the public's appreciation for a television or radio programme. This was the culture of the BBC: 'Yes, we're interested in how many people are listening, but equally important is whether they like or approve you.' Paul remembers that his rating was in the low seventies, pretty good, while someone like Simon Mayo was around seventy-six, which was very good. DLT, on the other hand, was off the scale at eighty-two.

Anyway, Paul asked if he could see Beerling. Paul had always found Beerling to be the perfect gentleman, which didn't make it any easier when he announced that he was resigning. 'I appreciate all you've done for me,' began Paul. 'But I have to leave. I'm going to follow my career as a hypnotist.'

'Oh, come on,' said Beerling. 'They all try this one. You'll get a better show later, don't worry. I've got plans for you.'

'It's not a play, I'm genuine about this. And this is one of the hardest things I've ever had to do.'

Paul could tell that Beerling wasn't happy about it, but he accepted the decision and the two men shook hands. As Paul closed the door behind him, he felt this twisting sensation in his guts. 'What the hell have I done?' he thought to himself. 'Nobody resigns from Radio 1!'

After his final show went out, Paul received a letter from Beerling: 'Paul, I heard your last show. I thought it was really good and, if things don't work out, the door is always open.'

Paul never forgot that kind gesture. It was typical Beerling.

DJs were always at the mercy of the vagaries of executive decisions. The show they were given was pretty much out of their control; it was whatever the management thought they were suitable for. Some DJs didn't take holidays, or very few, so worried were they about being replaced when they got back. But even Bruno Brookes was left scratching his head when he was asked to host the early weekday breakfast show, starting at 4 a.m. 'The obvious question was: "Who the hell is listening at that time?" I said to myself, "Christ, I can't believe I'm doing this."'

This meant the end for Bruno's show with Liz Kershaw. And while Bruno faced what was commonly known as the graveyard shift, it was worse for Liz as she was let go from the station. Both even had to work three months' notice, with their listeners fully aware of the situation. 'It was like being on radio's very own death row,' Liz complained in her autobiography.

Bruno had been moved because Capital's breakfast show was now on at an earlier slot and it was hoped that he would pump up the listenership in time for the start of Radio 1's breakfast show. He went about this by involving in the show the kind of people who were around at that time of the morning, such as van drivers and truckers. 'I thought, "Here's the chance for me to be the really cheeky Bruno, and a little bit risky." People would phone the show, real characters, from factory workers on a fag break to truckers. Just everyday people on a night shift. It was great radio with real audience interaction.'

About a year into the show, Bruno received a letter from Beerling. It was highly irregular to receive any communication from management in the post and Bruno feared the worst. In fact, it was a note of congratulations: his audience figures at 6 a.m. were bigger than the breakfast show at 6.30 a.m. 'What did I read into this?' he says. 'That maybe the breakfast show was right for me.' Bruno had always coveted the breakfast show. He did it a few times, covering for other DJs, but was never given the chance to really prove himself. 'I never owned it.'

Taking over the weekend breakfast slot from Bruno and Liz was Gary Davies. Gary had been on lunchtimes since 1984 and was still enjoying it, but accepted the view of management that things needed freshening up. 'Eight years is a long time, but it just flew by. It was the most fun you could have. It was an amazing job.'

Along with the weekend breakfast shows, Gary was given Sunday night between 10 and 12. 'That was my dream show. I produced it myself and played anything I wanted. It was like going back to when I first started on Radio 1 doing Saturday night, being able to just play quality music, a mixture of old and new and album tracks. All different kinds of music.'

There was the odd crisis, such as the occasion Gary played a song by Jamaican reggae duo Chaka Demus and Pliers called 'Tease Me' and received a heated phone call from executive Paul Robinson. 'What is this shit you're playing?'

'This is Chaka Demus and Pliers,' said Gary. 'It's great, isn't it?'

'It's terrible,' reiterated Paul. 'I don't want you to play that any more.'

Gary was having none of it. 'I'm sorry, it's my record of the week. I'll play whatever I want to play.'

The argument continued at that week's playlist meeting when Paul confronted Gary again with his views. 'That song is awful. People are going to switch off by the thousands. It's never going to be a hit.' Gary stood his ground. Two weeks later it reached number three in the UK charts.

★

Taking over from Gary on lunchtime was Jackie Brambles, who for the last couple of years had been on the drivetime show. Her two-year stint was to be her happiest on the network and she was most proud of bringing live sessions to lunchtimes, helped in part by her producer Jonathan Ruffle, who shared Jackie's love for guitar-led rock and the emerging grunge scene. 'There hadn't been the music to play before, indie or otherwise,' says Ruffle, 'because of the slurry pit that was late eighties pop. "China in Your Hand" by T'Pau does not a radio programme make. So, musically the world was dull. Then, in the opening chords of "Smells Like Teen Spirit", Nirvana changed all of that. At last we had some music we could talk about and love on the radio.'

The sessions kicked off with a lot of American bands, one of the earliest featuring Faith No More, but pretty soon Britpop began to bubble. 'We were riding a wave,' says Ruffle. 'If you've got punchier music, the show's better. It's as simple as that.' Some sessions took place in the studio itself, which, being so cramped, presented its own problems. When James went in to play live, only two out of the seven members could fit in, so they decided to do an acoustic set.

Of course, sessions were a feature of Radio 1 right from the start, but what made these special was Ruffle's desire to bring in the more established bands and artists.

> We took the idea of the session and made it big bands playing their biggest hits. That was very different from saying, 'Here's Norman Sprog, the new Ed Sheeran, and he's going to play you three songs none of us have ever heard before.' The policy was to say to the artist concerned, 'By all means play your latest single, but your three other tracks have got to be hits.' In Bryan Adams' case, it would have been, 'We know you hate "(Everything I Do) I Do It for You", but you are playing that record. Your ticket to appearing on this lunchtime show is that song.' In that way, we got some interesting alternative live takes of really, really big songs by big artists.

By and large, the sessions took place at the Maida Vale studios, as Jonathan remembers.

> You talked to the band down the line – that rather nice atmosphere where you go, 'Hello, Paul Weller. You're two miles away from us at the

288

moment. You're in the studios at Maida Vale, aren't you, and you've got the Paul Weller fan club there, haven't you. Give us a cheer, Paul Weller's fan club.' We'd invite Paul Weller's fan club to the studio, who'd be having the day of their freakin' lives, and they'd all cheer like bonkers. He'd play some new stuff and then a few classic oldies, and it would sound brilliant. It was taking the session idea and putting it into a totally different context.

23

Andy Peebles had been out all night. Still wearing his dinner jacket and an overcoat when he arrived at Egton House, he was informed that Johnny Beerling wanted to see him. Andy knew what was coming.

> I walked in and I remember saying to Johnny, with a grin on my face, 'OK, boss, let me make this easy for you. When am I leaving?' And Johnny stood up, shook my hand and said, 'Thanks for being so decent about it. It's with some regret that I have to tell you that we're not in a position to renew your contract.' I knew that I was nearing the end of my time at Radio 1. I could see what was going on. And thank God I got out when I did and that I didn't have to live through the nightmare of Matthew Bannister and Trevor Dann.

Thirteen years on the station was pretty good going by Radio 1 standards and Andy is proud of what he achieved. 'The greatest joy of my life is having met and interviewed some of my great heroes, having compered concerts by people like Marvin Gaye and Smokey Robinson, and sitting for three hours with Curtis Mayfield. These are utterly treasured memories.'

Much had changed at Radio I for Andy in those thirteen years. It had become much more aware of itself and more politically correct. 'There were things that had gone on in the old days that weren't going to be countenanced any more. Ranking Miss P arrived and Janice

Long. Suddenly we had more women on the station. So, it did change. Although some of what it did and the way it did it was still very old-fashioned. It was still very old-style BBC.'

That was about to change, too, in the most dramatic of circumstances.

That summer of 1992, Radio 1 celebrated its twenty-fifth anniversary. The highlight of the festivities was a huge Roadshow at Birmingham's Sutton Park, dubbed Party in the Park. With live acts including Del Amitri, Aswad, The Farm and headliners Status Quo, it's little wonder the event attracted a record-breaking crowd for a Roadshow of 125,000 fans. It was proof, if any were needed, that Radio 1's status as the most listened-to and popular station in the country was unrivalled.

All that didn't seem to cut any mustard with John Birt, who'd joined the BBC as deputy director-general in 1987. Birt came from commercial television, working for Granada and then London Weekend Television, where he became controller of features and current affairs, and, later, director of programmes.

His first day at the Beeb was inauspicious to say the least. Walking into Broadcasting House, he was duly accosted by one of the BBC commissionaires. 'Oi! What's your name?'

'Birt.'

'Yeah. Bert who?'

Before Birt's promotion to director-general in 1992, his influence and determination to change the way the BBC operated had begun to seep down to every level of the corporation and across to Radio 1. It was one of the reasons why producer Martin Cox decided to leave when the opportunity arose to move into film and documentary production. 'The mood had changed at Radio 1. It wasn't anywhere like as much fun and I didn't like the way things were going. I could kind of see what was coming.'

He was joined by Dave Atkey, who had risen to the rank of executive producer, in charge of marketing and promotions, the Roadshow and outside broadcasts, and one of five people then running the station. He left at the same time as Martin and for identical reasons:

'Radio 1 was going down the pan. I could see it coming. I thought, "I've got to get out of this."'

Producer Choice was one of the first things that came in that totally changed how programmes were made. Previously, heads of departments and producers had a budget to make their shows. Block deals were done where producers would negotiate with, for example, studios for live sessions or the various archives or how many outside broadcasts they were going to do in a year. It was a lump sum that was supposed to be managed. But it wasn't working. Dave Atkey recalls that he never had to deal with a budget.

When he first arrived at Radio 1, Paul Robinson was dismayed at the state of what was happening. 'As a programme director, I was responsible for budgets, so I asked, "What's my budget?" and they said, "Oh, don't worry about that. Just do what you need to do." No one knew what was being spent. Nobody had any idea. One thing Birt did was, he said, "We now need to know what things cost and we need to have an accountability because it's public money." I was very happy about that, but a lot of people weren't.'

The idea of Producer Choice was that there would be commissioners and suppliers. So, if drama or music programmes wanted to make a programme for Radio 4, the network had to buy it from drama or music and agree a price for it. Essentially what Birt did was create an internal market. 'And that did produce efficiencies,' claims Paul. 'But it was quite a big step for a lot of people. There was a lot of the old guard at the BBC.' Paul remembers one chap coming up to him and saying, 'Paul, you're a young man, you're in a bit of a hurry, but you really need to slow down and stop putting your head above the parapet. My advice to you is: have a gentle nudge on the tiller. That's all that's required.' The culture was: 'Don't rock the boat.'

There was nothing wrong with the BBC being more accountable to the public, who after all, through the licence fee, paid their wages, but the result of the reforms was to turn the making of programmes into another branch of manufacturing, like churning out baked beans or making car tyres. The system of internal charging brought with it a mass of administration, bean counters galore, finance managers and bureaucrats, focus groups and flip charts. 'The mentality of Birt was that every paper clip had to be accounted for,' says Chris Lycett. 'More accountants were coming in rather than creative or programme people. Up until that time, let's arbitrarily say my role was 80 per cent creative and man management and 20 per cent admin and corporate bollocks. Birt's internal market and Producer Choice turned that on its head. The transition was absolute purgatory. It really did change the culture.'

What sums all this up perfectly was the change made to the record library. For years, if a DJ wanted a record from the gramophone library, they phoned up Dave Price, the ex-Radio 1 man who ran it, and, within five or ten minutes, he'd bring it to them in a little box. Then with Producer Choice it was: 'Well, actually that's a service being provided to Radio 1, so we will charge a fee for Dave to bring that record over to your studio.' For many producers and DJs, it was cheaper to go to a shop and buy the bit of vinyl themselves. One wag at a meeting said, 'Fuck me, Our Price would be cheaper than Dave Price.'

Obviously, people stopped using the record library, with the inevitable result that there was no longer sufficient income to maintain what had been the best library of its type in the world: they had every single record that was ever issued. 'This precious bit of BBC silver was lost for ever,' laments Beerling. The same thing happened with the reference library and news information service. If a DJ was interviewing, for example, Elton John, they could have a file of press clippings about him for the last ten years delivered to their office so that they could do their research. 'Many valuable services like this were curtailed or lost,' says Beerling. 'It was very sad.'

Chris Lycett recalls the very first big meeting with John Birt when he unveiled his grand scheme. He'd already presented his vision to the bigwigs at television, and now it was the turn of radio. About fifty people – all the high-flyers of BBC radio – gathered in the council chamber at Broadcasting House, with portraits of past heads staring down at them from the imposing wood-panelled walls. Chris was there in his new capacity as head of programmes at Radio 1, a job that required him to manage all the production teams. 'There were a few tut tuts,' he remembers, as Birt spoke. When the director-general reached the end of his speech, he asked if there were any questions. 'I thought, "Well, I'd better make my presence felt," so I put my hand up and said, "I notice that you mentioned 'change' several times in your speech. Can you just give us any idea how long this period of change will last?" He looked across this vast table at me and said, "Well, Chris," and there was this long pause. "It will be for ever." That marked me down as one of the reluctants.'

There were other malcontents, too. During the meeting, Birt had used the phrase 'tainted by experience'. Chris was sitting next to John Drummond, head of Radio 3 at the time. 'When Birt said "tainted by experience",' Chris remembers, 'I could hear John Drummond harrumph and almost see his blood pressure rise. Drummond was a fastidious dresser. He always wore Savile Row suits with a matching tie and hanky out of the top pocket. At the very next meeting, gone was the matching tie and hanky, replaced by a T-shirt, the sort you got made at the end of Brighton Pier, that read: "John Drummond, tainted by experience, and proud of it."'

Now that Chris Lycett was head of programmes, he could start to implement his own set of plans. One of the things that he'd always wanted to achieve was more fluidity between the two strands of Radio 1, the musos and the showbiz jocks. Out of that lofty ambition came the left-field idea of putting the king of nighttime, John Peel, onto a daytime slot. 'No, Lycett,' said Peel when it was broached to him one afternoon. 'I wouldn't be able to play what I wanted.' The two men always used to call each other by their surname in mock pretence that they were still in some minor public school. 'Look, Peel,' said Chris. 'If I produce it, would you consider it? And I promise you, not necessarily deliverable, but as long as you play the game, I will make sure that it doesn't dilute your style.' The answer was still no.

As it happened, Jackie Brambles, who was then doing the lunchtime show, was set to go on leave for about a fortnight, and Chris managed to persuade Peel to deputise for her. 'What I said to John was, "These are the playlist records, so if you can just grit your teeth and put your fingers in your ears." We got through it very well and we got great feedback saying it was great to hear John on daytime.'

While to a large extent Peel was mollified, he dug his heels in when it came to certain records, usually on the playlist. There'd be a bit of haggling, most often when they were just about to go on air when Peel would suddenly announce, 'I'm not playing that!' On one occasion, the record in question was Bryan Adams. 'Come on, play it, please,' implored Chris. Peel cued up the song, introduced it and banged the play button. The opening lyric was 'Can't stop me now', Peel lifted the stylus, opened his mic and said, 'Oh yes, I can.'

Despite these occasional bumps in the road, Chris thinks Peel had a great time doing those two weeks. 'He loved it. We all have egos, don't we, and he loved it; though he never admitted it.'

At the other end of the spectrum from Peel was Alan Freeman. In the summer of 1993 when Radio 1 celebrated the twentieth anniversary of the Roadshow at Derby's Markeaton Park, Alan was guest of honour, having hosted the very first Roadshow in 1973. The event was another spectacular success. 'I think we had over 100,000 people there,' recalls Gary Davies. 'The motorway was just completely jammed for miles around with people trying to get there.'

Alan had been with the network on and off since the very beginning. He'd gone to Capital in 1979 before returning to Radio 1 a decade later to front a revised *Pick of the Pops*, this time playing a retro chart format. There was also the *Saturday Rock Show*. But his days were numbered and by the end of the year he was gone.

Paul Robinson worked briefly with Freeman towards the end of his Radio 1 career and found him to be an absolute sweetheart.

He was one of the most professional broadcasters. I remember saying to Alan, 'You never make a mistake on the air. You've got all these cartridges and bits of music, all really fast-paced.' He said, 'I rehearse, Paul. And then I rehearse again and then I rehearse again.' He was in the studio two hours before a show started, making sure everything was done. And this is a man who'd been doing this for thirty-forty years and he's in there working and getting it right. Steve Wright was the same. He was on the air at three in the afternoon, but he was in the office at half past eight in the morning. This was why these guys were good. They were very talented broadcasters, but they also did their work.

Alan and *Pick of the Pops* did return to the BBC, this time to Radio 2 from 1997 until 2000, when Alan bowed out from the BBC and from broadcasting, wrapping up a remarkable career. However, underneath the pop persona that he'd built up successfully over the years was a deeply vulnerable and insecure human being. All the 'Greetings, pop pickers, not arf' was an act. It was a performance. Sometimes in the studio he would shake with nerves, and constantly seek reassurance that what he'd done was good enough. Tim Blackmore was Alan's manager from 1983 until his death and reveals that the DJ once suffered an emotional breakdown. 'He was in a bad way,' remembers Tim. 'I sent him to a psychiatrist just to have a few discussions and the psychiatrist called me into his office. He said, "I don't understand Alan at all. I've never met anyone with such a low estimation of his self-worth." That summed Fluff up. He could never believe that he was successful.'

Nor did Alan properly come to terms with his homosexuality; sadly, during the course of his life he never established a permanent relationship. During his breakdown, Tim visited the private hospital where he was staying for a week. Walking into his room, Tim witnessed Alan sobbing in bed and asked what the matter was. 'I wish I hadn't been gay,' Alan said.

'Why do you feel that, Alan?'

'I wouldn't have ended up so lonely.'

Tim cherished their friendship. As his manager, he looked after both his business affairs and work commitments. When Alan first asked Tim to look after him, he said, 'There's one difficult thing you will have to do one day. You'll have to tell me when it's time to go.' And it did happen, when Tim had to tell his friend that it was time to stop doing *Pick of the Pops* because it was getting to a point where the show required too much editing. 'The speed of the thing was too much for a man who was in his early seventies.' He had also begun to suffer from arthritis, which badly affected his fingers and made it difficult to operate the studio equipment. Alan Freeman quietly passed away at his London home in 2006.

By the end of his time at Radio 1, Alan's style and demeanour, through no fault of his own, had become open to ridicule. This was epitomised in the characters created and performed by comedians Harry Enfield and Paul Whitehouse on *Harry Enfield's Television Programme*. First appearing in 1990, Smashie and Nicey, a pair of naff and cheesy DJs working at Radio Fab FM, were thought to have been modelled on Blackburn and Fluff. Blackburn later went on record saying how he always found them quite amusing, although he knew of one or two DJs who thought it was modelled on them and didn't find it funny. Dave Lee Travis was particularly touchy about it. 'Dave got quite shirty and failed to see the joke,' said David Hamilton. 'He felt they demeaned us all.'

According to Johnny Beerling, the whole thing started after Harry Enfield was a guest on Steve Wright's show and observed Alan Freeman in the next studio. Whatever the origins of the characters, Beerling thinks the sketches, broadcast on BBC TV, were harmful to Radio 1. 'It drew attention to an image that I was trying to move away from.' And while these characters were very much a stereotype of eighties Radio 1 DJs, their popularity couldn't help but highlight a general feeling around Broadcasting House that Radio 1 was perhaps too stuck in the past, living off former glories and out of touch with the younger listenership.

The fact that teenage audiences were being lured away to the new commercial radio stations sprouting up, like Kiss FM, was of particular concern. The feeling was that some DJs were no longer appropriate for Radio 1 and the youth market, and that they'd grown old as indeed the network itself had along with its audience.

At first, a lot of people working at Egton House thought Smashie and Nicey was nothing more than an amusing adjunct to Radio 1. 'We didn't realise that Smashie and Nicey was the death knell of Radio 1,' says Jonathan Ruffle. 'Because obviously it was.' Some Radio 1 shows even referred to the characters and played up on the spoof, like the one

Ruffle produced with Liz Kershaw and Bruno Brookes. 'I bet if you listen to those shows you'll hear us all doing Smashie and Nicey impressions and using those names. How numbnuts can you get and not notice what's happening? There was an avalanche around the corner and I didn't spot it,' Ruffle admits.

24

Rumours of a revamp had begun to circulate around Egton House as early as the summer of 1992. The Beeb as a whole was filling up with more Birt appointees – on not insubstantial salaries. 'This new intake knew nothing of entertainment or populist broadcasting,' says Adrian Juste. 'They were there with an agenda – there were social issues to be forced home, revisionist mantras to be preached. The fact that the Great British Public didn't want to listen never deterred them in the slightest!' But, in the new Kingdom of Birtdom, they were 'on message'.

Lots of people were starting to feel depressed with the turn the BBC was taking. Adrian Juste remembers going to see Johnny Beerling, who dejectedly informed him that everything they'd worked so hard for was being overturned by the new guard and that it would soon be time for them to go. 'I said thanks, but the writing on the wall was writ extremely large and I'd keep going till they fired me.'

Bob Harris was to recall in his autobiography being ushered into one of the offices by Dave Lee Travis. After taking a quick shufty around him to make sure they couldn't be heard, Dave said, 'They're taking us all off Radio 1.'

'What on earth are you talking about?' said Bob, unable to believe it. 'Things are going really well.'

'You don't understand, Bob. I've been talking to top management and they're going to reposition the network and get rid of us all. You and I will be the first to go.'

Bob was in shock. 'But what about Johnny Beerling? He won't let it happen.'

Travis was adamant that what he was saying was true, and, as a friend, wanted Bob to know and advise him to start looking for other options, 'Because your days here are numbered.'

The first sign that things were going to change arrived when it was announced in June 1993 that Johnny Beerling was giving up his position as controller. Before any leaks or press statements were made, Beerling scheduled a staff meeting and broke the news. He was amazed at the reaction. 'John Peel cried and John Walters made an impassioned spontaneous speech.'

For the most part, Beerling kept his powder dry about his departure until the Radio Academy's annual conference in 1994, after he'd left the station, when he didn't mince his words about the changes going on inside the network. 'Life at the BBC had become like working under communism,' he declared. He went on to say that he left 'because he could not work under such a totalitarian regime, where his job had less to do with creativity and more to do with bureaucracy.'

With the benefit of hindsight, Beerling accepts that it was the right time to go. He was 54 and had been with the station since the opening day. Perhaps he wasn't the man after all to bring Radio 1 into the new younger times. 'Johnny really loved Radio 1,' says Paul Robinson. 'He lived and breathed Radio 1. If he had any faults, he didn't build a bond with John Birt, so ultimately Johnny was seen as not the right man.' This was despite the fact that Paul felt Beerling was evolving the network, and was always open to new ideas. For example, Paul came across an artist called Apache Indian, who was mixing traditional bhangra music with reggae, and asked Beerling if they could do a show with him. 'Yeah, yeah, do it,' he said. 'So, I booked him,' says Paul. 'And I brought in various other DJs and Johnny was always very happy to let me get on and do that.'

This is probably what irritated Beerling the most: that a lot of his work over the years had gone largely unheralded by his superiors. He recalls the occasion John Birt said to him, 'I can't hear any difference between Radio 1 and Capital Radio.' Slightly taken aback, Beerling replied, 'You must be deaf then,' as he cited the amount of public service he was providing, such as increasing the news coverage and social action projects, documentaries that he insisted went out in peak time rather than being marginalised to the evening, along with the live sessions and concerts that they were covering and the promotion of new artists, none of which Capital was really doing at the time. 'Johnny was let go because he was seen as part of the problem and not the solution,' says Paul. 'And that wasn't fair.'

The new controller of Radio 1 was a former *Newsbeat* journalist called Matthew Bannister. Just a year earlier, John Birt had hired Bannister in order to compile and write a document called 'Extending Choice', which amounted to a manifesto about the future role of Radio 1. Its most significant finding was that Radio 1 had to be younger and cooler, and if it lost a few million listeners in their thirties and forties, well, so be it, because that's not what the network was for any more.

Both Paul Robinson and Chris Lycett applied for the top job, but everybody soon realised that the advertising of the Radio 1 controller's job had just been window dressing: the post had been filled months previously – from on high. Beerling himself wasn't in the least surprised by the choice. 'I knew how close Matthew's editorial thinking was to that of John Birt,' he wrote. 'In Matthew, John knew he would have a safe pair of hands who would introduce the sort of changes John felt were needed.'

Born in Sheffield in 1958, Matthew Bannister studied law and went to work as a reporter at Radio Nottingham and then Capital. He joined Radio 1 as a *Newsbeat* presenter in 1983. When he left, he teamed up with another Radio 1 exile, Trevor Dann, and conquered local radio with Greater London Radio (GLR), which burst onto the London airwaves, fronted by a young and vibrant roster of presenters like Chris Evans, Chris Morris and Danny Baker.

Bannister admitted to being no great fan of Radio 1. 'It wasn't exactly the station of hip youth,' he said. 'It was the station your mum listened to.' His first real encounter with the station was during one of their 'weeks out' in Derby, when he was invited to a disco event in the evening. He was disappointed by the fact that there were no live bands, just music from records. When a whole bunch of Radio 1 DJs came onto the stage in various states of fancy dress, including Dave Lee Travis riding a mini motorbike, his disappointment was replaced by a sense of sheer bemusement. He just didn't understand it: was this meant to be entertainment?

When Bannister took over as controller, he found an organisation 'out of touch with its public service role and its young audience' and he was in no doubt about what he had been tasked to do. John Birt had reached the conclusion that despite being the nation's most listened-to station, Radio 1 was not sufficiently different and distinctive from its commercial competitors. The decision was made to reposition the station to serve a younger demographic. The target audience was now 13 to 25 rather than 13 to 40. It was to be the most radical overhaul in the twenty-six-year history of Radio 1.

Bannister knew from the start that he needed to take the staff with him by persuading them of the necessity for change. But upon his arrival he was shocked at how entrenched the culture was. Pretty much at the top of priorities was a cull of those who had been tarnished by the Smashie and Nicey tag, along with those who were a bit long in the tooth. 'There were a number of DJs who were older than the prime minister, the director-general and the Archbishop of Canterbury,' argued Bannister. While never intending to be ageist, it was clear that management perceived these DJs to be massively out of touch with youth culture and that was clearly a problem.

Egton House was alive with rumours. 'We knew it was coming,' says Gary Davies. 'Ever since John Birt took over, we knew changes were afoot, that things weren't going to be the same. There was a period of about eighteen months where it was really uncomfortable working at Radio 1.'

Obviously realising that his number was up, Dave Lee Travis was the first to go that August, announcing live on air to his 15 million listeners that he was quitting. 'Changes are being made here that go against my principles,' he said, 'and I just cannot agree with them… The only option is very regrettably for me to leave – so that is what I am doing.'

Travis hadn't planned to make a speech at all. He just got angry and out it all came. For him, he was speaking on behalf of the hardworking people behind the programmes who didn't have a voice. Travis expected to honour the few months he had left on his contract, only to be told that he wasn't going back on the air again. 'I didn't have a chance to say goodbye to my listeners,' he said, 'which after twenty-seven years was a bit tough.'

This was followed a month later by the resignation of Simon Bates, who must have realised the writing was on the wall. 'I'm a great believer in saying "I'm off" two days before they're going to say "Goodbye".' Bates had presented the morning show for thirteen years and built up a following of nine million listeners. It was after falling on his sword that Bates was told by Bannister that his contract wasn't going to be renewed anyway. Bannister then asked if Bates could leave by a side entrance after his show to avoid the growing melee of reporters outside. Bates purposely left by the main doors.

Also axed were Alan Freeman, Tommy Vance and Bob Harris, all of whom had been great servants to the station. 'They were just dismissed as if they were nothing,' said Adrian Juste. 'As if they were something on the bottom of your shoe.'

Bob Harris knew the game was up when a call came through that Bannister wanted to see him in his office. The two of them had never met before. It was a swift two-minute meeting by the end of which Bob's career at Radio 1 was over. Opening the door to leave, Bob turned back. 'Just to let you know, I won't be going to the press to slag you off, or anyone else for that matter,' he said. 'I've loved it here. It's as simple as that.'

The atmosphere at Egton House was now toxic, with DJs wondering where the axe was going to fall next, and whose neck it was going to be. 'I avoided the night of the long knives of Matthew Bannister,' says Johnnie Walker. 'Chris Lycett rang me up. "Johnnie, you're not included. We've never considered you a Smashie and Nicey DJ." It was incredible the difference that Harry Enfield and Paul Whitehouse made. They absolutely revolutionised Radio 1, through comedy. Those DJs had passed their sell-by date, and that style had passed its sell-by date.' Mike Smith put it even more dramatically when he claimed, 'I actually think that Smashie and Nicey are probably responsible for the wholesale destruction of Radio 1.'

John Peel was safe, despite having had his detractors over the years. 'If Beerling had had his way, he wouldn't have had Peel on Radio 1,' claims Chris Lycett. 'Derek Chinnery just went with it. But they would always wheel Peel and Walters out if ever they wanted to prove their public service credentials.' It was the same when the new regime took over. They cited both Peel and Andy Kershaw's programmes as being the kind of model others should follow. That went for Annie Nightingale, too, now an enthusiastic champion of the dance music scene. Like Peel, her survival rested on the fact that she always insisted on playing her own selections, and playing the music she was passionate about.

Peel's producer John Walters, however, was not enamoured with what was taking place. After his retirement, he'd make the odd trip back to his old stomping ground from his home in Surrey, lamenting the changes instigated by what he described as 'the evils of Birtism and yuppiedom'. Andy Kershaw recalled one of his trips when he complained that the place was overrun with 'children, reeking of Perrier'.

Watching his colleagues scythed down wholesale, Gary Davies started to get nervous. He'd always known that the closer he got to 40, then his days were probably numbered. 'The thing about Radio 1, it was always really a young person's radio station and nobody had a divine right to stay there for ever,' Gary recalls. He was still bringing in big audience figures, though. 'My problem was they weren't 14 or 15-year-olds, they were probably late twenties and thirties. That's the problem the BBC had then and still has now: they've got to attract a younger audience.' He'd been reassured by Bannister that everything was going really well with his Sunday night show. 'But I knew he was talking bullshit. I knew it was just a matter of time.'

If he was going to get the chop, Gary had pretty much decided that after Radio 1 he didn't really want to carry on broadcasting, since it just wouldn't be the same. 'I'd seen all these amazing DJs in the past from Radio 1 now working on these gold stations being treated like shit and it must have been soul-destroying. I never wanted to be in that position.' Yes, he would do a bit of radio part-time, which is what he ended up doing on Virgin, but his main focus was on accomplishing something else with his life, and that was setting up his own music company.

By the close of 1993, Gary found out he was indeed being dropped. Because it didn't come as too much of a surprise, the disappointment was in the way the whole thing was handled. For weeks, Bannister continued to tell Gary that his show was great, until he asked for a meeting one evening at a hotel near Euston Station. They met in the bar and Bannister told him that it was all over. 'I thought that's why you wanted to see me,' said Gary. 'Why didn't you say this to me a few weeks ago?' Bannister said that he couldn't, that his hands were tied. 'You lied to me,' said Gary. 'Why would you lie to me?'

A year later, the two men bumped into each other at an industry function and Bannister made a point of going over to Gary to apologise for the way he'd overseen the DJ's exit.

And so, in the end, Gary did leave with some bitterness. Working at Radio 1 had been something he'd loved doing. 'What an incredible job to be able to listen to music all day and play amazing songs and communicate,' he says. 'It was the best job in the world.'

For many people working within Egton House, there was sadness and anger that a sledgehammer was being used to crack a nut, carried out, in the words of Chris Lycett, who was thoroughly jaded by it all, 'with a missionary zeal'. There's always a danger that somebody wants to make their mark. 'Matthew's view of management, in those days, was very much, "You will do this because I say so,"' says Trevor Dann. 'It was a case of saying, "My colleague John Birt says we have to change things and I am his henchperson and I will do this."'

Most people accepted and understood why some of the DJs needed to be removed, but surely the better solution, since the likes of Bates, Travis, Gary Davies et al were still hugely popular, should have been to keep them within the BBC family and shunt them across to Radio 2. That should have been their natural home, instead of being thrown out into the open market and snapped up by commercial stations who got themselves a ready-made star DJ.

When Johnny Beerling was negotiating his way out as Radio 1 controller, he proposed the idea of running Radio 2 and taking all the ousted Radio 1 jocks with him. 'We'll use the power of the BBC's marketing machine to switch the audience across to Radio 2,' he suggested. 'Then you can make Radio 1 young and sharp.' The powers that be baulked at that idea. 'Oh no, no,' they said to Beerling. 'We don't want to do that. It will disadvantage the existing Radio 2 audience.'

At the time, the musical gap between Radio 1 and Radio 2 was unbridgeable. 'There was no way our listenership would have gone over to Radio 2,' says Gary Davies. 'They were playing stuff like Kenny Rogers. The gap was huge.'

In the mid- to late seventies, Radio 2's output had resembled Radio 1's to such a degree that some people within the BBC had dubbed the station 'Radio 1 and a half'. During the eighties it went much more middle of the road. 'I think there was some missive from management that said that they had to sound less similar,' reveals producer Martin Cox.

David Hamilton had recently quit the station complaining of its 'geriatric' music policy. The last straw came with a memo headed 'Whistling & Wurlitzers'. David asked for a meeting with Radio 2's controller, Frances Line. 'I said, "You've got panpipes, but there's no mention of Motown." She said, "What do you mean by Motown?"'

Chris Lycett received much the same response when he, too, suggested taking the ousted Radio 1 jocks over to Radio 2. 'The then controller of Radio 2 was a bit of a folkie and I remember her publicly saying, "I don't want any of that boom-boom music on Radio 2."' Adrian Juste, who was trying to get his programmes out as usual while keeping one eye on the next swing of the Grim Reaper's scythe, had already done a demo tape for Radio 2. 'It came back faster than a Sampras volley: "Although you are a big success on Radio 1, we feel that it wouldn't work... et cetera et cetera" Mind you, they were still playing Perry Como and Vera Lynn in those days!'

So that was it: what could have been a much more natural transition was rejected, leaving Beerling particularly angered. 'They didn't have enough foresight.' A few years later, Jim Moir became Radio 2's new controller and did exactly what Beerling and others had called for, playing classic rock and pop aimed at a more mature audience than Radio 1, but still embracing new music. It also meant that the newer generation of Radio 1 jocks were able to gravitate more smoothly to Radio 2. The new thinking was: 'If you've got talent at Radio 1, it should be possible for that talent to then go to Radio 2, to stay at the BBC; why should they be lost to the BBC?' All this meant, of course, that Radio 2 in essence became the old Radio 1, or as Steve Wright claims, 'It's the family radio station that Radio 1 used to be.'

Having made wholesale personnel changes, Bannister began bringing in new blood: Jo Whiley, Mark Radcliffe and Mark Riley, Steve Lamacq, and, from his former station GLR, Emma Freud and Danny Baker. Bannister was a huge admirer of Baker's talents in particular. The broadcaster was working on the newly launched BBC Radio 5, presenting a football chat show, when Bannister brought him over to Radio 1 and put him on the air. Some thought Baker's highly individual style just didn't fit, not least Dave Lee Travis, whose weekend slot Baker had filled. Adrian Juste was in his studio ready to go on after when a call came through. It was Travis ringing from home and sounding heartbroken on the other end of the line, 'Are you listening to this crap?'

'Oh, Dave, don't upset me any more,' answered Adrian. 'I've got to go in and try and do a comedy show.'

307

Bannister's original idea was to give Danny Baker the top job on the breakfast show. It was Paul Robinson who managed to talk him out of that one. Paul had been promoted by Bannister to managing editor, effectively becoming his deputy. But he wasn't happy with some of the changes that were being implemented. 'Some I persuaded him not to do, and some I couldn't persuade him and he did anyway,' Paul says. 'Some were probably right but I didn't agree with everything he did.' Paul thought Danny Baker was better suited to a more specialist-type show and so didn't agree with him taking over from DLT, either. 'I didn't particularly like the DLT show, but a lot of people loved it and his numbers were very good. I knew putting Danny Baker on instead, that audience was going to leave in droves, and, of course, they did.'

Bannister stood by his man ('I thought what the BBC should do was to be able to support people who were inventive and surreal and different'), even when the press gleefully reported that his listening figures were tumbling. It wasn't just Baker, though. Bannister's other new signings were struggling to attract that hallowed new younger audience, while the older listeners were switching off after reaching the conclusion that it wasn't their station any more.

For Paul, putting Emma Freud on lunchtime was another mistake. Like Baker, Emma was another talk jock. She took over the slot vacated by Jackie Brambles, who'd left Radio 1 to pursue a television career in America. What Bannister wanted from Emma was a kind of news/music hybrid show, but what Brambles was doing with the lunchtime session was exactly where Radio 1 needed to be. 'Jackie should never have been allowed to go,' insists Paul. 'Emma was more Radio 4 than Radio 1. Being a music jock was not her thing, so another disaster, but Bannister insisted on doing it.'

It's fair to get rid of some of the people who had been there for so long, but they weren't being replaced with enough of the right sort of people. And the fact that the Bakers and Emma Freuds were being asked to take over from seasoned pros like Bates and DLT, without the tools or experience, merely compounded the situation. 'These guys like Bates and Travis had been doing those shows for Christ knows how many years,' says Jonathan Ruffle. 'You suddenly put somebody else on in that slot and they don't know how to do that show. Why would they? Why would somebody coming in know how to do that? You've got to learn that.' The practice at Radio 1 had always been to bed in new DJs so they weren't on every day, or they did early or late-night shows, maybe subbed for a DJ on holiday. They weren't exposed too soon as they learnt the ropes, but eased into the schedule. 'But was that happening to any of the poor sods who came in and replaced those DJs on Radio 1 under Matthew?' says Jonathan. 'I don't think so.'

Just as bad, as Adrian Juste recalls, was that all new recruits to the station were ordered not to befriend the old guard. 'We had a nice friendly atmosphere, everybody knew everybody. And then none of the new influx were allowed to speak to us. "Don't speak to them, just ignore them." You can't run a bloody radio station doing things like that.'

The result of all this: listeners began to desert in their millions. There were press reports that audiences were down two million and others that stated the network was haemorrhaging seventeen listeners a minute. The likes of Dave Lee Travis felt that the BBC were just throwing these people to one side and wanted to forget about them. 'That annoyed me,' he says, 'because we had spent twenty-odd years building them up.' All the hard work shaping, developing and creating Radio 1 as this big brand was being dismantled in front of everyone's eyes. 'No commercial radio station in the world would allow that audience to just disappear,' says Gary Davies. 'You'd be fired.'

It seemed as if it would be just a matter of time before Bannister himself was given his marching orders, but he was carrying out orders given to him by the BBC hierarchy, who therefore had no choice but to stand by him. The next eighteen months, though, were dark days as audience figures continued to look bleak. Speaking in 1997, Johnny Beerling explained why he thought so many listeners switched off. 'Listeners are very slow to forgive. If you change one of their friends, they might forgive you. If you change, as Matthew Bannister did, all their friends in three months, that's what the audience didn't forgive, and that's why it dropped so quickly.'

Watching all this from the sidelines was Bannister's former colleague at GLR, Trevor Dann. 'I thought Matthew had fucked it up,' he says. 'It was pathetic frankly. He didn't really know what he was doing. It was sad to watch because Radio 1 definitely needed change, but… his recruitment and his identification of new talent was very flawed, and I think that's because he wasn't a music radio person.'

Bannister had never been a DJ. After working as a reporter for *Newsbeat,* he'd joined Capital Radio as a journalist and then been promoted to head of news and talks. Perhaps the problem lay in the fact that he could never talk to the Radio 1 jocks in a language they could understand. He didn't get the game. It was a little bit like a cricket coach going into a premiership football team. He didn't understand the sport or the culture. 'They just didn't trust him,' claims Dann. 'They thought he was a pompous git.'

Dann was surprised not to have been asked to come in with Bannister right at the start; instead he'd continued his job at GLR. When a little over a year into Bannister's reign his services were required, Dann had half a mind to refuse, largely because a headhunter was sent to recruit him rather than Bannister picking up a phone and asking for him personally. Then Dann thought, 'This is a fantastic opportunity. If I can get this anywhere near right, this will be a good thing to be seen to have done. It may not be terribly enjoyable at the time, but I'll be proud of it if I can pull it off.' He accepted. 'But from day one it was made very clear to me by Matthew that I was to know my place. There was no sense of: "Let's put the old team back together." It was now: "I'm in charge and I've slightly reluctantly agreed that I need an old bruiser in to help me, but I'm not going to put my arm around you and take you on side." And he never did.'

Dann had been brought in to look after the in-house production department and admits that when he arrived there was a terrible atmosphere about the place. 'Nobody would talk to me. There was a real sense of "What are you doing here?" It was most unpleasant until I could start recruiting my own team.' Behind the scenes at Radio 1,

Bannister had kept the producing staff intact, thinking he only needed a bunch of new DJs. Dann believed that was the wrong approach and what they really needed to do was get some young staff in there to make the programmes and change the atmosphere. His big idea was to abolish the role of executive producer, which meant that suddenly five or six people were redundant. They were all let go. 'It was a horrible thing to do but I just felt that it needed to be done. It was like getting rid of the old footballers in your team who are complacent because they may have won the FA cup last season but they weren't playing very well any more.' Not for nothing did Dann earn the nickname around Egton House of 'Dann Dann the Hatchet Man'. 'He fired the bullets that Bannister made,' says Adrian Juste.

Suddenly the network had a group of forward-thinking people who didn't owe anything to the past regime, and some of them, such as Rhys Hughes, later head of live music and events, and Ben Cooper, who became controller, ended up running Radio 1. 'There was a big change of atmosphere and vibe,' says Tony Wilson, 'with lots of new people brought in to freshen the whole place up. I just felt that I wasn't able to carry on the way things had been.' Tony left the BBC with a heavy heart; it had been his sole employer since leaving school thirty-one years earlier. 'Working at Radio 1 had been great. It was doing something that I loved, working with music every day.' He went into freelance production and, with some colleagues in the late nineties, opened up his own rock station called Rock Radio Network. Including input from Tommy Vance, the network eventually became Total Rock.

Someone else leaving who'd been with the station since its inception was Jeff Griffin. Jeff had nothing personal against Matthew Bannister, although, as he admits, 'I was slightly rude about him at my leaving do. I talked about the listening figures sliding down the bannister when he took over and people fell about. A bit embarrassing because he was there and, as Johnny Beerling pointed out to me, "Bannister's paying for a lot of this." I said, "I don't care. It's still true."'

A few months after his departure, Jeff was having drinks with some friends when one of them raised the subject of Radio 1. 'You must be really pissed off about what's going on there.' Jeff had to stop him. 'What makes you think that I would be listening to Radio 1 now after having worked there for so many years? It would just be silly.' As young producers, Jeff and his colleagues had come in with new, bold ideas and Radio 1 had changed as a result. Now Jeff acknowledged that it was another generation's turn. 'If I was listening to Radio 1 now and enjoying it,' he said, 'then they would be doing something wrong.'

As things were changing behind the scenes, Bannister made the bold move of taking Steve Wright off his highly successful afternoon slot and putting him on at breakfast. About to turn 40, Steve had his own doubts about the switch. 'I thought, for a 40-year-old to be on and to be able to relate to young people was probably not the thing.' Steve was still holding his own at the station and bringing in good numbers. He was even voted the nation's most popular DJ by readers of *Smash Hits* magazine in a 1994 poll. But he didn't agree with many of the things happening at Radio 1. 'There was a little bit of panic on the go and several people were let go. They started to make a couple of mistakes here and there with the playlist. They also made the changes too quickly. The trick is to always gradually bring people with you and make the changes rather slowly... That's why I decided to just step out of it, maybe for a year or two, and then maybe come back. So, I quit.'

Steve tried to arrange a meeting with Bannister and Dann – 'who I quite liked. I had nothing against them personally' – but, unable to see them, he wrote a letter of resignation. 'It just said, "I've had a really nice time here," which I'd had, I'd been there fifteen years. "I just feel that it's probably time for me to go." I learnt later that they had no intention of firing me and were very happy with what I was doing. But I thought, "Sooner or later, I'm going to have to go anyway."' Unlike a few others, Steve didn't talk to the press or bad-mouth the station in public. He went to work for the newly launched Talk Radio (later Talk Sport), before Jim Moir asked him to work for his revamped Radio 2.

Bannister took Steve's resignation like a bullet to the chest. 'I thought we would be in big trouble,' admitted Trevor Dann. 'I very rarely saw Matthew look worried, but he did that day.' There was plenty to be worried about. The papers had got hold of the story and Bannister held crisis talks that went late into the evening. The headlines next morning didn't make for comfortable reading. One ran: 'New crisis throws pop station into desperate chaos.' It wasn't an over-exaggeration. Bannister was stuck, unsure which direction to take. At the same time, the BBC governors were getting itchy fingers and wondering whether to pull the trigger on his reign.

It was Chris Evans who came to the rescue. Beerling had first hired Evans in early 1992 to host a Sunday afternoon show, lasting just six months. Since then he'd gone to GLR and become one of the hottest broadcasters in the country with his own Channel 4 show, *The Big Breakfast*. Bannister made his move and Evans bit.

Getting Evans on board was a real coup. It was a way of saying, 'We're a station that you need to listen to, that's going to be different. It's going to do something you didn't expect.' But it came at a hefty price. Evans' eight-month contract cost a reported £1 million. It was a pay deal that broke the pay structure at Radio 1. 'We really were civil servants,' says Paul Gambaccini. 'Nobody made money being on air until Chris Evans. He was the first to make big money. In his first year, he got paid more than I'd been paid in my entire Radio 1 career up to that point.'

Something else, too. Bannister had been unable to persuade Evans to work with the in-house production department. He would only come if he could be an independent. What this meant was that Radio 1 no longer had any control over the breakfast show, seen by many as its jewel in the crown. This would prove problematic in time. 'But he was absolutely desperate,' claims Trevor Dann. 'It was the last shake of the dice. If he hadn't managed to get Chris, I think he might have gone.'

Evans' arrival as a freelance operator within the BBC caused problems for Trevor Dann. He'd spent all this time convincing the staff to stick with the project, that it was all going to be great – and then suddenly the flagship show was taken away. 'Not just taken away from us,' he says, 'but given to a bunch of people that had no respect for any of the rules. We could say, "This is the playlist and you have to follow it." And they would say, "Not going to, because we don't work for you."'

By the time Evans began his breakfast show in April 1995, the final cull had taken place of those DJs who'd managed to slip through the net the last time. Looking at the roster of DJs in the building, one might have thought it would be easy enough to write on a piece of paper in two columns those who had to go and those who had a future. But it wasn't quite as clear-cut as that. Bannister and his chief assistant Andy Parfitt recruited a cutting-edge marketing agency to carry out work for them. Part of it was audience research they'd done on what the public thought about Radio 1's DJs. And the overwhelming result was that Simon Mayo had to go, because he represented everything the audience hated: he was smug, he was middle-class. And then, no more than three months later, the same piece of work was done, and the result was: you can let everybody go but not Simon Mayo because he's the one everybody loves. Maybe there was a lesson to be learnt there about the reliability of market research.

The latest cull had begun just before Christmas. Adrian Juste was sitting in the studio getting his show ready, when the phone rang. It was one of Bannister's assistants. Adrian knew what was coming. 'Do you want Matthew to call you back?' went the voice. 'No, don't bother,' Adrian said resignedly. 'I've got a show to get out. Just wish him a Merry Christmas and tell him to fuck off, will ya.' As far as Adrian was concerned, being sacked on the phone was not the BBC that he'd joined and he was glad to get out. Sixteen years, though, wasn't a bad run and he'd enjoyed pretty much all of it. 'After a show I used to go for a bagel and coffee on Regent Street, and if I'd done a good show – you did about one good programme in every three – I'd think, "Yeah, I've made a few million people laugh." You got a nice sense of satisfaction off that as a performer.'

But the final show on New Year's Day was tough. 'I thanked the techies as usual, and said tearful goodbyes to John Peel and Andy

Kershaw (both faithful listeners I'm proud to say!). Then, after heartfelt goodbyes from the BBC commissionaires, who we'd got to know really well over the years, I made my way out of Broadcasting House reception into the fading gloom of Regent Street for the last time.'

The last big name to go was Bruno Brookes. Still a prominent voice on the station, doing the Top 40, he'd come into Egton House for his early breakfast show as usual. 'I've got a pretty good sixth sense about things and on this particular morning I felt a bad spirit in the building,' he says. It had just turned five o'clock and Bruno was busy with his show when Matthew Bannister came into the studio, asking if he could come and see him after the show. 'I knew there was going to be trouble.' And there was when Bannister dropped his bombshell. 'Bruno, I know you've got a contract, but we've been thinking and we want to change a few things around, so really we want to give it another few weeks and then let's call it a day.'

'Completely?'

'Yeah. We think the time's right.'

'OK,' said Bruno. 'If that's the way it's got to be.'

There followed a brief discussion about how to handle things in terms of the press. Bannister was happy to go along with Bruno's wishes that nothing be made public until nearer the time. Bannister agreed to this and they shook hands. Bannister then left as he was due to speak at a university in Liverpool that evening. Bruno had his own plans. He was flying that night to a holiday home he owned in Ireland. Arriving at Shannon, Bruno saw that his housekeeper had come to meet him and immediately sensed something was up. 'There's people from the papers all around the front gate,' she said. 'They came knocking on the door offering big money for the story.' What was going on? Bannister had announced Bruno's departure during his speech in Liverpool, which just happened to be in front of a class of media students; news inevitably leaked out.

Bannister's immediate announcement of Bruno's departure, just after he'd agreed to keep it quiet for a while, left a bitter taste as the DJ worked towards his last day. During his tenure on the early breakfast show, he'd become something of a cult figure amongst the nation's truckers, driving the lonely highways at dawn with Radio 1 and his voice coming through the ether. He'd even appeared as a special guest at numerous truckfests. 'On my last day at Radio 1 there was a whole line of trucks parked down Regent Street as a kind of goodbye,' he remembers. 'They had the classic picket-line braziers, were doing bacon and egg sandwiches and invited me out to join them... They were not best pleased I was leaving because we had really created an amazing bond. It was a friendship with a community.'

Perhaps the biggest change required at Radio 1 wasn't so much jettisoning the old guard but changing the music policy. 'What was blindingly obvious was that we were playing the wrong records,' says Trevor Dann. 'We were still trying to be all things to all people.' There was no point in telling a 15-year-old that Radio 1 was cool if he was walking into his own kitchen and seeing his parents listening to the station. 'It wasn't focused enough on the audience we knew we had to get,' says Trevor. 'It had now reached the point that if a new record came out by a group or an artist that were considered heritage, like Status Quo or Cliff Richard, one had to take a stand and say, if we are really a station for 15- to 20-year-olds, this is completely irrelevant to them. Radio 2 should be playing this. We should be playing Blur and Oasis, Supergrass and Pulp.' Trevor Dann deliberately put 'Firestarter' by The Prodigy on the playlist almost as a way of saying to the older listener: 'Go away.'

However, there were still some at the station who retained a sense of 'Why is there a potentially popular record that we're not playing?' An emblematic moment arrived when it was decided not to put the new single by Status Quo on the playlist. What Trevor Dann didn't know at the time was that the band had made a deal with Johnny Beerling in 1992 when they headlined at Radio 1's twenty-fifth birthday concert. Quo's then manager agreed the band would top the bill if Beerling guaranteed their records always being on the playlist. Nothing was written down; it was a verbal agreement only, but obviously Quo took umbrage about not being on the playlist and went to the press, leading to headlines galore about Radio 1 banning Status Quo. The group even appeared in front of the media outside Broadcasting House. Trevor went on radio to say he recognised a publicity stunt when he saw one. 'They sued me for saying it was a publicity stunt,' he adds, 'which in itself was a publicity stunt.'

The whole press furore over the 'banning' of Quo's single was a turning point for Radio 1. 'It completely turned our image on its head,' says Trevor. 'That was saying, "We're not like that any more. We do actually value new British music more than we value this old shit."' This change in music policy, Trevor believes, out of all the things that happened, was probably the most fundamental change. It certainly turned out to be a hit with young listeners, coinciding with the explosion of the Britpop movement of the mid-nineties, which Radio 1 played a significant part in. Indeed, they fed off each other.

There was also the emerging rave culture, and hip DJs were brought in like Tim Westwood and Lisa I'Anson as the station began to radically veer towards dance. Radio 1 had always kept dance music at arm's length. 'In our era, we weren't quick enough or determined enough to embrace dance music,' admits Chris Lycett. 'Probably because of our age: we'd had Pete Tong tucked away on a Friday evening.'

It's amusing to note how this rebranding of Radio 1 towards the controversial yet flourishing sounds of house, techno and jungle came about in part because of a John Birt directive. In order to compete in a more cutthroat and commercial media world, Birt wanted the BBC to outsource much of its programming to independent producers and production companies. By a curious coincidence, one of the companies producing shows for Radio 1 was run by a former DJ at the network, Jeff Young. Before joining Radio 1, Jeff had a very brief spell at Capital and found the atmosphere there much more alive than at the BBC. 'I think it's because it was commercial and they had to react to things fairly quickly,' he says, 'whereas at the BBC there was a little bit of plodding going on.' Birt's idea of outsourcing was something Jeff found to be a positive change as it allowed Radio 1 to react much more quickly to new trends. 'When drum and bass suddenly became a fixture, they got themselves a drum and bass show relatively quickly, like five or six months,' he says, 'whereas previously they might have waited eighteen months or something.'

Through all the chaos, the bitter recriminations, the attacks in the press and from within, Bannister did feel vindicated that the changes he made laid the foundations for the Radio 1of today, a station that has remained an engine room for new talent and music. 'But it was done in what looked like a very cavalier and frankly careless way,' claims Trevor Dann. 'People who felt they'd put their lives into this product were treated in a very shabby fashion.'

Bannister has always argued that his job was made that much harder because the BBC should have acted sooner with regard to Radio 1, and so what might have been a gradual change had to become a very sudden and dramatic one. Paul Robinson argues that Beerling was evolving Radio 1, although not nearly quick enough, but not the revolution of Birt and Bannister. 'Revolution doesn't work in radio because people have got relationships and if you change too much too quickly audiences get upset and go away,' Paul says. 'And that's exactly what happened.'

25

We now live in an era where television is a multi-tasking medium. The majority of TV watching now involves people using personal devices at the same time as they're watching the square box in the corner, or the monolithic cube hanging on the wall. But of course, Radio 1 was the perfect multi-tasking medium. 'You could listen while you were doing your housework,' says Noel Edmonds. 'You could listen while you were doing your homework. You could listen in your car. It was part of the fabric of life for millions and millions of people and as a result people like me became part of their lives.'

And yet their masters, the BBC, never quite lost that disdain for the station which started in 1967 when it was first imposed on the broadcaster by the government. 'It was always looked down on,' says Johnnie Walker. 'When I joined BBC Radio 5 in 1990 and did a magazine show for them, I was suddenly invited to the governors' Christmas drinks party up on the top floor. It was the first time ever. I never got invited when I was at Radio 1. A lot of people within the BBC were sort of embarrassed about Radio 1; [to them] it wasn't a proper BBC station. There was a lot of snobbery. And yet they delivered the BBC their biggest-ever radio audience.'

It's very different today. When Broadcasting House underwent a massive renovation programme, the Radio 1 offices claimed the prime location on the eighth-floor penthouse. It was an acknowledgement

319

that Radio 1 had come of age, and finally been accorded the respect that it deserved within the BBC.

The DJs who worked at the station over the years look back on their time with justified pride. Even today they are recognised. People come up to them wanting to share a special moment or incident from Radio 1's past. It's hardly ever a burden but proof of the effect they had on the public. They're treated like an old friend who was a welcomed visitor for so many years in their homes. 'Working at Radio 1,' says Bruno Brookes, 'being in that building, everyone felt it was the hit factory. Every time you walked in or out, there were fans waiting for autographs. It was a fun place. It didn't feel like a business. And everyone knew how to make great radio.'

In 1996 Radio 1 left Egton House for the final time. The building had always been considered an eyesore, especially by those who worked there, but it was home and it was sad to have to leave. Sadder yet was the decision to demolish it in 2003 as part of renovation plans. Johnnie Walker was there the day the bulldozers moved in. 'I watched this wrecking ball at the end of this crane knocking down Egton House and I thought, "My God, all the memories, all the great times we had in there, all the great programmes that came out of that building. And all the people I met in there." Unbelievable memories and it's gone in an afternoon.'

Radio 1's fiftieth anniversary celebration in 2017 was a rather muted affair. If there was to be no 'official' celebration, producers Martin Cox and David Atkey took it upon themselves to organise their own party. As they began to send out invitations, there was just one stipulation: only people who worked up until 1992, or, as they called it, 'the golden years', were to be asked to attend. 'Because after 1992,' says David, 'it wasn't the same radio station.'

The venue chosen to hold the function was perfect: no fancy ballroom or grandiose chamber within Broadcasting House, this 'unofficial' knees-up was at a Wetherspoons pub in the middle of the City of London, just behind the Old Bailey. Having once been a bank, it was spacious enough to hold several hundred people. And it took place on a Sunday. 'We didn't want to draw attention to the party,' says Martin. 'It had to be a private party, rather than a media stunt.'

When Martin and David started putting the party together, they expected maybe a hundred to turn up; a month before the event they'd heard from 350 people and had to stop taking any more applications. So, unfortunately not everyone who wanted to be there was allowed to. The event turned out to be a special evening with old friends reunited after many years. 'To all be back in the same room, it was fabulous,' says Martin. 'You saw old plugger mates that you couldn't remember the names of, old producers and secretaries. It was such a lovely catch-up and a really good example of the camaraderie of Radio 1's spirit in those days.'

As part of the celebrations, Martin organised some video presentations, including clips about the Roadshow and old jingles. A decision was also made to produce a montage simple called 'Sadly missed but not forgotten' – a tribute to those who'd passed away, including producers, studio managers, secretaries, executives, pluggers, record company people and, of course, the DJs, all to the melancholic sound of George Michael's song 'Praying for Time'. 'When Martin played it to me, I found it very emotional,' recalls David. 'We showed it to Johnny Beerling and he actually walked out in the middle of it. We stopped and when he came back in, I asked him why he'd left. "I just found it too emotional," he said.'

After Beerling's reaction, David was worried how the video was going to be received on the night. 'But it got an amazing response. It went down a storm and stopped everyone in their tracks.'

Those who couldn't make it sent in video messages. Mike Read hosted and Beerling made a speech. It was a memorable evening for everyone there. Made all the more memorable by a specially invited guest, Roy Wood. After all, it was his song, 'Flowers in the Rain', that had started it all off back on 30 September 1967.

References

Author Interviews

David Atkey, Johnny Beerling, Pete Brady, Bruno Brookes, Tim Blackmore, Ric Blaxill, Tony Brandon, Paul Burnett, Dave Cash, Martin Cox, Trevor Dann, Gary Davies, Pete Drummond, Noel Edmonds, Paul Gambaccini, Jeff Griffin, David Hamilton, Paul Hollingdale, Adrian Juste, Phil Ward-Large, Chris Lycett, Paul McKenna, John Miles, Frank Partridge, Andy Peebles, Chris Peers, Mike Read, Paul Robinson, Emperor Rosko, Jonathan Ruffle, Keith Skues, Gary Stevens, David Symonds, Robbie Vincent, Johnnie Walker, Tony Wilson, Steve Wright, Jeff Young.

Books

Johnny Beerling, *Radio 1: The Inside Scene*, Trafford Publishing, 2008.
Tony Blackburn, *My Life in Radio*, Cassell, 2007.
Bob Harris, *Still Whispering After All These Years*, Michael O'Mara, 2015.
James Hogg & Robert Sellers, *Hello, Darlings!: The Authorized Biography of Kenny Everett*, Bantam Press, 2013.
Andy Kershaw, *No Off Switch*, Serpent's Tail, 2011.
Liz Kershaw, *The Bird and the Beeb*, Trinity Mirror Media, 2014.
John Peel & Sheila Ravenscroft, *Margrave of the Marshes*, Bantam Press, 2005.
Terry Wogan, *Is It Me?*, BBC Books, 2006.

Documentaries

Blood on the Carpet: Walking with Disc Jockeys, BBC, 16 January 2001.
Man Alive: The Disc Jockeys, BBC, 11 February 1970.
The Radio 1 Story, BBC, 20 September 1997.

Podcasts

'Radio Moments: David Jensen', Davidlloydradio.com, 5 October 2019.
'My Radio 1 with Shaun Tilley', BBC, 29 December 2017.

Articles

Chris Charlesworth, 'What's wrong with Radio 1?', *Melody Maker*, 18 July 1970.

John Clarkson, 'Interview with Janice Long', pennyblackmusic.co.uk, 24 March 2013.

Olga Craig, 'Tony Blackburn interview: "So what if people call me cheesy?"', *Daily Telegraph*, 3 October 2010.

Simon Garfield, 'The nation's favourites', *Guardian*, 16 September 2007.

Jane Graham, 'Simon Mayo interview: "Radio is full of shy people"', *The Big Issue,* 11 November 2015.

Joe Ingham, 'Interview with Annie Nightingale', oxfordstudent.com, 26 March 2014.

Jane Martinson & Jamie Grierson, '"Serious failings" at BBC let Jimmy Savile and Stuart Hall go unchecked', *Guardian*, 25 February 2016.

Kevin Young, 'Richard Skinner interview: Why Radio 1's DJs hated Newsbeat', *BBC News*, 24 September 2007.

Deborah Willimott, 'Interview with Janice Long', 1stwomenuk.co.uk, 15 June 2019.

'Annie Nightingale – respect to Radio 1's first female DJ, still going strong 40 years on', *Radio Times*, 28 October 2013.

'Dave Lee Travis trial: DJ "said groping behaviour was norm"', *BBC News*, 24 January 2014.

'Radio 1 turns 50: Annie Nightingale on pirates, sexism and the sound of the underground', *Daily Telegraph*, 25 September 2017.

Bernie Andrews quotes from the Bectu History Project interview, 1 February 2007.

Index

John, Elton 65, 70, 75, 90, 147, 206, 236
Johnny Arthey Orchestra 98
Johnson, Duncan 15, 28
Jones, Griff Rhys 242
Jones, Tom 264–5
Junior Choice 17, 39–40, 179
Juste, Adrian: Bannister's revamp 303, 307, 309, 311; comedy output 148, 162, 265; departure 314–15; early career 145–6; Egton House revamp 222; Jimmy Savile 162; John Birt's reforms 299; management relations 254–5; Our Tune success 139; popularity and job satisfaction 147–8; producer/DJ relations 239–40; Radio 1 football team 148–9; Radio 1 recruitment 146; Radio 2 move rejected 307; Roadshows 149

Kaye, Paul 149–50
Keating, Caron 257
Keen, Alan 11
Kennedy, Bobbie 36–7
Kershaw, Andy 229–31, 269, 304
Kershaw, Liz 251, 254–5, 256, 264–5, 286
Kid Creole 178
Kidd, Eddie 118
King, Carole 77
Kinks, The 157
Korgis, The 206
Korner, Alexis 136

Labour government policy 7–8
Lamacq, Mark 281, 307
Lander, Judd 85
Late Night Extra 40
LBC (London Broadcasting Company) 106, 107, 108
Led Zeppelin 30, 64–5, 74
Lennard, John 149
Lennon, John 31, 90, 181–2, 248

Lennox, Mike 15, 40
Lewis, Roger 114, 234, 273
Lewis-Smith, Victor 266–7
Lightfoot, Gordon 70
Lindisfarne 77
Line, Frances 306
Live Aid 223–9
Long, Janice 149, 199–200, 201, 214–15, 226–7, 256; *Top of the Pops* 166, 214
Love, Adrian 190–1
Lovejoy, Roy 126
Lycett, Chris: Bannister's revamp 304, 305; BBC bureaucracy 42; dance music 317; early career 73–4; engineering problems 48; engineer to producer 169–70; *In Concert* sessions 74; John Birt's reforms 293–4; Lapland trip 237–8; Live Aid 223, 227, 228; Peel's controversies 29, 59, 60; Peel's daytime cover 294–5; Peel/Walters partnership 197, 231, 304; promotion denied 301; punk music 136; Radio 1's detachment 41; Radio 1 to 2 transfers 306–7; record censorship 83; record pluggers 84, 85; Roadshows 105; *Walter's Weekly* 197–8

MacLean, Donald 61
Madness 174
Madonna 273–4
Mandela, Nelson 274
Margereson, Dave 45
Marine Broadcasting Offences Act 1967 7, 11
Marley, Bob 91–2, 195–6
Martin, George 15–16
Mary Whitehouse Experience, The 267
Matthew, Brian 17, 89, 206–7
Matthews, Al 220

Doreen Davies 83; engineering problems 47–8, 49; *Friday Rock Show* 159–60, 185–6; John Walters 60; producer/DJ relations 101–2; *Saturday Rock Show* 101–2; Teddy Warwick 155

Windsor, Tony 69

Wishbone Ash 75

Wogan, Terry 15, 23, 40–1, 59, 100, 112

Wonder, Stevie 30

Wood, Roy 321

Wood, Victoria 265

Wright, Steve 102, 179–81, 187–8, 232, 240–3, 268, 307, 312

Wurzels, The 104

Wyatt, Tessa 139–40

Wylie, Pete 214

Yentob, Alan 41

Yes 74

Young, Jeff 251, 252–3, 281, 317–18

Young, Jimmy 11, 15, 36–8, 96

Zappa, Frank 147